Praise fo

'I am a great wine lov
broaden my choice'

*M.G., Sheffield*

'My husband was given a copy of *Superplonk 1997* . . . Life has not been the same since – supermarket shopping has been attractive – more power to your elbow (and ours!)'

*Mrs A.H., Ratby, Leicestershire*

'Malcolm Gluck, in his manifestation as *Superplonk*, has been a welcome, cheering and inebriating presence in my family since his first appearance'

*Mr G.G., Newton Abbot*

'Ever since I was given a present of your *Superplonk* book and thereby discovered your weekly column, I have not once been disappointed by your recommendations'

*Mr J.W., Oxford*

'It is a great help to be able to be pointed in the direction of a good "glug" rather than stand dazed in front of rows and rows of appealing-looking labels . . . Wine is fun and so are your books'

*Mr P.B., Shrewsbury*

'Thank you again for the drinking pleasure your selections give us'

*Mr A.W., Colchester*

'Thank you for *Superplonk 1997*, essential reference for a totally ignorant wine buyer'

*Mrs D.G.N., Uxbridge*

'Incidentally, I treated myself pre-Christmas to a copy of the High Street guide, which I find equally enthralling! I fear that this will also become another annual "must have"'

*Mrs B.F., Beckenham*

'The moment you give a wine the magic score of 16 or above, it disappears entirely from the shelves'

*Mr N.W., Cambridge*

'May I sincerely thank you for a number of things: *Superplonk 1997*, *Streetplonk 1997* and *Gluck, Gluck, Gluck* . . . For the working man on a limited income as well as a person who appreciates value for money, your book has provided me with a genuine improvement of the quality of my life'

*Mr R.J., Stoke Gifford*

## *About the Author*

Malcolm Gluck is the wine correspondent of the *Guardian*, mitigating the effects of tasting several thousand bottles of wine a year by cycling in all weathers all over London. He writes a weekly Saturday column, *Superplonk*. Last year he presented his own BBC-2 television series – *Gluck, Gluck, Gluck*. When he is not raising a glass, he helps raise a family.

# Streetplonk 1998

Malcolm Gluck

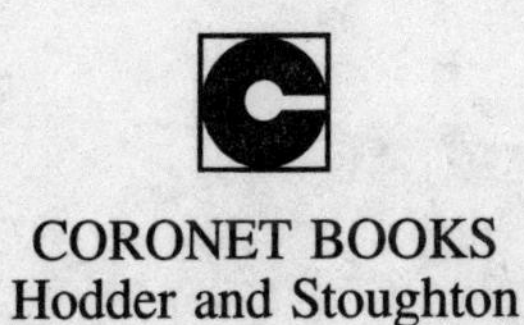

CORONET BOOKS
Hodder and Stoughton

First published in Great Britain as
a Coronet paperback original in 1997



10 9 8 7 6 5 4 3 2 1



British Library Cataloguing in Publication Data

Gluck, Malcolm
Streetplonk. – 1998
1. Wine and wine making – Great Britain – Guidebooks
I. Title
641.2'2'0296'41

ISBN 0 340 66625 0

Typeset by Palimpsest Book Production Limited,
Polmont, Stirlingshire
Printed and bound in Great Britain by
Mackays of Chatham PLC, Chatham, Kent

Hodder and Stoughton
A division of Hodder Headline PLC
338 Euston Road
London NW1 3BH

To Syd, sorry the flowers didn't take

# CONTENTS

‘I think the British have the distinction above all other nations of being able to put new wine into old bottles without bursting them.’

*Clement Attlee*

Streetplonk 1998

# INTRODUCTION

'What two ideas are more inseparable than Beer and Britannia?' wrote the Reverend Sydney Smith, but if he's keeping an eye out for trends from his tomb in Kensal Rise cemetery he will know just how much the alcoholic inclinations of his country have changed since the 1800s. Today, what two ideas are more inseparable than *Wine* and Britannia? A vast river of vinous liquid streams into the UK market regularly quenching the thirsts of some 70 per cent of the drinking population (whereas in the Rev. Smith's day it was less than 2 per cent who indulged the habit).

The year when Britain has handed back its last remaining overseas dominion seems an appropriate moment to consider Britannic images and reflect on our colonial past. Appropriate time, perhaps, you may say, but is this an appropriate book? This tome, scrap, offering, high street boozer's *vade mecum* – call it what you will – is devoted to the contents of the nation's leading wine shops. Surely, the wines they sell have very little to do with Clive of India, Captain Cook, Hong Kong or the Pitcairn Islands. You would, however, be wrong to think this. The links are not tenuous, but vivid and healthy. Indeed, there has always been something which can be characterised as colonial with regard to this country's dealings in wine. Even though the days of Empire were in reality over and done with long before Chris Patten and Prince Charles sailed off into the sunset this last July, Britain's enduring international influence in the wine business has remained and still remains strong, and has even enjoyed something of a resurgence in the past few years.

Recalling the days of Red Splashes on the World Map is

relevant here because the same pioneering, entrepreneurial and mercantile driving force which built the British Empire has also been responsible for numerous overseas conquests in the wine business. One has only to travel to Oporto, the home of port, or to Jerez, the centre of the sherry business, or to Bordeaux for that matter, to see the evidence of British influence, most noticeably in the proliferation of British names above the doors of bodegas and negociants alike. Not surprisingly after so many years the direct links have been eroded. Many of these companies are now owned by multinationals and some of the families are no longer involved in the business. What remains, however, is the fundamental reason why these companies were set up in the first place: the fact that Britain is a major importer not only of sherry and port but almost every other form of alcoholic beverage apart from whisky which, depending on your view, we either make ourselves or import from another colonial possession.

It was consumer demand for a reliable supply of quality wine that led the likes of George Sandeman, William Offley and Thomas Osborne to set up their businesses out in the known wine regions of the eighteenth and nineteenth centuries. And although the modern wine business is structured in an entirely different way, there is in essence little difference between what the major retailers are doing today and the function of such wine shippers 200 years ago. Indeed, the developments over the past ten years in the wine business make the parallel even stronger.

For while none of today's wine retailing chains directly owns wineries in any of the countries they import from they are today more closely involved with the planning, creation and development of the products they sell than ever before. Just like the early wine shippers, many of the retailers in this book involve themselves heavily in the regions of production by visiting the vineyards and wineries regularly, participating in blending the wines they will eventually be selling and discussing at length with winemakers and their agents how the wines are to be made. Retailers have wines made to a brief, special labels are designed and in some cases names are created or resurrected from dusty archives to meet a particular demand or fill a certain niche in a retailer's range.

This is very different from how wine retailers operated even ten years ago and represents a key part of what has been effectively a revolution in wine marketing and retailing in the UK, inspired in part by the Australians' radical approach and by market forces which resulted in retailers shipping most of their wines directly from the regions of production. In the pre-revolutionary wine market, retailers would buy much of their wine 'off the peg' through importers in the UK. There was much less in the way of tailoring wines to particular drinkers or developing new and interesting concepts, such as unusual grape varieties, indigenous traditional varieties from lesser-known regions, or innovative branded ideas. The retailers concerned themselves with catering for the stock generic sectors – claret, muscadet, chianti and so on – and satisfying all the important price points. But innovation was extremely limited. It wouldn't be an exaggeration to state that innovation and British wine retailing was a joke, an oxymoron, a risible contradiction in terms.

The main catalyst for change came also from a colonial connection, albeit a lapsed one, when at the end of the 1980s Australian wine producers began to target the UK with considerable gusto and no little panache. Until then, Australian wine was regarded in the same lampoonist's light as the Swiss navy. Many is the time, out and about doing intensive research in various Soho dives with friends during the late sixties and seventies, we would pass the Australian Wine Shop at the Shaftesbury Avenue end of Greek Street and without fail one of our number would pass an unkind comment. Did we ever venture inside? We didn't dare risk the ridicule. This was about the same time, you may recall, that we Brits were also in stitches about the imbecilic Japanese who were attempting to make inroads into the UK car market with a vehicle sharing a name with a well-known brand of light bulb. A little later, as Australian wine began its first moves from its obscure corner on the wine shelves that it shared with tonic lotions designed to fortify the over-nineties, I remember the guffaws which also greeted the lunatic notion that foreign footballers might soon come in droves to pollute our national sport. Are all these cosmopolitan imports somehow, one wonders, related? Be that as it may, Australian wine, hitherto regarded as a joke, suddenly became a tipple to take seriously and a much more rosy prospect for the ambitious wine retailer. This was not only because the wines were tasty and hit the pocket with as soft an impact as the fruit in the bottle but equally because the Australian producers were so enthusiastic and eagerly prepared to listen to what the retailers said and give them what they asked for. By contrast with the cobwebbed bastions of European wine production, set in their ways, sometimes arrogant and staggeringly complacent, this was not only a pleasanter way to do business (in the same language), it was so agreeably and profitably revolutionary.

The rest, as they say, is history. Australian and New Zealand wine have taken off; as have Chilean, South African, Californian and now Argentinian. They've taken off and orbited successfully, with aplomb, and show no signs of crashing to earth. Accompanying this, wines from Eastern Europe have also prospered in a wine market which has grown more eclectic and diverse by the year. True, the Bulgarian wine explosion pre-dated the arrival of the Australians by some years but their progress has been all the same price level, until last year, and there has been no evidence of anyone ever meeting an actual Bulgarian winemaker. I myself never have; though I hope to rectify this when I visit the country sometime soon. Australians speak English to a reasonable degree of fluency and so it was easy for them to make nifty progress simply by picking up the phone.

Unquestionably the consumer, the drinker, you and me, that is, has been a major beneficiary in all this. There is now far more choice and variety available. Quality has risen across the shelf, up the shelf, down the shelf, and all over the shop, as Old World has tried to match New World in improvements in vinification, viticulture, and in the introduction of new products. (A part of the introduction to the sister book to this one, *Superplonk*, goes into a little detail about certain new filtration methods which have done away with old-fashioned, unsympathetic treatments and as a result we are drinking healthier wines than ever before, as well as cheaper ones.) By feeding this demand for better-quality wines from increasingly diverse places, the major retailers have also progressed. Over the same period, most of the retailers in this book have expanded numerically, albeit sometimes at the expense of other smaller merchants. But more importantly most have enhanced their retail surroundings and improved in-store service and they have all increased the range and choice of wines they have to offer. One of the topics of every conversation I have with vignerons, wine growers, grape producers and wine makers when I am abroad is the astonishing choice and quality of choice to be seen in every wine shop, high street wine chain and supermarket to which these professionals are naturally drawn whilst on holiday in the UK or on a business trip here.

## *MADE TO ORDER – never mind the price tag, feel the depth*

It is not simply the greater variety which is notable, but the fact that the retailers now get far more involved in the creation and development of the wines. In much the same way as their predecessors in Jerez and Oporto did, the likes of Victoria Wine, Thresher and Oddbins are out in the regions of production working with the producers in order to obtain precisely the wines they and their customers are looking for. The analogy ends there because today's wine retailers do not own the wineries, though it is interesting to note that both Oddbins and Victoria Wine are part of international conglomerates which do own wine production. The Oddbins parent company, Seagram, actually owns Sandeman in addition to wine interests in California, Champagne and Bordeaux, while Allied-Domecq, which owns Victoria Wine, still has wineries in France, Spain, Portugal and the US. These links, however, are not of great significance with the possible exception of Seagram's success with Mumm Cuvee Napa whose favourable reception in the UK was built at the outset on support from Oddbins. Indeed, it was precisely to achieve decent distribution of its brands in this country that Seagram purchased Oddbins in the first place. It is a tribute to Seagram's managerial style that Oddbins has retained its colourful in-store ethos and not had this submerged beneath an anonymous grey blanket (as happens with many another US-owned UK subsidiary when the parent's fundamentalist intolerance suffocates individualism).

The extent to which wine retailers have become involved in tailored projects varies from retailer to retailer. The major supermarkets are all extremely involved and, in the high street, Oddbins, Victoria Wine and Thresher are the most active. Oddbins reckons that it has had some involvement in the development or styling of 60–70 per cent of the wines it carries. Thresher estimates that around half of the wines on its list have either been made at its request or blended to its specifications. Victoria Wine has also been busy in this area and says as much as one third of its turnover comes from wines which it has had a hand in. With the exception of Majestic, which does take a markedly different approach from its competitors, the rest of the retailers have all been involved in either commissioning wines or having them made to a certain brief.

'We work with producers before the grapes are even harvested, sometimes before the vines are even planted,' says David Howse of Thresher, before reeling off a list of products which have been made with Thresher's stylistic input. 'We suggest directions that they should go. We give them the security to experiment and innovate by commissioning ranges of wine. Any partnership that is robust and productive is equally beneficial to both parties.' The Thresher view on this subject, with which most of the other retailers concur, is that the retailer is the expert in the market, and the winemaker knows about wine. In essence, it is nothing more than pooling their respective grey matter. 'We are knowledgeable about the market, not oenology. We don't tell them how to make it or ask them for impressions of a wine from another country. It would be as daft as hiring a great chef and then telling him what ingredients to use and how to cook them. Better to just tell them the style of food that you like and that you like to discover new tastes too.'

## *THE NEW GENERATION – 'masters of the future by not being slaves to the past'*

The parallel with the wine shippers of old, venturing forth to distant vineyards to satisfy their well-to-do customers back in Britain is, I believe, striking. The modern UK wine retailer is carrying on a tradition centuries in the maturing. What the retailers nowadays do in terms of styling and developing products is in many cases carried out in collaboration with wine agents. It is only natural that the wine shops should take the plaudits for the increase in choice and range and the innovative products on their shelves – a result of competitive pressures encouraging attitudes which are much more open and adventurous than ever they were – but behind much of this innovation there are some relatively unsung heroes. I am not talking here about the winemakers (in any case, as I will explain further on, their personalities are very much to the fore in the modern wine market). I am referring to the middle-men. Middle-men, historically, used to side-step the spotlight and consciously avoided its glare. Clandestinity was part of their mystique. In general, the last decade has seen the middle-man suddenly becoming a recognisable personality in his own right. (Middle-women don't seem to figure much; peculiarly, like spies, the majority of these characters are men.) Nowadays, in fields of endeavour like sport or fashion for example, the agent or middle-man is often more famous, more notorious, than the clients he represents.

This kind of tawdry glamour does not attach itself to the wine industry. Perhaps it might be more fascinating for my readers if it did. Nevertheless, I shall press on since my aim in this introduction is not to fatigue you with a dry treatise on how the *fin-de-siècle* wine industry of these islands is structured but to try to give you a genuine glimpse of the far-reaching changes which have taken place. Behind all the most visible of these changes, which we can see on the shelves in the shape of more varied and interesting products from increasingly widespread locations (China, Zimbabwe, Malta and Uruguay are perhaps the least likely of the new hot spots), an interesting history has evolved and continues to develop and expand. These changes have had a direct bearing on the broadening of choice for drinkers and so I am extremely mindful of and passionately interested in these developments. In sum, retailers now buy their wines direct, ex-cellars, without bringing in the wines through a third-party importer. When this became increasingly popular, it looked as though the days of the wine importer/agent were numbered and in fact many did go to the wall never to be seen in the same guise again. But those nimble-footed companies which adapted quickly to the new structure of the UK wine world have, contrary to pessimistic predictions, actually flourished in recent years. Today's most successful middle-men by and large do not hold any stock in the UK and will act purely as agents, strengthening the link between the retailer and the area of production. Today's retail wine buyers now see these links as vital to their business.

Companies such as Western Wines, Thierry's, Bottle Green and Guy Anderson Wines, for example, are unlikely to be familiar names to wine drinkers but the wines with which they are involved ('source' is the trade term) most certainly will be and one of their bottles may well have been the choice number you drank at dinner last night. These companies have played a key role in broadening drinkers' choices, introducing new product ideas, innovative concepts, wines from different countries and regions and generally raising quality levels, always working very closely with the retailers in this book.

Their survival was not solely based on being 'lean and

mean' at a time when the middle-man was being squeezed. Simply servicing the retailers' requirements would not have been enough. To prosper, these companies had to be on-the-ball, dynamic, pragmatic, and original, and provide something that the retailers could not easily find themselves. Most importantly, they have themselves gone out into the regions of production, often preposterous and initially inhospitable destinations, and set up joint ventures and wine projects, and commissioned wines to be made to a brief. They are therefore more than wine agents, they are in many cases actually wine producers.

'The traditional middle-man, graduate of the old-school wine trade, has died since the late 1980s,' says Jerry Lockspeiser, the man behind Bottle Green, which works to a greater or lesser extent with all the retailers in this book and has doubled its sales every year for the past three years. Bottle Green employs two full-time winemakers, but tries to work with local rather than flying winemakers wherever possible. It is directly involved in production in Hungary, France and Spain. The Hungarian project alone amounts to some 600,000 cases of wine a year, producing wines to different specifications for Fullers, Spar, Victoria Wine, Thresher and Unwins. It not only supplies the Spar Danube Red and Danube White, but also the Moravian Vineyards Czech wines.

Underlining the pioneering spirit of these companies, Bottle Green is also keen to buy or commission wines from relatively unfamiliar places, and by working with local producers come up with wines which are drinkable for the consumer and marketable for the retailer. The company was for instance responsible for Domaine Cigogne Moroccan Red which it introduced through Victoria Wine. The labels for this wine were designed by Bottle Green and Mr Lockspeiser himself goes to Morocco to supervise blending. I liked this wine enough last year to give it 14.5 points, but I gather it is soon to be de-listed by Victoria Wine. In addition, the company is involved with a range of Maltese wines, though the only retailer who has taken these is, interestingly enough, the generally conservative Unwins. 'We work with the buyers to find or directly produce the kind of wines they want,' says Mr Lockspeiser. 'What I set out to do is to work closely with the buyers. We look at their range and try to come up with things they haven't got. We propose things and we try to find what they want. The key to it is being creative and, to use the horrible jargon, to be market-led. To put ourselves in the retail buyer's chair and to think of things before they do.'

Chris Ellis of Western Wines has a similar professional style. He believes that the primary task of an agent in today's wine market is to 'add value to the supply process', something his company has most certainly done. This company too has grown enormously in the past few years and now has a turnover of some £-millions, the annual fruit, at the last harvest, of some 3-million cases of wine. Being involved in wine production and developing new wines is central to the business. Western Wines employs three full-time winemakers and is directly involved with production in Italy, South Africa, Spain, France and Chile. The company works with all the major wine shops. It was responsible for Thresher's Las Colinas Chilean range, as well as a number of other Thresher exclusives. For Victoria Wine, the company came up with the Spanish wines, Ed's Red and Ed's White, as well as more recently El Liso (absolutely no pun intended, Mr Ellis assures me) which is a barrique-aged tempranillo from La Mancha. Chris Ellis reckons the company probably supplies Oddbins with between twenty and thirty wines on a bespoke basis.

Arguably the most important element in what these companies have to offer is their close links with the areas of production which give them their edge and, in particular, the ability to spread innovative and successful winemaking ideas from one region to another, most importantly perhaps from the sophisticated to the less developed parts of the wine world. 'It's using experience in winemaking techniques and cross-fertilising ideas with regions of production to come up with things that set us apart, that are new and innovative and providing good value for money,' says Guy Anderson of Guy Anderson Wines, another of the new breed, who works in France, Argentina and Zimbabwe. 'My role would be to really understand clearly what the consumer and the retailers want in Britain and then use my knowledge of the vineyards to come up with the wines that suit.'

## *CAT'S PEE AND FAT BASTARDS – name your poison (or poison your name?)*

The sophistication in our tastes and the retailers' desire to market wines which meet them have resulted in the creation of many wines, the like of which would have been inconceivable a few years back. The idea of launching a fancy chardonnay called Fat Bastard, the brainchild of Guy Anderson and Thierry Boudinaud, would have been not just ridiculous but unacceptable when Mad Maggie was on the Throne of Westminster (I speak of her time – I do not presume to judge of her nominal moral outlook). The first vintage of this Vin de Pays d'Oc, the 1995, was seen in the UK in Fullers stores and was very successful – I enjoyed it to the extent of giving it 16 points – and the 1996 is, at time of writing, being sold through Fullers, Majestic, Victoria Wine, Bottoms Up and Greenalls. Like many of the very best names it was not the fruit of a marketing team brainstorm, but came about by chance remark. The winemaker, Thierry Boudinaud, was in the cellar going through a tasting of various samples with Guy Anderson, and referring to one particularly fleshy beast, remarked, 'That is one fat bastard of a chardonnay,' and the name stuck.

I am told by Guy Anderson that he and some of the retailers concerned received many letters about this wine and though one can imagine such a moniker raising eyebrows in the more genteel parts of the land only two out of some 350 epistolic responses were disapproving. One came from Tiverton and the other from a lady in Annan in Scotland. So incensed was this latter tippler that she wrote to the retailer, in this instance Victoria Wine, to protest at confronting such an offensively named bottle on the shelves. When she did not receive full satisfaction from the retailer, she did what any outraged citizen would do. She called the cops. The Annan constabulary duly arrived to inspect this affront to public decency, bought six bottles, and left. Nothing more has been heard. As when Radio 1 bans a risqué record, such moral outrage seldom produces the effect the reproachers are looking to achieve. It is of course instructive to muse that a similar reaction would not have been forthcoming had that lady seen the French inspiration for the Fat Bastard pun. Fat Bastard, however much Monsieur Boudinaud innocently may claim otherwise, is surely a jocular reference to Batard-Montrachet, a white burgundy emanating from the eponymous village the especially fatty, vegetal style of whose wines the Fat Bastard punsters must have thought their wine resembled. This was true, to my palate at least, of the '95. It was less so with the '96, but it might develop some Montrachet characteristics as it ages. Certain things, whatever their taste, can, it seems, appear the height of respectability and the reverse of repellent simply because the name is in a language perceived to be glamorous. Batard-Montrachet has been seen for decades on the highest and swankiest dinner tables in the land and there is no record of a single diner stomping off into the night in outraged protest (well, not in response to the name on the label at any rate).

Guy Anderson seems to have a knack of sourcing unusually named wines. He was also responsible for bringing in the Big Frank's wines. Once again, there is a solid – in this case particularly solid – foundation to this name. Frank is an American chemical engineer of Polish extraction who by a convoluted series of events – including crashing his boat into the bedroom of a luxurious New York harbour-front property – landed up making wines in Minervois. Apart from being true, this is the kind of story that you wouldn't make up. What is more, Frank is big, in girth and character, and apparently can only just squeeze into an extra large-sized Fat Bastard T-shirt (though you could hang such a tee-shirt from the ends of Frank's moustache).

Far from being a marketing creation emanating from the Victoria Wine nerve centre in Woking, Big Frank's Red was actually being marketed locally in Minervois where Guy Anderson discovered it while playing snooker with someone called Fast Eddy. (I did say it was the kind of story you wouldn't, yawn yawn, make up.) Big Frank's Red was then listed by Victoria Wine and the range has subsequently been expanded with the addition of a white, a rose – Big Frank's Deep Pink – and a Viognier. Most recently, Victoria Wine has introduced a Big Frank's Sticky. It has been suggested that Big Frank might make an interesting proposition as a flying winemaker, to which Mr Anderson's response was that he did not really feel the rest of the world was yet ready for him.

There is, then, a real man and a genuine personality behind these wines and that, in Guy Anderson's view, is crucial if the concept is going to work. He believes wines with such outlandish names have to have some foundation in reality or else they will seem too gimmicky. (This, let me point out, from a man who has also recently introduced a rather tasty tongue-tingler called Wild Pig Red.) 'I think ultimately unless there is some solid basis in these things it will never hold up,' he says brazenly and with a straight face. 'If there was no Frank, if it was pure fiction, the whole project would not hang together. If you went to a retailer with Big Sally's Chardonnay with no Big Sally in sight and no reason for calling it that why would they bother?' Just in case you are curious, Wild Pig Red is claimed to owe its name to the fact that it is made from extra-ripe grapes. Well, of course! In the Gard region where the wine grows the longer you leave grapes on the vines the greater the chance of wild boars coming down from the hills to take their pick. (Slight clearing of throat to be heard from sceptical wine writer, but let it pass.) I must comment that the wine would splendidly accompany a wild boar (roasted and well seasoned). Other wines from this region have also inspired the do-or-die punster. A Co-op wine buyer, Mr Paul Bastard, was an early exponent of this art with his Bad-Tempered Cyril (red) and Fair Martina (white) – names which owed their relevance to their respective grape varieties: syrah and vermentino. One is forced to wonder how Mr Bastard's vivid imagination would transform, on label, such varieties as Tinta Negra Mole (which helps to make Madeira) or Pineau d'Aunis – a fast-disappearing Loire red grape less inspirationally known as Chenin Noir.

The main rationale behind such products is that a wine like Cat's Pee on a Gooseberry Bush will sell better than if it were simply called New Zealand Sauvignon Blanc. In a conversation with one wine buyer about a similar so-called 'concept' wine, the man remarked: 'It's been incredibly successful. If it was a £5.99 Vin de Pays d'Oc it would sell OK but not shift like Cat's Pee.' This does not augur well for the hidebound quaffers of Annan and other strongholds of conservatism. I wish I could say I had no sympathy with their point of view, but though I approve of lots of the new ideas flooding into the world of wine and find many of the names amusing and apposite, I have a sneaking suspicion an anti-reaction will set in if sheer silliness proliferates in the name of conceptual marketing or the wines in the bottles don't always come up to scratch. It is illuminating here to listen to Mr Chris Dee, who is wine buyer for the bijou chain of northern supermarkets Booths (now an entry in the *Superplonk* book). Mr Dee could not be called conservative or lacking in chutzpah. He is responsible, after all, for Booths £3.49 Spanish tempranilllo called Scraping the Barrel which features a cartoon character's head stuck in a cask. 'I think wine buyers should be selectors. Not blenders or makers of wine. They should buy finished products only. I think wine buyers can become too attached to their concept wines at the expense of quality. Such ranges of wine can become static fixtures.' He believes that 'quality to the customer suffers' if the wine buyer becomes so besotted by the concept surrounding the wines that making it work and continuing to sell it takes precedence over finding the best fruit to place in the bottle. He makes a very good point and he makes it tellingly. Wine buyers should bear in mind the advice of the literature don and mystery writer Sir Arthur Quiller-Couch. Q, as he was known, told budding writers to 'Murder your darlings'. For many years I had this commandment, in bold letters, stuck to the pinboard behind my typewriter. I have lost it. But I have not lost the instinct to kill phantoms with which I foolishly fall in love.

In terms of innovation, one trend has been for retailers to carry wines which are New World-style but in fact emanate from Eastern Europe or Germany. Innovation, wacky names and creative packaging are fine if the wines fit the concept and can carry it off, but fashion is a fickle thing. Bottle Green developed a French wine for Kwik Save called Skylark Hill which Mr Lockspeiser now believes may have been ill-advised. 'I thought it was a good idea at first but I have gone off it since because people like French names. We did it in this case because the French name was unpronounceable. I don't think it's a good idea any more.' On the other hand, with some of the serpentine and gruesomely unpalatable Hungarian names he believes more approachable names will give drinkers reassurance, thus making the wines far more marketable.

## *THE CULT OF THE WINEMAKER – 'remember the time people only knew the names of the stars of the film, never the name of the director?'*

A key part of the revolution in the wine market in the past few years has been the advent of another kind of peripatetic pioneer, namely the flying winemaker. To clarify the definition of this term, this is a winemaker who may well have made a reputation for him or herself in one country, who is now in demand as a winemaker in other countries. Increasingly, these people are marketed directly to the consumers. We are, I think, becoming increasingly aware of them. A few years ago, the names of winemakers even at the most prestigious chateaux would have been unknown to the people who drank the wines. The flying winemakers, however, have increasingly become personalities, known to the consumer at large rather like designers at fashion houses. Men such as Hugh Ryman, Kim Milne, Jacques Lurton, Geoff Merrill and Peter Bright are anything but distant and obscure figures and their names feature on wine labels.

The evolution of the flying winemaker also owes much to the popularisation of Australian wine and the New World style. In the first place, many of them are Australian. But more importantly, Australian wine production in general tends to place far more emphasis on the winemaker as the individual creator, whereas the European system is focused first and foremost on the area or particular vineyard that the wine comes from, its climate and other differentiating factors; the *terroir* as the French call it, a term for which, like *bon appetit*, there is no direct English translation. I also learned from the Australian winemaker, Peter Bright, that the term 'winemaker' is not a direct equivalent of oenologue in French or oenologist in English, which explains why a cult or identity is more easily developed. Oenologists work on the wine in the winery or in the laboratory whereas a winemaker is responsible for the whole process, translating the product from the vineyard to the bottle.

In the years since the Australian boom it has become much more common for wines to be marketed using the winemaker's identity and personality. According to Hugh Ryman, 'It helps humanise wines and gives consumers something to recognise.' All the wines he makes, wherever they are destined and however they may be marketed, bear the HR initials on the capsule.

In recent years, able and renowned winemakers, well versed in vinification methods which produce wines with the bold, upfront fruit expression that underpinned the Australian success, have increasingly moved around to different regions all over the world. They frequently travel to areas with potential to produce excellent fruit but which have been held back by poor and old-fashioned methods or out-of-date equipment. A prime example would be one of Hugh Ryman's earliest and most successful ventures in Hungary. Hugh began to import his Hungarian Gyongyos Estate wines back in the early 1990s.

It had been quite obvious for years to anyone who visited the area that it was capable of producing all kinds of fruit, not just grapes, of a very high taste intensity. These Hungarian wines were sold through Thresher and several of the supermarkets and, coming at a time when there was a shortfall in supply from France as a result of spring frosts, they were a great commercial success. Seventy thousand cases were sold in the first four months. Thresher also backed Hugh Ryman's venture in California where he aimed to demonstrate that high-quality wines could be produced in the Central Valley region (known, to me at least, as the Ever Producing Oven, such is the ferocity of the Valley's torrid climate and consequent high yield from its vines). This project led to the creation of the King's Canyon brand. These wines are still sold through Thresher and the most recent vintages are rated in this retailer's section.

Hugh Ryman still works on *ad hoc* projects on behalf of retailers and wine companies but his business is now based in Bordeaux and he concentrates on producing wines under his own brand-names, focusing on four main areas: South of France, Spain, Argentina and Moldova, as well as working in South Africa and Hungary. The fact that Hugh Ryman has made this adjustment in his business suggests that he may concur with what one or two wine critics have been hinting at in the past couple of years, which is that the flying winemaker idea is reaching the end of the road. To infer this generality from Mr Ryman's individual business stance is erroneous, in my view. If anything, the flocks of flying winemakers will increase I would have thought. The surface of their potential has barely been scratched let alone worn thin. True, it has been said that some of these overactive winemakers spread themselves too acrobatically and are compelled to be in so many places at once that they cannot give individual projects their wholehearted attention and this, it is claimed, means the winemaker is merely autographing wines which have been made to his specification by other people. But if the wines are better than what has gone before who is the loser here? Certainly not you or me. And most certainly not the wineries which acquire invaluable insight into modern techniques.

Hugh Ryman believes his business has evolved beyond just being a flying winemaker, but it is still fundamentally based on his reputation and prowess as a winemaker. His business is now split evenly between the UK, continental Europe and the US, but much of his early work was channelled through the UK multiple retailers, specialists and supermarkets, who have been keen customers for flying winemaker projects. Mr Ryman is now an established internationalist. This is good.

(G K Chesterton would approve. 'Good men are international,' he said. 'Bad men are cosmopolitan.')

Through the offices of one of the new breed of wine importers, International Wine Services, another flying winemaker, Kim Milne, has also been in great demand with the multiple retailers. Among Mr Milne's creations have been the Winelands South African range at Thresher which now numbers eight or nine wines, Cape View, and another South African range at Victoria Wine. Both of these ranges were developed in collaboration with the retailers, to the specific style demanded. 'Usually I will do the initial blending and submit samples for them to look at,' Mr Milne says. 'Sometimes they actually come out to the projects and will be there at the blending.' Oddbins and Majestic also list a number of Kim Milne's creations, often taking small quantities. Arguably Kim Milne's magnum opus has been his project in Puglia, now in its fifth year. This produces a range of more than twenty different wines retailing from £3.99 to £6.99 which are widely available in the wine shops in various guises. Kim Milne wine is the originator of Spar's Italian Rondolle duo and was also the creator of the two new Italian wines, Original Zin and Original Sin, complete with blue bottles and crown seal capsules, now being sold at Thresher. End of the road? Piffle. These Puglian wines really show the flying winemaker as genuine business innovator and Italy is a big place with openings for new ideas everywhere you care to look.

Kim Milne's background is not unlike a number of the

other flying winemakers currently doing the rounds. For a start, he is Australian. Many of the flying winemakers are blessed with this saintly birthright. Is this because of the inbred market-aware approach of Australian wine producers or the itinerant tendencies of Australians in general? One thing leading to the other is the simple answer. For Kim Milne, who went to work for Berry Estates in Australia straight after graduating in oenology from Australia's leading wine university, Roseworthy, it has clearly satisfied an inner urge. 'I always intended to travel so this is a nice way to combine my work with doing just that,' he says. Didn't Darwin say much the same thing?

On the one hand the flying winemaker idea can be seen as international and eclectic, but some critics consider that the idea of a group of Australians with similar wine backgrounds travelling around the world making wines to suit the British palate, generally meaning smooth if not anodyne tannins, soft and juicy fruit expression, and relatively low acidity in the whites, results in a sameness of everything they touch. This runs counter to the prevailing idea that the drinker today has a far broader range of products and countries or regions of origin to choose from. Kim Milne, like all his flying winemaker co-conspirators, firmly rejects the accusation. 'Complete nonsense,' he protests. 'It shows they haven't tried many of them. If you taste the wines I have done in the south of Italy compared with the wines made in the north of Italy from the same varietals they are completely different wines. We do not do exactly the same thing wherever we go.' He agreed that what the wines tend to have in common is that they are modern style with fresh fruity flavour and are ready to drink. 'The UK consumer seems to like freshness, fruity flavours, drinkability and particularly in the under £10 bracket what they are looking for is something that can be consumed when they buy it. So the wines are made to that style.'

When I met another Australian flyer, Geoff Merrill, who has worked extensively in Italy, last year he made a very similar and vehement defence against this accusation. Geoff Merrill, a graduate of Roseworthy in 1970 some ten years before

Kim Milne, said what he was striving for was total fruit expression with very soft tannins achieved by, among other things, removing grape stems to avoid the stronger tannins that they contain. He was not, for instance, looking to 'Australianise' Italian winemaking. Even though he uses the same vinification methods in different countries, the wines are different because the fruit is different because it grew in different soils and under differing climatic conditions.

Nevertheless, a key part of what the flying winemakers and some of the agents discussed earlier are doing is transplanting successful ideas in wine production to other areas. Taking this idea further, one company is even as we speak working on wines which are made from a blend of wines from two different countries. The white will be a blend of Chilean Sauvignon Blanc and South African Chenin, while the red will be an Argentinian Malbec/Syrah blended with a Chilean Merlot. It sounds like a challenging marketing proposition certainly and it will be even more fascinating if it holds up in tasting. We shall see. It would seem an horrific idea to the French – as unattractive and blurred a concept as those wines on sale in some continental hypermarkets which announce amidst the smallprint on their labels that they are a 'product of different countries of the European Community'. But – and it is a significant but – if the resultant blend is a terrific sum of its parts, widely available, and inexpensive, we drinkers, yet again, will be the gainers and no winery will be the loser.

## *HISTORY REPEATING ITSELF – rule Britannia, Britannia rules the wines*

So as retailers, agents and flying winemakers steadily extend their sphere of influence into both established and relatively untested wine-producing regions, I am left to ponder just how comparable are their activities with those of British merchants in the eighteenth and nineteenth centuries. For some insight into this it is instructive to turn to George Sandeman, a descendant of the George Sandeman who, aged twenty-five, founded the famous port and sherry business back in 1790. Although the House of Sandeman has been part of Seagram since 1980, George Sandeman still works for the group, running the Sandeman port and sherry companies. He is therefore the seventh generation of the eponymous Sandeman clan to work for the company.

Because port and sherry, as well as claret, were the dominant styles of wine being drunk in Britain donkey's years back, it is not surprising that most of these early pioneers were centred on the regions where these wines are made. There are records in Jerez of wines being shipped abroad as early as 1485, though there are references in Chaucer, writing in the 1380s, to the strong white wines of Andalusia. Sherry Sack was established as a favourite drink of English imbibers by Elizabethan times. In fact, one of the early sherry importers, though rather informally, was Sir Francis Drake. During his daring raid on Cadiz in 1587 – the renowned singeing of the King of Spain's beard – he stayed in the port for three days and, according to Julian Jeffs's delicious book *Sherry*, made off with some 2,900 pipes of wine, much of which had been intended for the Armada.

Like many of the famous British shippers, the early Sandeman founded his company in London, having moved down from Scotland. He was clearly a man of no little ambition. When urged by his sister to return to the bosom of his family, he wrote back: 'I shall remain where I am, till I have made a moderate fortune to retire with, which I suspect will be in the course of nine years; which to be sure is a long time, but some lucky stroke may possibly reduce it to five or six.' However, he did not stay where he was, but was soon travelling to Spain and Portugal to visit winegrowing areas (just like some latterday Oddbins or Victoria Wine representative). According to Rupert Croft-Cooke's book *Sherry* (1955), during the two years after 1790, Sandeman travelled extensively to Spain and Portugal, before deciding that port and sherry were the two wines he would deal in. These wines became the heart of his business, though he did not effectively create the Sandeman brand until around 1850. There is evidence of Sandeman being closely involved with blending the wines to the specific requirements of his customers, wine merchants in Britain, and elsewhere. Now where have I heard this idea before? And aren't there dunderhead critics still claiming it's an idea which has run its course?

Some of the correspondence from Sandeman's original customers survives in the company's archives. For instance, a merchant from Amsterdam wrote in January 1890: 'We have observed that the taste of people here has changed, and that they ask now for wines less sweet than those they drank formerly.' The extant George Sandeman reveals that travelling around the regions making blends to the specific requirements of particular merchants was an important part of his ancestor's business.

Some 200 years later, modern retailers have come to a very similar conclusion. What the two strategies have in common is the recognition of the value of a strong connection with the region of production. The retailers, by and large, agree that the comparison with the likes of George Sandeman is a fair one. As Thresher's David Howse puts it: 'None of it is very complicated. All we are after is quality, innovation, excitement and character. It is like the old days of Empire and British pre-eminence but with a modern tinge.'

This tinge is a fresh shading to a deep dye which vividly and benignly colours the British national character. The latest wheezes, this 'modern tinge', is merely a new slant on an established historical bent. We're born to meddle with wine. It's in our blood. We Brits can't resist establishing influences over the mercantile activities of other nations where wine is concerned and, give or take the inconvenient hiatuses of two world wars plus the odd local belligerent skirmish with a wine-producing country, we've never stopped poking our noses into the wine made abroad and, incredibly, our judgement on it has always been anxiously sought and our approbation courted. The styles of the great European wines of old were all deeply influenced by the British palate and by what the British wine drinker wished to drink with his food and to consume in company to demonstrate his status with his peers. Wine today is simply a new demotic. We all drink it. We all pronounce on it. We all enjoy it and we all know what we like.

It may be fashionable to believe that things aren't what they used to be, that the country has gone to the dogs, that tradition is dead, and all the usual tripe, but as far as this drinker is concerned we've never been better off and we're simply doing – us British wine drinkers – what we've always done: making the world's wines sing to our tune. We've been at it for hundreds of years. There isn't another nation on the face of the planet which is remotely in the same league. Chin, chin!

## Health Warning!

I get a few letters a week from readers (both column and book) telling me that a wine which I have said is on sale in a certain wine shop is not there and that the wine has either sold out or the branch claims to have no knowledge of it; I get letters telling me that a wine is a bit dearer than I said it was; and I get the odd note revealing that the vintage of the 16-point wine I have enthused about and which my correspondent desperately wants to buy is different from the one listed.

First of all, let me say that no wine guide in the short and inglorious history of the genre is more exhaustively researched, checked, and double-checked than this one. I do not list a wine if I do not have assurances from its retailer that it will be widely on sale when the guide is published. Where a wine is on restricted distribution, or stocks are short and vulnerable to the assault of determined readers (i.e. virtually all high-rating, very cheap bottles), I will always clearly say so. However, large retailers use computer systems which cannot anticipate uncommon demand and which often miss the odd branch off the anticipated stocking list. I cannot check every branch myself (though I do nose around them when I can) and so a wine in this book may well, infuriatingly, be missing at the odd branch of its retailer and may not even have been heard of by the branch simply because of inhuman error. Conversely, the same technology often tells a retailer's head office that a wine is out of stock when it has merely been completed cleared out of the warehouse. It may still be on sale in certain branches. Then there is the fact that not every wine I write about is stocked by every single branch of its listed supermarket. Every store has what are called retail plans and there may be half-a-dozen of these and every wine is subject to a different stocking policy according to the dictates of these cold-hearted plans.

I accept a wine as being in healthy distribution if several hundred branches, all over the country, not just in selected parts of it, stock the wine. Do not assume, however, that this means every single branch has the wine.

I cannot, equally, guarantee that every wine in this book will still be in the same price band as printed (these bands follow this introduction). The vast majority will be. But there will always be the odd bottle from a country suddenly subject to a vicious swing in currency rates, or subject to an unprecedented rise in production costs which the store retailer cannot or is not prepared to swallow, and so a few pennies will get added to the price. If it is pounds, then you have cause for legitimate grievance. Please write to me. But don't lose a night's sleep if a wine is 20 pence more than I said it is. If you must, write to the appropriate retailer. The department and the address to write to is provided with each retailer's entry.

Now the puzzle of differing vintages. When I list and rate a wine, I do so only for the vintage stated. Any other vintage is a different wine requiring a new rating. Where vintages do have little difference in fruit quality, and more than a single vintage is on sale, then I say this clearly. If two vintages are on sale, and vary in quality and/or style, then they will be separately rated. However, be aware of one thing.

When *Streetplonk* appears on sale there will be lots of eager drinkers aiming straight for the highest-rating wines as soon as possible after the book is published. Thus the wine buyer who assures me that she has masses of stock of Pillar Box Red and the wine will withstand the most virulent of sieges may find her shelves emptying in a tenth of the time she banked on – not knowing, of course, how well I rate the wine until the book goes on sale. It is entirely possible, therefore, that the vintage of a highly rated wine may sell out so quickly that new stocks of the follow-on vintage may be urgently brought on to shelf before I have tasted them. This can happen in some instances. I can do nothing about this fact of wine writing life, except to give up writing about wine.

Lastly, one thing more. And let me steal from myself yet again:

'*Wine is a hostage to several fortunes (weather being even more uncertain and unpredictable than exchange rates) but the wine writer is hostage to just one: he cannot pour for his readers precisely the same wine as he poured for himself.*'

I wrote this last year and it holds true for every wine in this book and every wine I will write about in the years to come (for as long as my liver holds out). I am sent wines to taste regularly and I attend wine tastings all the time. If a wine is corked on these occasions, that is to say not in good condition because it has been tainted by the tree bark which is its seal, then it is not a problem for a bottle in good condition to be quickly supplied for me to taste. This is not, alas, a luxury which can be extended to my readers.

So if you find a wine not to your taste because it seems pretty foul or 'off' in some way, then do not assume that my rating system is up the creek; you may take it that the wine is faulty and must be returned as soon as possible to its retailer. All the retailers in this book will listen to any sensible complaint and provide a refund or a fresh bottle for any faulty wine returned. I am not asking readers to share all my tastes in wine, or to agree completely with every rating for every wine. But where a wine I have well rated is obviously and patently foul then it is a duff bottle and you should be compensated by getting a fresh bottle free or by being given a refund.

## *How I Rate a Wine*

Value for money is my single unwavering focus. I drink with my readers' pockets in my mouth. I do not see the necessity of paying a lot for a bottle of everyday drinking wine and only rarely do I consider it worth paying a high price for, say, a wine for a special occasion or because you want to experience what a so-called 'grand' wine may be like. There is more codswallop talked and written about wine, especially the so-called 'grand' stuff, than any subject except sex. The stench of this gobbledegook regularly perfumes wine merchants' catalogues, spices the backs of bottles, and rancidises the writings of those infatuated by or in the pay of producers of a particular wine region. I do taste expensive wines regularly. I do not, regularly, find them worth the money. That said, there are some pricey bottles in these pages. They are here either because I wish to provide an accurate, but low, rating of its worth so that readers will be given pause for thought or because the wine is genuinely worth every penny. A wine of magnificent complexity, thrilling fruit, superb aroma, great depth and finesse is worth drinking. I would not expect it to be an inexpensive bottle. I will rate it highly. I wish all wines which commanded such high prices were so well deserving of an equally high rating. The thing is, of course, that many bottles of wine I taste do have finesse and depth but do not come attached to an absurdly high price tag. These are the bottles I prize most. As, I hope, you will.

20 Is outstanding and faultless in all departments: smell, taste and finish in the throat. Worth the price, even if you have to take out a second mortgage.

19 A superb wine. Almost perfect and well worth the expense (if it is an expensive bottle).

18 An excellent wine but lacking that ineffable sublimity of richness and complexity to achieve the very highest rating. But extraordinary drinking and thundering good value.

17 An exciting, well-made wine at an affordable price which offers real glimpses of outstanding, multi-layered richness.

16 Very good wine indeed. Good enough for any dinner party. Not expensive but terrifically drinkable, satisfying and properly balanced.

15 For the money, a good mouthful with real style. Good flavour and fruit without costing a packet.

14 The top end of the everyday drinking wine. Well made and to be seriously recommended at the price.

13 Good wine, true to its grape(s). Not great, but very drinkable.

12 Everyday drinking wine at a sensible price. Not exciting, but worthy.

11 Drinkable, but not a wine to dwell on. You don't wed a wine like this, though you might take it behind the bike shed with a bag of fish and chips.

10 Dead average wine (at a low price), yet still just about a passable mouthful. Also, wines which are terribly expensive and, though drinkable, cannot remotely justify their high price.

9 Fit for parties for failed Conservative candidates.

8 On the rough side here.

7 Good for pickling onions or cleaning false teeth.

6 Hardly drinkable except on an icy night by a raging bonfire.

5 Wine with more defects than delights.

4 Not good at any price.

3 Barely drinkable.

2 Seriously – did this wine come from grapes?

1 The utter pits. The producer should be slung in prison and the key buried.

The rating system above can be broken down into six broad sections.

Zero to 10: Avoid – unless entertaining a stuffy wine writer.

10, 11: Nothing poisonous but, though drinkable, rather dull.

12, 13: Above average, interestingly made. Solid rather then sensational.

14,15,16: This is the exceptional, hugely drinkable stuff, from the very good to the brilliant.

17, 18: Really wonderful wine worth anyone's money: complex, rich, exciting.

19,20: A toweringly brilliant world-class wine of self-evident style and individuality.

## *Prices*

It is impossible to guarantee the price of any wine in this guide. That is why instead of printing the shop price, each wine is given a price band. This attempts to eliminate the problem of printing the wrong price for a wine. This can occur for all the usual boring but understandable reasons: inflation, economic conditions overseas, the narrow margins on some high street wines making it difficult to maintain consistent prices and, of course, the existence of those freebooters at the Exchequer who are liable to inflate taxes which the supermarkets cannot help but pass on. But even price banding is not foolproof. A wine listed in the book at, say, a B band price might be on sale at a C band price. How? Because a wine close to but under, say, £3.50 in summer when I tasted it might sneak across the border in winter. It happens, rarely enough not to concern me overmuch, but wine is an agricultural import, a sophisticated liquid food, and that makes it volatile where price is concerned. The price banding code assigned to each wine works as follows:

## *Price Band*

| | | |
|---|---|---|
| A Under £2.50 | B £2.50 to £3.50 | C £3.50 to £5 |
| D £5 to £7 | E £7 to £10 | F £10 to £13 |
| G £13 to £20 | H Over £20 | |

All wines costing under £5 (i.e. A–C) have their price band set against a black background.

## *ACKNOWLEDGEMENTS*

*I have an assistant, Linda Peskin, to run the computer system behind this book and check every wine in it and I thank her (indeed, I thank her every day of my working year). I am also blessed by a lovely editor, an uncomplaining typesetter, a superb copy editor, and lots of dedicated people backing up my efforts at Hodder & Stoughton. I must also, therefore, express my gratitude to Kate Lyall Grant, Helen Dore, Martin Neild, Kerr MacRae, Jamie Hodder-Williams, Karen Geary, and Katie Gunning. As ever, I am also grateful to Felicity Rubinstein and Sarah Lutyens. I am fortunate in other respects as well. Ben Cooper, who does much of the research work for the introductions, has been assiduous and painstaking and the retail wine buyers who have freely given of their time to help him have my thanks. I'd also, perhaps unusually for a journalist, like to thank certain secret agents who must remain nameless – but these press and public relations people know who they are. These are the ones who have NOT been spinelessly smarmy but genuinely helpful without making a nuisance of themselves. I am grateful for their indulgence of my obsession with my readers' interests, rather than theirs.*

# FULLERS

It is now three years since Roger Higgs first parked his feet under the wine buyer's desk at Fullers. He was made an offer he couldn't refuse, he says. As the directors of this somewhat traditional, family-owned west London brewery are unlikely to have been dangling Mr Higgs by his feet from Hammersmith Bridge at the time, one can fairly assume that it was the attractiveness of the challenge that lured him away from Oddbins where he was an assistant buyer. As he promised he would, Mr Higgs has overseen significant changes at Fullers in those three years. (His modesty constrained him from adding he might be the instigator of these changes.)

The main task as he saw it was to enhance Fullers' credentials as a wine merchant. He wanted to bring the entire estate up to the standards of the company's top forty flagship wine shops. Some of the dowdier 'beer and fag' shops have had to go, closing when their leases expired, while new shops have opened. The chain overall has grown and now numbers seventy-one links. The Higgs Project, as one might term it in Hollywood parlance, also included developing staff wine knowledge and in-store communication and the achievements in this area, as reported in last year's book, are highly creditable.

But important though these considerations are, it is in the quality and style of the product range itself that the fruits of Mr Higgs's orchard must surely first be judged. This is not simply a question of whether he is a good judge of wine. As Mr Higgs himself points out, wine buyers today have to be far more than just good wine tasters. A wine buyer has to seek out the producers who are going to be able to supply products that will set the retailer apart. 'There are two types of business now,' says Roger Higgs of the people who make their living by selling him and other retail wine buyers their wines. 'There's the old-fashioned business where someone comes in and says, "Here's our price-list" and they show you a list of names. It's just, "This is what we've got and if by some fluke you happen to like it well that's great but if not we'll just keep pattern-bombing you with things that might be good for you or might not."'

I should point out at this juncture, if it has not already become apparent, that Roger Higgs is a down-to-earth sort of bloke who speaks it like it is. Exuding youthful enthusiasm and worldly discernment in roughly equal measure, when he sees a spade he calls it a spade, reserving rather more colourful vocabulary for those in the wine trade whose methods he perceives to be outmoded and obsolete. More and more he is looking for market-aware wine producers and agents who will provide the interesting, distinctive and value-for-money products which he believes today's consumers crave. He continues: 'Then there is the other type of business which is proactive. They will work with you on projects to produce what you want. People don't produce a car in Japan and then send it over here and find out that everyone's too tall to get in it. They actually go and look at the market and do some research and find out what people want and need and the more proactive people in the wine business are doing that. The good guys are the ones who are switched on and know where the business is going. They will bend over backwards.' Elasticity – isn't it what many a stiffened sinew of the British business establishment has been forced to acquire in the past five years?

At the moment wines that have been specially tailored to Fullers' requirements by enlightened suppliers still represent a relatively small proportion of the total range in the shops – perhaps no more than 10 per cent – but it is an area of the business which Roger Higgs wants to build up. And who can blame him when such collaborative ventures can produce such scrumptious wines as the Vina Caliza Oak-Aged Tempranillo.

This aromatic, velvety wine rates 16 points without trying and is embarrassingly good value at £3.99. But it only came about through close co-operation between Roger Higgs and his Valdepenas supplier, Felix Solis. Mr Higgs asked for this wine to be aged for just four months in brand-new oak barrels rather than going through a longer ageing in older oak barrels, as is customary in the Valdepenas region. 'They don't need to include the cost of the barrels in the cost of the wine because they would have had to buy those barrels for their traditional wines anyway,' says Mr Higgs with the sparkle of a man who likes to get value for money. In fact, it positively benefits the producer. Brand-new barrels generally have too much oak character for the longer-aged wines and have to be used judiciously at the outset whilst the stringent oak character ameliorates. Vina Caliza therefore represents a rather convenient way to soften up the barrels and make them less aggressive to wine which will languish therein for years.

It's a strikingly simple idea, almost ridiculously obvious once broached. But that is so often the case with bright ideas. They seem so simple after inception. 'Anyone could have borrowed that idea,' the cynics may sneer (adding that the practice has been routine in Rioja for years), but it still needs implementing and seeing through. In fact, Roger Higgs seems to have a knack for implementing simple ideas and turning them into successful projects. I am reminded of a story he once told me of his time at Oddbins when he simply took a bottle of unwooded Australian grenache to a producer in Navarra where the same grape variety, Garnacha, is grown, and said 'Make me a wine like this, sport, and it'll sell like hot cakes.' The result was a delicious bottle at a delicious price (not a black look from the producer and a stern request to please remove the filthy New World muck from his premises).

There are a number of other examples of innovative, collaborative projects between Fullers and its suppliers, though quite a few of them are so recent that some of the wines are only in the development stage. He has recently briefed the South African producer,

Bellingham, to produce a very limited edition barrel-fermented Chardonnay, just 250 cases. Roger Higgs admits that this is something of a 'pain in the arse' for Bellingham. (Pain in the butt would have been the politer, arguably wittier, term but Higgsy, as certain puerile wine hacks insist on calling him, is ever the straight talker.) The producer is, however, happy to oblige because of the spirit of partnership and co-operation which has blossomed between the two of them – something of a South African battle cry in other respects as well. Incidentally, a number of retailers have commented that the South Africans, possibly still lacking experience in the export game after years of isolation, tend to be less flexible than suppliers from other countries. A generalisation maybe, but not an accusation that can be levelled at Bellingham. Fullers demonstrates its commitment to the partnership by listing the Bellingham Shiraz, Chardonnay and the excellent 15.5 point Sauvignon Blanc. No doubt by now the producer's success in the UK market is regarded with green eyes by less happily married Cape wineries.

Also imminent is a commission by Fullers of a wine from New Zealand, blended and bottled under the name Okiwa Bay. The label design for this wine is a fish motif being derived from a traditional Maori design. The labelling and naming of wines is increasingly an area where buyers and producers hugely enjoy putting their heads together. As the first retailer in the UK to list Fat Bastard Chardonnay, Fullers is not short of risque humour on its wine shelves. Roger Higgs once espied an illustration on a bottle of Cotes de Gascogne depicting a man falling off a cliff. The label has subsequently been adopted for a Marsanne under the name Cotes d'Angereuses. It was while strolling with an Italian wine producer that the name of another Fullers exclusive was dreamed up. Having been shown the area where the grapes for his wine were picked, Mr Higgs asked what the area was called. 'Colle Lungo,' came the reply (tall or long hill?) and that was that; Fullers' Villa Pigna Colle Lungo Rosso delle Marche, a superbly rich and rustic tipple bursting with fruit and vibrant tannins, was christened. (Somewhat mundanely one has to admit. But we must be grateful the area wasn't called Colle di Cane Idrofobo – or Hill of the Rabid Dog. It might be baring its fangs at us on Fullers' shelves right now.)

Giving wines distinctive and humorous names and eye-catching labels is sound marketing and it is a sign of how far the wine market has come in the last five years or so that there is so much more of this innovative form of thinking. But Roger Higgs knows that the wine in the bottle always has to measure up. In fact, it may be even more important for a wine with a wacky name like Fat Bastard to deliver. 'The wine had to offer excellent value for money because if it didn't some journalist might turn round and say this is a cheap gimmick,' says Mr Higgs. 'But it isn't a gimmick. It is genuinely worth £5.99. People may buy it because of the label but they come back and repurchase it because they think it is delicious.' Yet another of the cynical persuasion, one not far from this very word processor, might respond here that it's a pity traditional French wine buyers don't bring the notion of deliciousness into the equation when they make a decision to buy a wine because of the words on the label. When was the last time you discovered scrumptiously drinkable riches in a bottle of white burgundy with the word *batard* on it? The very word, of course, upon which Fat Bastard depends for its punning effect. (A note of caution here. Bizarre nomenclature is fine when a wine, like Fat Bastard '95, is sufficiently reminiscent of a more renowned wine to make the idea work. But what of Fat Bastard '96? It is nothing like a Batard-Montrachet. Delicious, yes; elegant, without doubt; but far more lemony and less vegetal than any Batard I've ever drunk. In its defence, I suspect Thierry Boudinaud and Guy Anderson, respectively the winemaker and the English importer who jointly had the inspiration for the name, would simply say the '95 was the inspiration for a wine which will simply become a small brand which will *try* for a consistent style but not always achieve it due to differing vintage conditions.)

Another name on the Fullers shelves which may grab the eye

is a recent introduction from Burgundy itself. The unusually named Ultra 35 – sounds more like an alcopop than a serious wine – has been developed in collaboration with the Burgundian producer, Denis Philibert, with whom Fullers has worked for many years. Monsieur Philibert provides an example of co-operation and marketing nous which flies in the face of the generally held perception of Burgundian wine producers, but then Roger Higgs does believe he is 'one in a million'. Together with Mr Higgs, Denis Philibert has tasted his way through the Fullers range, sampling anything from Australian Cabernets to Chilean Pinot Noirs in the interests of research. He is reportedly a big fan of Cono Sur. Mr Higgs asked him to make a smallish parcel of barrel-fermented Bourgogne Chardonnay from restricted yield vines. Monsieur Philibert did not even balk when Roger Higgs said what must be virtually unthinkable treason to a Burgundian producer – 'It doesn't matter where it comes from; the name's not important.' What mattered for Mr Higgs was that Ultra 35 was trying to be (not entirely successfully in my view at nigh on nine quid a bottle) a good-value Bourgogne Chardonnay with full concentrated Chardonnay character and fresh oak undertones. For me, the wine finishes rather weakly but I applaud fully Mr Higgs's efforts and I suspect the wine will improve in further vintages. The concept involved making just thirty-five barrels, using 35 per cent new oak, and fruit from vines yielding less than 35 hectolitres per hectare. The name for the wine was, then, staring them in the face. So happy with the results is Roger Higgs that a stablemate, a Pinot Noir Ultra 15, using 15 per cent new oak, is now in the offing (which isn't yet ready to taste).

Where, one conjectures, will it all end? What do the stuffy line law strategists and academicians think of it all? I have been unable to winkle out a view from the authorities. These Frogs are, remember, the old farts (now there's a good name for a new style Nuits-St-Georges for you!) who frown on expressions like le weekend and le parking. At a different stage of historical relations between Britain and France one would have felt concerned for

Mr Higgs's head should he have wagged it within the environs of Paris.

Fuller Smith & Turner plc
Griffin Brewery
Chiswick Lane South
London
W4 2BQ
Tel 0181 996 2000
Fax 0181 995 0230

# ARGENTINIAN WINE RED

**Alamos Ridge Cabernet Sauvignon, Mendoza 1994**

Dry Bordeaux style without the austerity.

---

**Bright Bros Argentine Red, Mendoza 1997**

This is a bright red wine like lipstick: it leaves a bright red mark on the consciousness. A touch devious? Crude? Yes, but very soft and sensual.

---

**Bright Brothers Tempranillo 1996**

---

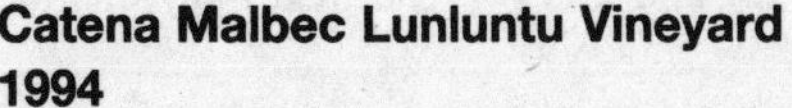

**Catena Malbec Lunluntu Vineyard 1994**

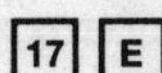

Vinified using the old shin pads of the Argentine footballer (Catena), this wine has majestic rusticity of leathery depth and richness and huge, huge fruit. But it's never coarse, always deeply elegant. A sensual wine of massive drinkability.

---

**Gran Lurton Cabernet Sauvignon 1995**

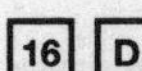

Smells like a grand cru classe Medoc of the 1950s (tobaccoey and woody). But the fruit is in much more lively array: rich, vibrant, immediate, deeply blackcurranty and polished. The final note is savoury.

---

**Malbec J&F Lurton 1996**

Ripe plums with a jagged edge. Good with food.

---

# ARGENTINIAN WINE — WHITE

**Alamos Ridge Chardonnay 1995** 

Big, chewy, terrific whiplash edge to the fruit making it good with food and in very good balance.

---

**Bright Bros Argentine Dry White, Mendoza NV** 

It seems basic as it approaches the palate but once safely tucked away down the gullet a gorgeous creamy feeling suffuses the soul.

---

**Catena Chardonnay, Agrelo Vineyard 1995**  

Very complex medley of fruit flavours – pineapple, pear – with nuts, cream, woodsmoke – and it is gorgeous texturally, neither overripe nor too oily.

---

**La Rural Pinot Blanc 1996**  

Clean and crisp with a lovely smack of tangy fruit undercutting it all. Better than Muscadet, Sancerre and so much else . . .

---

# AUSTRALIAN WINE — RED

**Basedow Barossa Shiraz 1994** 14 E

---

**Best's Great Western Dolcetto 1994** 15.5 E

---

**Best's Victoria Shiraz 1996** 11 D

So much livid fruit is surely a bit rich for a penny change out of seven quid.

---

**Chalambar Victoria Shiraz 1992** 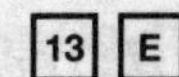

Interesting initially but . . . too ripe? Too anxious? Too pricey? Yep. All of these things.

---

**Four Sisters Grenache, McLaren Vale 1995** 

Interesting sisterly, slightly soppy quartet, armless but shapely, and if only it had more raciness to its conversation it might be better value.

---

**Grant Burge Old Vine Shiraz 1995** 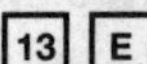

So ripe you could almost eat it with fruit cake.

---

**Hardys Bankside Shiraz 1994** 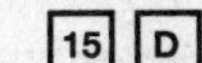

Soft yet rich and dry. Rather expensive but expressive.

---

**Hardys Nottage Hill Cabernet Sauvignon/ Shiraz 1995** 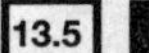

Hmm . . . okay, but a fiver?

---

**Jackdaw Ridge Shiraz/Cabernet 1996** 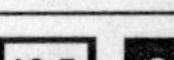

Very jammy and ripe with a hint of undergrowth where teenage louts stubbed their fags out.

---

**Lindemans Bin 45 Cabernet Sauvignon 1995** 13 D

I suppose one can imagine toying with a glass, but the wine tries to be liked so unimaginatively, it's embarrassing. I prefer more character in wine, as in people – especially at this price.

---

**Penfolds Bin 2 Shiraz/Mourvedre 1995** 15.5 D

Rich, dry, stylish, this has fluidity of fruit yet tannic firmness of tone.

---

**Penfolds Rawson's Retreat Bin 35 1995** 13.5 C

Respectable rather than raunchy.

---

**Peter Lehmann Barossa Grenache 1996** 14 C

Odd sort of fruit. You could try polishing your boots with it. Might get a shine there.

---

**Rosemount Estate Cabernet Sauvignon 1995** 14 D

Stylish and drinkable but a touch expensive.

---

**Rosemount Estate Shiraz 1995** 13.5 D

Plum and strawberry jam. Where's the tannin gone to? Oh, it's there. You just can't appreciate it under all that jam.

---

**Rosemount Shiraz/Cabernet 1996** 15.5 C

So soft and slip-downable it may be a crime.

---

**Rouge Homme Richardsons Red Block, Coonawarra 1994** 14 E

Curious lush rich finish on dryly undertoned fruit. Delicious.

---

**Rouge Homme Shiraz/Cabernet, Coonawarra 1993** 11 D

Touch too juicy to rate in the excitement zone.

---

**Scotchmans Hill Pinot Noir, Geelong 1995** 12 E

Oh come on! Scotchmen never tasted like this.

---

**Stonewell Shiraz, Peter Lehmann 1990** 14.5 G

Lot of money, £15. Lot of cheek to ask for it. But this wine is worth the price of an M&S gentleman's shirt. It has tannin at least, and complexity.

---

**Woolshed Coonawarra Cabernet/Shiraz/ Merlot 1994** 14 D

---

# AUSTRALIAN WINE — WHITE

**Basedow Barossa Chardonnay 1995** 15.5 E

---

**Green Point Chardonnay 1996** 13.5 E

Classy, rich, textured – but not worth ten quid.

---

**Hardys Nottage Hill Chardonnay 1996** 15 C

This elegant style of Aussie chardonnay is light years ahead of the blowsy blockbusters of yesteryear.

---

**Ironstone Semillon Chardonnay, W Australia 1996** 15 D

The minerally aroma leaps up the nose and the rich fruit pours over the palate restrained in its lava-like flow by the pert acidity. A big wine which is developing – and will develop – well in bottle, it is excellent with fish dishes.

---

**Jackdaw Ridge Semillon/Chardonnay 1996** 13.5 C

Touch gawky and ill-tempered.

---

**Katnook Sauvignon, Coonawarra 1996** 15 E

Typical grassy fruit from this estate, nicely balanced by the richness of the finish. A very classy wine for fancy fish preparation (i.e. anything you wouldn't eat out of newspaper).

---

**Madfish Bay Oaked Chardonnay 1995** 12.5 E

---

**Nottage Hill Riesling 1995** 14 C

Ripe and young, spicy, musky – and good with Thai and Chinese food – but also capable of greater excitement if cellared for a couple of years.

---

**Penfolds Rawson's Retreat Bin 21 Semillon/Chardonnay/Colombard 1996** 15.5 C

Loaded with flavour and rich layers of fruit, this is a wine to put heart into the drinker.

---

**Rosemount Estate Chardonnay 1996** 15.5 D

Opulence vinified. Rather grandly fruity, proud and rich.

---

**Scotchmans Hill Chardonnay, Geelong 1995** 11 E

Named after the 5000 brave Celts who facing fifty Aboriginal warriors were boomeranged to death in 1321. This wine is their memorial. If you believe that you'll pay a tenner for this wine.

---

## CHILEAN WINE RED

**Casa Lapostolle Cuvee Alexandre Merlot 1995** 17 E

One of Chile's finest merlots. It's magnificently well endowed with deftly interwoven fruit and tannin. Masterly.

---

**Concha y Toro Merlot 1995** 16 C

Hits the spot with leathery undertone and richness. Distinguished edge to this wine and an excellent food companion.

---

**Cono Sur 20 Barrel Pinot Noir 1995** 14 E

Love the texture! The fruit's better than many a £30 Cotes de Beaune, too.

---

**Cono Sur Cabernet Sauvignon 1995** 15 C

Forget the cabernet grape – this is an extra-terrestrial grape of richness, ineffable velvety texture and tremendous length of flavour. Lovely wine.

---

**Cono Sur Pinot Noir 1996** 14 C

Gamy aroma, good texture, wild raspberry edge to the fruit, a dry finish – this is an admirable pinot to please buffs as well as normal human slurpers.

---

**Cono Sur Pinot Noir Reserve 1995** 14 D

---

**Cono Sur Reserve Cabernet 1994** 14 D

Goodness, I havered over what rating to give this wine. It's the price which gives me the headache – not the fruit: is it reasonable? Well, it's a quiet rather than an exuberant bottle but it is in good order.

---

**Explorer Pinot Noir, Concha y Toro 1996** 16.5 C

I admit it, freely. Sentiment plays a part in rating this remarkable little wine: it reminds me of a Mercurey I drank looking into the eyes of a remarkably beautiful woman in June 1968. I married her. The texture, aroma and bitter cherry and nutty finish of this are delicious. Call me a romantic? Never!

---

**La Palma Merlot 1996** 15 C

No tannin? You might think so until a few seconds after the fruit (soft and cuddly) has gone down the throat – and then your lips start to pucker inside. Only subtle, this effect.

---

**La Palma Reserve Cabernet/Merlot 1996** 16 C

Ooh . . . just as you think this is standard Chilean fruit it turns a bit brutal and sarcastic as it goes down the throat. Got some character, this wine.

---

**Louis Felipe Edwards Reserve Cabernet Sauvignon 1994** 17 D

Sheer chutzpah: fruity, rich, chocolatey, consummately drinkable. Fabulous texture of suede and velvet.

---

**Pupilla Luis Felipe Edwards Cabernet Sauvignon 1997** 16.5 C

Captivating and haunting stuff. Has a lovely textured ripeness but the tone of the thing as it descends, and then lingers, is like Bach on the organ.

---

**Santa Ines Cabernet/Merlot 1995** 16 C

Lovely, dry, rich, savoury depth and balanced attack of elements. Great savoury edge – almost like an elegant, vinous Marmite.

---

**Terra Noble Merlot 1995**  C

Sensual in texture, eye-catching in colour, nose-enticing in aroma, throat-catching in fruit, this is a bottle of wine as wine ought to be at a fiver.

---

**Valdivieso Malbec 1996** 17.5 C

Wonderful wine! Quite wonderful! The texture is the softest velvet, the fruit is exquisite plum and blackberry, the balance is poised.

---

**Valdivieso Reserve Cabernet Franc 1995** 15.5 E

Loads of cherry/raspberry fruit with soft, rich tannins perfectly poised in attendance – ready but not servile. A gorgeous wine.

---

**Valdivieso Reserve Cabernet Sauvignon 1994** 13.5 D

---

**Valdivieso Reserve Pinot Noir 1995** 12 D

Too ripe and slaphappy.

---

# CHILEAN WINE WHITE

### Concha y Toro Gewurztraminer 1996 

A sipping gewurz, not a spicy food one. The smell is of rotting melon gone haywire and spicy in the sun. The fruit is boyish and flirty, with a suggestion of spice not fully achieved on the finish. Overall an untypical gewurz, quite delicious.

---

### Errazuriz Sauvignon Blanc 1996 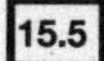 

Surprisingly delicious and richly textured and yet whilst it runs away in the fruit stakes – way out in front of other sauvignons – it has enough nous to offer a hint of classic crispness amidst all that opulence.

---

### La Palma Chardonnay 1996 

Delicate yet effusive – can Chile manage this every year? This offers such soothing fruit, this wine, it's like lying in a hammock.

---

### Tocornal Chardonnay 1996 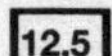 

Soon to be replaced by the 1997.

---

### Valdivieso Chardonnay 1996 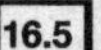 

Don't take Prozac! Drink this wine. Let the aroma stroke the nostrils, the fruit stoke up the fires of the tastebuds and the genteel texture warm the heart as it refreshes the throat.

---

### Valdivieso Reserve Chardonnay 1995 

Ignore the mish-mash of a label. The fruit is the thing: textured, ripe, rich, double-pronged, decisive and very lingering.

---

# FRENCH WINE RED

**Carignan Vieilles Vignes, Lurton VdP d'Oc 1995**

---

**Chateau Cazenuve Les Terres Rouges Pic St-Loup 1995**

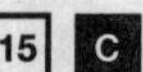


Delicious oddity. Touches of old mountain ham to the fruit.

---

**Chateau de Lancyre Coteaux du Languedoc 1996**

Lovely ripe cherry finish. Ripe fruits, hints of leather footwear and herbs, and very juicy in texture.

---

**Chateau de Lancyre Grande Cuvee Pic St-Loup 1995**

Soft, ripe, more gooey than the other Pic St-Loup wines at Fullers but this in no way damns it. It triumphs, where many Aussies fail, in the soft, ripe stakes.

---

**Chateau Grand Renouil Canon, Fronsac 1994**

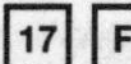


Very classy, classic claret with a touch of coffee. Great dry herbiness, big rich tannins, and that tobacco-edge to it all is just wonderful. A brilliant posh roast-lamb dinner-party-with-candle-light wine. Twelve quid very well spent here.

---

**Chateau Haut Bages Monpelou, Pauillac 1994**

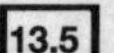

Touch disappointing with the texture. It sags on the finish, gently – even though the tannins grip.

---

**Chateau Les Pins, Cotes du Roussillon Villages 1995** 15.5 D

Elegantly labelled as it is fruited: rich, dry, herby, only marginally rustic . . . but the finish! It goes on forever.

---

**Chateau Ste Agnes Pic St-Loup 1995** 18 D

Brilliant stuff. Rates only a half point less than last year which was world class. What did I say last year? 'The flavour just goes on and on. It lingers like a rich remark by Peter Ustinov and it is just as remarkably fat, individual, deep, highly intelligent and immensely rewarding company. Fantastic value at seven quid.' The '95 is not a let-down.

---

**Domaine de l'Ameilland Cairanne, Cotes du Rhone Villages 1995** 15.5 D

Shoe-leather aroma leads to beautifully brisk-edged yet soft-finishing, rustic red of class and richness. Delightful thwack of dry concentrated fruit on the finish.

---

**Domaine de Serame Syrah, VdP d'Oc Lurton 1995** 15.5 C

---

**Roq Dur Unfiltered Syrah VdP d'Oc 1996** 15.5 B

The three black-robed monks on the label, thinly disguised as rakes, refuse to show their faces and this is a pity. Whoever made this classy yet rich rustic masterpiece should be feted in public.

---

**Touraine Gamay, Paul Buisse 1996** 12 C

Useful bottle, when empty, to keep under the bed in case burglars break in – especially Frenchmen trying to charge too much for their wine.

---

**Valreas Domaine de la Grande Bellane, Cotes du Rhone Villages 1996 (organic)** 13.5 D

Is this getting juicier? Or am I just getting crustier?

---

**Winter Hill VdP de l'Aude 1996** 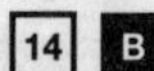

Light, dry, very demure, very drinkable.

---

## FRENCH WINE WHITE

**Bourgogne Chardonnay, Joseph Bertrand 1996** 13.5 C

Respectable stab at excitement but it barely breaks the skin. More passion next vintage, s'il vous plait.

---

**Bourgogne Chardonnay Ultra 35 1995** 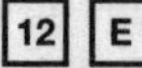

I wish the fruit were as heavy as the glass used to make the bottle.

---

**Chateau de Lancyre Pic St-Loup, Coteaux du Languedoc 1996**  

A perfect little rose. Delicate yet food-friendly, fresh yet fruity, stylish yet easily approachable.

---

**Chateau Haut Grelot Premieres Cotes de Blaye 1996**  

Hints of grass amongst the mineralised, faintly saline fruit. Excellent fish wine of some class.

---

**Chateau Lacroix Merlot Rose 1996**  C

Not indecent if not entirely wanton.

---

**Chateau Les Quints Sauternes 1994 (50cl)** 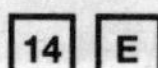

---

**Coteaux du Layon Chaume, Domaine de Forges 1996** 16 E

I love wine like this: touches of wet wood, earth, honey, mineralised acids and glycerine-rich edges. But it isn't everyone's cup of tea – until, perhaps, 2008 AD, when it might well rate 18 points.

---

**Domaine des Martins Terret/Sauvignon, VdP d'Oc 1996**

Terrific fish wine of some style. Has faint touches of earthy character but it's mainly clean and fresh.

---

**Domaine Vieux Manoir de Maransan, Cotes du Rhone 1996**

A modern version of the earthy Rhone-style white – it's fruity, bustling, polished, and crisp to finish.

---

**Fat Bastard Chardonnay VdP d'Oc 1996**

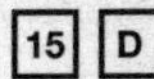


I went out and bought a few bottles of this wine after I'd tasted it. Its lemon edge and subtle melon richness were perfect for a fish dish I planned to cook. N.B. if a wine writer spends his own money he really likes a wine.

---

**J F Lurton Domaine des Salices Viognier, VdP d'Oc 1994**

---

**James Herrick Chardonnay VdP d'Oc 1996**

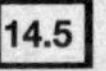


New World restrained by Old World coyness. A chardonnay of subtlety and crisp fruit which is always nicely understated.

---

**Macon Davaye Domaine des Deux Roches 1995**

Terrific white burgundy for the money. Shows opulence without fatness, vegetality and great subtlety and style.

---

**Pouilly Fuisse Clos du Chalet 1995** 13 E

Amusing presumption.

---

**Rhone Valley VdP de Vaucluse 1996** 14 B

Clean, crisp, very fresh and terrific with shellfish.

---

**Sancerre Cuvee Flores, Vincent Pinard 1996** 12 E

Oh come on, Roger! Over nine quid for this wine isn't on – please fax Sancerre immediately.

---

**Sancerre Domaine Durand 1996** 13 D

Oh well – what do you expect of sancerre nowadays?

---

**Sauvignon Cotes de Duras 1996** 15 C

What a knife-edge fresh sauvignon! It's more cutting and decisive than many a higher-priced chic beast from the Loire.

---

**Winter Hill VdP de l'Aude 1996** 15.5 B

Difficult, with this wine's assertive mineral-sharpened fruit, to imagine anything tastier with fish grimily blackened from the grill.

---

## GERMAN WINE WHITE

**Kirchheimer Schwarzerde Beerenauslese 1994 (half bottle)** 15 C

---

**Serrig Herrenberg Riesling Kabinett, Bert Simon 1995** 13.5 D

More fruit than acid but quite complex in both departments. I'd be inclined to drink it in 2005 – when it should rate 16 points at least.

---

## HUNGARIAN WINE — WHITE

**Eagle Mountain Irsai Oliver 1996**

B

Has the hint of peachy fruit and an undertone of muscat grapiness. A delicate aperitif.

---

## ITALIAN WINE — RED

**Briccolo Cabernet del Friuli 1995**

D

Like it up-front – don't see it justifying six quid on the finish.

---

**La Luna e I Falo, Barbera d'Asti 1994**

There are times when the drinker, wishing to avoid the heavy demands of an affair or even marriage, requires a light but meaningful flirtation with fruit. Here it is.

---

**La Luna Nuova Montepulciano d'Abruzzo Casalbordino 1995**

So drinkable you could bathe in it and drown. Lots of soft fruit here.

---

**Villa Pigna Colle Lungo Rosse delle Marche 1995**

Gorgeous cherry/plum/blackcurrant fruit with vibrant tannins. Brilliance of texture, richness of fruit and overall superb style. It has a terrific rustic polish.

---

## ITALIAN WINE WHITE

**Carato Chardonnay Barrique, Bidoli 1996** 15 D

Who says Italy can't produce a chardonnay with Old World texture and New World fruitiness? This is individual, balanced, deeply satisfying wine.

---

**Pinot Grigio Pecile, Friuli 1996** 13.5 C

Trim figure to the fruit but not a lot of flesh or rich curvature.

---

**Sauvignon Pecile, Friuli 1996** 15 C

The ultimate style of clean fish and shellfish wine. The tongue feels like a razor has flitted across it. Delicious! Extraordinary!

---

## NEW ZEALAND WINE RED

**Sacred Hill Basket Press Cabernet 1995** 13 E

Should be sacred at nine quid a bottle.

---

## NEW ZEALAND WINE WHITE

**Hunters Sauvignon, Marlborough 1996** 15 E

Elegant and lush – a beautifully manicured lawn from end to end. Not a weed in sight.

---

**Kemblefield Chardonnay, Hawkes Bay 1994** 14 D

---

**Okiwa Bay Sauvignon Blanc 1996** 14 D

Earthy, grassy, finely individual, and wonderful with a spiced crab cake and green beans with grilled almonds.

---

**Oyster Bay Marlborough Sauvignon Blanc 1996** 15 D

Richer style of Marlborough fruit with the herbaceousness tightly controlled. Rates half a point more than at Majestic, where it's slightly more expensive.

---

**Sacred Hill Barrel Fermented Chardonnay 1996** 14 E

Deliciously difficult. Is it rich? Maybe. Is it fresh? Perhaps. Is it worth the dosh? Just about.

---

**Te Awa Farm Chardonnay, Hawkes Bay 1996** 14 E

Delicately virtuous but it does flirt with being a bit of a savage.

---

## PORTUGUESE WINE — RED

**Baga Bright Brothers 1994** 14 C

---

**Quinto do Crasto Douro Tinto 1995** 15 D

It's very opulent and fruity, very soft, but never squashy or antipodeanly soppy. Gorgeous, full, amusing all the way through.

---

## SOUTH AFRICAN WINE — RED

**Bellingham Shiraz 1994** 13.5 C

---

**Clos Malverne Auret Cabernet/Pinotage 1995** 15 E

What an interesting character. Combines, on the palate, touches of rioja, barolo and the northern Rhone but, for all that, it *is* true to itself. Only South Africa would make such a wine.

---

**Fairview Cabernet Franc/Merlot 1995** 16 D

This is one of those wines the parent of teenage children retreats with to escape friction. Here, unmolested by angst, the adult can feel enthralled, entertained, titillated, and well-fruited – and the kids can go to hell.

---

**Fairview Zinfandel/Cinsault 1996** 15.5 D

Rich yet never so deep it clogs the tastebuds or the imagination. It is multi-layered and impish, very high in alcohol yet not brutal. Elegance with power here.

---

**First Cape Cinsault 1996** 14 C

Joyously bold fruit with a lovely edge. Drink it soon! It won't keep.

---

**Jacana Merlot 1995** 16.5 D

Goodness, if the texture doesn't stun you with its thick, knitted multiplicity, the fruit takes your breath away with its sheer richness yet fluidity and elegance. A wonderful merlot.

---

**Woodlands Pinot Noir 1994** 11 D

---

## SOUTH AFRICAN WINE WHITE

**Bellingham Sauvignon Blanc, Paarl 1996** 15.5 C

Terrific value for such crispness of fruit, gentle nuttiness, good balance and invigorating personality. Real class for relative peanuts. Why pay for, or drink, sancerre at twice the price?

**Bouchard Finlayson Chardonnay 1995** 13 E

As you inhale it seems to have everything. The fruit is decent, too, if a bit loose on the palate. But then it goes down and you think: hmm . . .

**Fairview Chardonnay 1996** 15 D

Now it isn't as fancy and wooded and pretentious as the Bouchard Finlayson chardonnay but it is so much more honest, well textured, and richly drinkable a wine. And it's a lot cheaper.

**First Cape Chenin Blanc 1997** 13.5 B

Fresh but not devoid of fruit. A pleasing aperitif.

**Jacana Old Bush Vine Chenin Blanc 1996** 15.5 C

What lush class here. Has demure richness, slightly creamy and smoky, and a lovely devil-may-care touch as it descends.

**Jordan Chardonnay 1995** 16.5 E

Hugely ripe, multi-faceted fruit of finesse yet great flavour and depth. Superb fruit/acid balance. Extraordinarily delicious.

**Neil Ellis Chardonnay 1996** 14 E

The finish seems unfocussed but the complexity of the fruit does provide a little excitement.

**Neil Ellis Sauvignon Blanc 1996** 14 D

Grassy and rich, most individually compacted. Difficult to rate but 14 about does it. It needs seafood.

# SPANISH WINE RED

**Berberana Oak Aged Tempranillo Rioja 1995** 13.5 C

Has a hint of rawness to it – just an edge but it does give the fruit slightly less appeal.

---

**Enate Cabernet Merlot, Somontano 1995** 14.5 C

Not quite as rampant as the aroma might suggest but the flavour is very deep and, boy, does it linger . . .

---

**Enate Reserva, Somontano 1993** 13 E

Like the tannin, don't go for the juice on the finish.

---

**Marques de Grinon Dominio de Valdepusa Syrah 1994** 16 E

A bit headmasterly at first meeting but this brusqueness turns into a dry sense of humour once the rich personality of the wine is revealed and the peppery side controlled and softened. A wine of great potency and depth. Teaches you a lesson about Spanish wine (i.e. don't underestimate it).

---

**Marques de Grinon Merlot 1994** 16 C

Rich, dry, deep, very classy, terrifically priced, this is smashing merlot of real style. It has a simple aroma but the fruit is multi-layered. The finish is profound. Good tannins here yet food-friendly.

---

**Tierra Seca Tempranillo/Cabernet Sauvignon 1995** 15.5 C

---

**Vina Caliza Oak-Aged Tempranillo 1993** 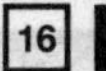

This is a really delicious wine. And I mean scrumptiously drinkable. It is aromatic, rich but not too alcoholic or soupy, finished off with touches of velvet, and it has a hint of a louche pedigree.

## SPANISH WINE — WHITE

**Castillo de Montblanc Chardonnay 1996** 

Such elegance, such texture, such fantastic value for money. This is modern Spain: fruity, crisp, soft, rich, insouciant.

**Nekeas Barrel Fermented Chardonnay, Navarra 1996** 

Wow! This is woody stylishness for you and it lingers, excites delicately and really coats the palate and the throat.

## USA WINE — RED

**Schug North Coast Pinot Noir 1995** 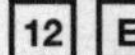

Oh well. Silly name for a wine anyway.

**Thornhill Barbera NV** 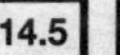

**Thornhill Pinot Noir NV** 

What a pity the juiciness of the final film fails to clinch the excitement of the trailer.

# USA WINE — WHITE

**Fetzer Bonterra Chardonnay 1995** 14.5 E

Lovely musk of melon aroma, rich and inviting, which leads to unhurried fruit of charm and poise, finishing the melony fruit with vague hints of pineapple and firmer hints of lemon. A fine, well-textured wine.

---

**Redwood Valley California Reserve Chardonnay** 13 D

---

**Schug Carneros Chardonnay 1995** 14 F

Yes, it's an absurd price to pay for a bungalow in Cleethorpes let alone a bottle of wine but it is impressively rich and well flavoured. But you can't live in it.

---

**Thornhill Chardonnay NV** 

Extraordinary grilled edge to the melony fruit. Makes a fascinating change from the usual chardonnay.

---

# FORTIFIED WINE

**Grahams 1983 Vintage Port** 17 H

A beautifully textured port of great depth, richness and softness. It finishes wonderfully with masses of flavour so insistent it is at home with blue cheese.

---

**Stanton & Killeen Liqueur Muscat (half bottle)** 15.5 D

Extraordinary balsam. Has figs, roasted hazelnuts, honey and scrapings from the strawberry jam jar thickly entwined and it's a brilliant wine for Christmas cake.

---

# SPARKLING WINE/CHAMPAGNE

**Champagne Brossault Brut NV** 16 F

This champagne is not found in any cocked hat. It is just perfect for the price.

---

**Champagne Brossault Brut Rose** 13 F

---

**Champagne Pommery 1990** 14.5 H

One of the most delicately delicious champagnes around. It is in the class of the finest bubblies from Marlborough, New Zealand. It is, alas, more than twice the price of them.

---

**Chateau de Boursault Champagne Brut** 13.5 G

Some elegance here but the price tag itches when it should soothe.

---

**Joseph Perrier Champagne NV** 13 G

Well, I'd much rather drink Fullers' cheaper champagne.

---

**Pommery Brut Royal (Champagne)** 13 G

---

**Seaview Pinot Noir Chardonnay 1993 (Australian)** 15 E

Classic styling, fresh, clean, hints of yeast on the finish, this is excellent value for money.

---

**Shadow Creek Californian Blanc de Noirs** 14.5 E

See that cocked hat? See how sodden it is? That's the champagne this terrific bubbly has knocked there.

---

**Sonoma Pacific Brut NV (USA)** 14 E

---

# MAJESTIC

It is the exception which proves the rule, as the oft-quoted and seemingly contradictory maxim has it, the idea being that it is the exception which tests the existence of the rule. I have been suggesting that there has been something of a revolution in the wine market which has transformed the way retail buyers go about their business. They are much more 'proactive', to use a sloppy business buzzword. They have wines made to order to fit what they believe their customers are looking for. They are extensively and intimately involved in the job of creating the wines. Then one comes to Majestic Wine Warehouse which doesn't really do any of this. The exception.

That is not to say that Majestic is any less clear about what its customers are looking for. Quite the contrary. But Majestic believes its job is to find interesting wines which provide quality and value for money for its customers. This may involve using the widest range of sources possible, but it does not extend to creating the wines themselves. All retailers want to give value for money, but for Tony Mason, trading director, buyer and a founder of Wizard Wine which bought Majestic in 1989, it is at the root of the credo. 'I would say that we are substantially different from most of our competitors,' he says, clearly revelling in the fact. 'I have always regarded Majestic as fundamentally a trading business. We are concerned with the relation between price and quality. If there is a good deal for the punter we will go and buy it.'

Punter? Given that the word, punt, is a wine term, meaning the bottom of the bottle where the adept wine pourer often places his or her thumb, I am moved to ponder if by any remote chance this word is related to the epithet for one who purchases wine from a Majestic Wine Warehouse. I have always thought that an important gauge of the quality of a bottle is how satisfying it is to nestle one's thumb in its punt. Big, heavy bottles with enormous cavernous punts feel fantastic, while cheap, light bottles with virtually no hollow at all are far less rewarding. Of course, the former are more expensive to produce and to transport and often push up the price. Since over the years I have found many excellent wines in containers that do not do them justice, I would have to conclude that the quality of the bottle tends to say more about the cost of a wine than its value. But what of a possible connection between the words 'punt' and 'punter'? Punt is a shortened form of punty which is both the word for the iron rod used to manipulate hot glass, and also for the small, circular or oval hollow which is left on glassware when the punty or pontil is removed. The original 'punter' however was one who laid a stake against the bank in baccarat, faro or basset. As one might have predicted, no connection whatsoever. So not only have I digressed, but done so fruitlessly. But that's Majestic all over. It makes you wander and dream, just like its warehouse style operation where I have seen grown men spend hours pondering over bottles, picking them up, scrutinising labels back and front, tut-tutting at this set of bottles, humming and hawing over that set. Yes, there is no doubt about it. Majestic isn't like any supermarket wine retailer or high street merchant.

Naturally enough, then, Majestic is less bothered about creating new wine concepts and marketing them to the consumer than its competitors. If a wine is exclusive to Majestic it is very often because the company has bought up the entire parcel rather than having the wine made to order. 'We spend a vast percentage of our buying budget on parcels and tranches of stock and deliver very good value for money for our customers,' Mr Mason continues. This virtue, if it is such, was even enshrined in the offer document published to encourage the purchase of shares in the company following its flotation on the Alternative

Investment Market and conversion to a PLC last November. It read: 'In addition to a core range of some 360 wines, Majestic specialises in purchasing one-off parcels of wine, which offer the customer both additional variety and value.' Any shareholder will be cheered to note that Majestic's sales are 60 per cent up on last year's and one suspects that the five new stores opened are just the trickle in a measured flood of expansion.

For a perfect demonstration of the company's cute buying policy at work, you need look no further than its current range of Swedish clarets. Swedish clarets? Yes, indeed: rare things. Have we just entered the Twilight Zone of winemaking where tannic and complex red wines can be produced in the frozen tundra? It is definitely time to be taking global warming seriously if Cabernet Sauvignon is now flourishing in Scandinavia. Allow me to clarify. The Swedish clarets of which I speak are those which Tony Mason has cleverly acquired from the Swedish State Monopoly which is selling off surplus stock in advance of privatisation, at silly prices. There are as many as seven different Bordeaux wines on the Majestic list which have been acquired by this route and in many cases the silly prices are being passed on to its customers.

Certain Scandinavian white spirits or 'akvavits' complete their ageing by being transported in cask around the world in the hold of a ship, the combination of gentle rolling and climatic change giving them their unique character. Whether shipping claret to the UK via Sweden has the same improving effect I cannot say, but among the wines which Majestic has purchased through Mr Mason's Swedish connections there are some real crackers. Look out for Chateau Coufran Haut Medoc 1990, ready-to-drink with plenty of fruit but character and backbone too; it rates 14 points. The 1992 from the same chateau was even more vibrant and tannic and scored 15 points. The Chateau de Lisse St Emilion 1989 costs £7.99 but it's a classic St Emilion, dry and fruity but not intimidating, earning 15 points. It is in finding such obscure gems that Majestic looks to set itself apart rather than in the creation of new products. As Tony Mason puts it: 'We are traders. The wine business is enormously fragmented. There is always someone that wants to turn wine into cash.'

It is only on very rare occasions that Majestic will request a wine to be made to a certain specification. One recent example was a request for Guy Anderson to produce Big Frank's Viognier. Guy Anderson also worked with Majestic in Bordeaux, coming up with the Claret Lot 278 and the more recent Sauvignon Lot 279. Both were wines specifically produced for Majestic. The retailer is now looking at the possibility of having some wines made to order in South Africa. However, such examples are fairly few and far between.

But what of the 'new generation' of wines? Is Majestic being left behind by not sending flying winemakers to La Mancha to create luscious Cabernet/Tempranillo blends with take-the-piss labels? Not in Tony Mason's view. He believes that the creation of all these wines is something of a bandwagon and while some very good wines have been made, there is a 'sameness' about some of the so-called innovation. 'There is a good parallel with the car business,' he explains. 'If all cars are designed in a wind tunnel then all cars will look the same.' Mr Mason may have a point. If all buyers go looking for wines with similar characteristics, such as soft tannins, full fruit and low acidity, then the likelihood is that the wine market will begin to homogenise. 'You end up with claret tasting like Languedoc-Roussillon and a Languedoc-Roussillon tasting like a wine from Australia. You are getting a sameness running through the industry.'

Tony Mason says the Majestic range has been influenced by general trends in the wine market and the more hands-on approach of other retailers. As supermarket and off licence buyers have demanded new styles of wines, these styles rapidly become the norm in the wine industry. 'Both in style and presentation we pick up some of the things that the supermarkets have achieved. For us it is a question of emphasis.'

The emphasis at Majestic is on the more traditional end of the market. This always seems at odds with a retailer which in so many other ways seems to have such a bright and breezy attitude. The ambience in Majestic's 'no frills' stores may be informal but measured by what is on the shelves they are wine toffs through and through. Over 50 per cent of its range is from France. Majestic sells 100,000 cases of burgundy a year, more than its sales of Australian and New Zealand wines combined. I am not privy to the intimacies of retailers' sales data but I am assured that if there is any other retailer in this book who flogs more Burgundian wine than Australian then my research assistant, Ben Cooper, is prepared to eat his hat covered in chilli sauce whilst standing starkers on Clapham Common.

In fact, in terms of its range Majestic has far more in common with the old-fashioned kind of wine merchant and that, says Mr Mason, should not be surprising. 'We are modern traditional wine merchants,' he says, to a degree confirming that contradiction between the retailer's outward image and its choice of wines. As I have previously written, this traditional style of wine merchant, frequently a pin-striped dinosaur, has become virtually extinct because it has lost its core market, its natural habitat, of predominantly male, middle-class professionals. Majestic's research, coupled with the fact that the chain has grown from thirty-eight stores to fifty-nine in the past five years, suggests that these consumers have not all taken the vow but are now shopping at Majestic where Tony Mason sees that they are well catered for. 'Their tastes are probably a bit more classic than the twenty- to thirty-year-old supermarket consumers,' he says, carefully adding that Majestic aims to cater for those consumers' needs as well. But crucially this does not mean selling wines that have been 'conceived' to appeal to those tastes. 'We want winemakers to present us with wines they think we can sell, ready made and ready to sell. It isn't a buyer's job to spend weeks with the winemaker. The best winemakers understand what their consumers want. We do sell wines which have been made by winemakers with the UK market in mind but our fundamental job as a retailer is to know what our customer base is and buy wines for them.'

It is therefore not surprising that Majestic wine buyers tend to spend less time out in the wine regions than those from other retailers. Majestic estimates that its buyers travel for about one month in a year, whereas other retail buyers may be away on average one week in every month. Majestic wine buyers do not claim to be 'frontiersmen' of the wine business. 'We are not crusaders in areas of wine production,' says Jeremy Palmer who has responsibility for South America, South Africa, New Zealand, California, the more 'down-to-earth' French wines and Eastern Europe. 'We are pragmatic merchants rather than pioneers.' And even though Mr Palmer and his colleagues do find themselves in far-flung, exciting and awe-inspiring locations, the retailer does most of its final wine selection back in the less picturesque setting of its tasting room at Majestic HQ in Watford. This is probably no bad idea. I can vouch for the fact that tasting a wine on the veranda of a palatial villa overlooking Tuscan vineyards and olive groves or a carefully landscaped South African estate can do wonders for a wine. If, however, the wine still stands up when being sampled in a rather cramped tasting-room where formica surfaces and polystyrene tiles have replaced oak and marble, it is probably pretty decent. It also allows the Majestic buying team to taste as a panel.

But while it is clear that Majestic is capable of finding very decent wines which fit its quality and value requirements, it is remarkable that it has so little need for tailored projects, especially when one considers how wine marketing has changed. After all, when the other retailers have wines specially made for them, it is not just the liquid in the bottle which concerns them, but also the outward appearance, the packaging, the name – the concept as it is grandly called. While Tony Mason concedes that in this regard not being an active 'commissioner' of wines could be to Majestic's disadvantage, he remains sceptical about such marketing innovation. 'Packaging and presentation is important and what looks good sells,' he says. 'Whether looking good is calling something Fat Bastard I wouldn't know.' This is a reference to that fine wine from the South of France, Fat Bastard Chardonnay, which incidentally Majestic sells.

While he clearly values high standards in packaging and labelling, one gets the impression that Tony Mason can live with bottles having a slightly drabber on-shelf appearance if value and quality are being maintained. His thinking here is that specialist wine retailers have staff on hand to point customers in the right direction with 'informed, intelligent advice', so wines do not necessarily have to shout their case from the shelves with eye-catching and colourful labels. 'If we find a good wine with a grotty label we would still buy it because we have the staff who can sell the wines,' he says. 'That is what being a specialist ought to be about.' The thought also occurs that the stores themselves are clearly not designed with visual appeal as a priority. People are not attracted to Majestic by its looks, but by its mind. 'Over 80 per cent of store staff are graduates,' I seem to remember reading in the share offer document. As it happens, the fact that the stores often look a little untidy adds a certain cluttered charm and may even put customers at their ease.

Tony Mason is reassuringly consistent. He flies in the face of almost every convention which has emerged from looking at the buying policies of the major wine chains. While his opposite numbers have spoken at length of the importance of establishing long-term partnerships, Mr Mason prefers to keep himself more aloof. As a trader, he wants to move around freely from supplier to supplier, one might even call him promiscuous, and if he does end up working with people over a long period of time it would appear to be more by accident – and the fact that they have continued to meet his demands on quality and price – than by design. 'I am very suspicious of long-term partnerships,' he says. 'Traders want to trade and that is what makes the business hum. When people start talking about nebulous relations that go on for years I am a touch sceptical.' The wine market and the choice of wines is constantly developing, and this is naturally reflected in the make-up, appearance and style of Majestic's wines, though to a markedly lesser degree than some other retailers. The difference perhaps is that Majestic is not consciously looking to change the world it inhabits and, always guided by its consumers, is happy to move along at its own pace.

I am very happy with that pace, speaking as a Majestic customer myself. Not only is Majestic the source of my favourite calvados, it is also the place where I get my favourite mineral water (Badoit). Once, in a mad moment, I even bought some half-bottles of a lovely German wine there. What greater accolade can a wine retailer receive than that it be the place where that ultimate *parasite du vin*, the wine writer, spends his own money?

MAJESTIC WINE WAREHOUSES
Odhams Trading Estate
St Albans Road
Watford
WD2 5RE
Tel 01923 816999
Fax 01923 819105

**SEE STOP PRESS SECTION AT END OF BOOK FOR LAST-MINUTE ADDITIONS TO THIS RETAILER'S RANGE.**

## ARGENTINIAN WINE RED

### La Rural Malbec 1996

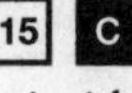


In spite of its brassy beer-labelling appearance, the wine inside is more respectably clothed in velvet-textured deep scarlet. Has a real flourish in the finish.

---

### La Rural Merlot 1996

It's the satin texture which grips the imagination as forcefully as the fruit lashes the tastebuds. Elegant yet a touch raunchy, and improving nicely in bottle. Fab.

---

## AUSTRALIAN WINE RED

### Angove's Classic Reserve Cabernet Sauvignon 1994

---

### Angove's Classic Reserve Shiraz 1995

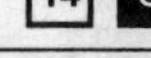

All soft, soppy soup.

---

### Cape Mentelle Cabernet Merlot 1994

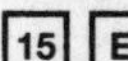

It's the texture! It's so perfectly flavour-enhancing to the fruit. Like the perfect frame to a picture.

---

### Ironstone Cabernet/Shiraz 1994

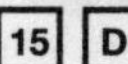


Soft as woolly socks but far more soupy and drinkable. It's very soggy in the middle but this could be said to be mere approachability. But it's decidedly flavour-packed.

---

**Lindemans Bin 45 Cabernet Sauvignon 1993 (half bottle)** 15.5 B

Splendid half of perfect food wine yet also eminently gluggable. Dry yet richly flavoured, deep, handsomely textured. Good meaty finish. A soup of a wine.

---

**Lindemans Bin 45 Cabernet Sauvignon 1995** 13 C

I suppose one can imagine toying with a glass, but the wine tries to be liked so unimaginatively, it's embarrassing. I prefer more character in wine, as in people – especially at this price.

---

**Penfolds Bin 2 Shiraz/Mourvedre 1995** 15.5 C

Rich, dry, stylish, this has fluidity of fruit yet tannic firmness of tone.

---

**Penfolds Rawson's Retreat Bin 35 Cabernet/Shiraz 1995** 13.5 C

Usual decent turnout.

---

**Preece Cabernet Sauvignon, Mitchelton 1994** 14 D

Now, this is soup. Pour it into a ladle and throw it over the teeth. It hasn't escaped from a wild animal enclosure, it's too tame for that, but it does have a tame, doggy manner.

---

## AUSTRALIAN WINE WHITE

**Angoves Classic Reserve Chardonnay 1996** 15 C

Good aroma, lovely plump texture, rich hints of melon and strawberry on the finish (subtle though this is).

---

**Cape Mentelle Semillon/Sauvignon Blanc 1996** 14.5 E

A combo of Aus/NZ and California. Thus we have grass, richness, and vegetal warmth.

---

**Ironstone Semillon/Chardonnay 1996** 16 D

Ooh! What a succulently fruity beast of richness, flavour and great depth yet amazingly cheeky freshness. Starts off like smoky melon and pineapple and finishes with a hint of creme brulee. But this is not all custard, this wine. It is palate arousing and very vibrant.

---

**Lindemans Bin 65 Chardonnay 1996** 

Delicious combination of butter, hazelnuts and melon undercut by a perfectly weighted uptide of acidity.

---

**Mick Morris Liqueur Muscat (half bottle)** 

Rich as a honey bee-hive concentrated into a single teaspoon of flavour. Has the texture of tarmac. Wonderful with Christmas pudding!

---

**Penfolds Barrel Fermented Chardonnay 1994** 15 D

Rich but balanced, sane but with an exciting eccentric undertone of exoticity subtly underpinning the more conventional top layer of fruit, this is a delicious bottle of wine.

---

**Penfolds Rawsons Retreat Bin 21 Semillon/Chardonnay/Colombard 1996**  

Richly textured, warmly fruity (some complexity on the finish where the acidity is most pertinent), this is an excellent vintage for this wine.

---

### Preece Chardonnay, Michelton 1995 — 14 D

Nutty and highly drinkable. Touch expensive for the style, which is certainly not tidal, flood-gate chardonnay. Nevertheless, has commendable elegance.

---

### Rosemount Roxburgh Chardonnay 1993 — 17 G

Yes, 17 points, 17 quid. No justice, is there? This wine is simply one of the best chardonnays in the world. It is a perfect melding of wood, fruit and acid into a delicately rich, lingering, superbly textured work of huge charm and great finesse.

---

### Rosemount Show Reserve Chardonnay 1995 — 16 E

The haute couture of this – one of Oz's most incisively delicious chardonnays – is fully in evidence. An impressive wine of assured demeanour and manner.

---

### Wynns Coonawarra Riesling 1996

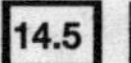

Richly energetic, developing but needing a year or more to flower fully, this is an interesting wine. Good with fish now, in a while it'll be tremendous.

---

### Yalumba Family Reserve Chardonnay 1995 — 14 E

If this is the family's reserve how come we get to try it? It's rich and deep and very good with mussels.

---

## CHILEAN WINE — RED

### Arlequin Merlot, Maipo 1996

Utterly delicious: ripe, dry, polished, rich, deep and so drinkable you wonder if it shouldn't carry a health warning.

---

**Carta Vieja Antigua Cabernet Sauvignon 1994** 14.5 C

A faraway hint of rich custard on the soft, easy-going fruit. Very easy to like such friendly wine.

---

**Carta Vieja Merlot 1996** 15.5 C

---

**Carta Vieja Vino Tinto 1995** 16 B

Fabulous wine to get everyone roaring at Christmas. Beautifully fruity, great fun to drink, brilliantly priced.

---

**Felipe Edwards Cabernet Sauvignon Reserva 1994** 16.5 D

It makes you wonder what the cabernet fruit does to make itself so smooth, beautifully textured, finely flavoured, classic yet drinkable. Made from grapes grown on another planet.

---

**Santa Rita Reserva Cabernet 1994** 15 C

---

**Undurraga Cabernet Sauvignon 1996** 14 C

The final flourish of fruit leaves it very late as it goes down the throat. Very drinkable and dry yet cosily rich.

---

**Undurraga Merlot 1995** 14 C

Not tasting so well as it was last year. Seems rather mild and unadventurous.

---

**Undurraga Pinot Noir 1995** 14 C

Not exactly classic pinot but it is firmly in the camp of wines it is a great pleasure to quaff with or without food. Piles on the richness and flavour most agreeably.

---

## CHILEAN WINE WHITE

**Carta Vieja Antigua Chardonnay, Maule 1996** 13 C

**Carta Vieja Vino Blanco 1996** 15.5 B

Utterly delicious sauvignon with a cleanness of fruit, picked out by a subtle melonyness and undercut by crisp, gently herbaceous acidity. Brilliant.

**Undurraga Chardonnay 1996** 13 C

**Undurraga Chardonnay Reserva 1995** 14 D

Good frontal attack of aroma (very opulent). Finish needs smartening up. But very classy in ambition.

**Undurraga Sauvignon Blanc 1996** 13 C

## FRENCH WINE RED

**Bourgeuil Grand Mont, Druet 1990** 10 F

**Bourgeuil Rouge Les Cent Boisselees, Druet 1995** 13 E

**Bourgogne Pinot Noir Delauney 1995** 11 C

**Bourgogne Rouge, Leroy 1993** 10 E

Far too expensive. Far too.

**Cabernet Sauvignon VdP du Gard Les Garrigues 1995** 14.5 B

Fruity, dry, hints of classic cabernet stalky pepperiness and dryness. Brilliant value drinking and food companionship.

---

**Chateau Calissanne 'Cuvee de Chateau', Coteaux d'Aix en Provence 1995** 15 D

Very cleanly defined fruit which has tannins and acidity to give it weight, structure and richness – yet it possesses individuality and a herby edge. It has a suggestion of sumptuousness yet it is very slurpable.

---

**Chateau Calissanne 'Cuvee Prestige', Coteaux d'Aix en Provence 1995** 13.5 D

Not as exciting as its cheaper brother.

---

**Chateau Cantemerle Medoc 1990** 13 H

---

**Chateau Corbin-Michotte, St Emilion 1988** 14.5 G

Excellent aroma and concentration of rich fruit but only the tannin stays on the teeth – the fruit has given up. With food, this flaw will be mitigated.

---

**Chateau Coufran, Haut Medoc 1990 (half bottle)** 14 C

Delightful fruit here. Immediately drinkable and smooth yet not untypical (i.e. has some character and backbone).

---

**Chateau Coufran, Haut Medoc 1992 (half bottle)** 15 B

More vibrancy and greater tannic alertness and food versatility than the '90. Very dry.

---

**Chateau Coufran, Haut Medoc 1993 (half bottle)** 13.5 C

Somewhat vegetal and austere.

---

**Chateau de Birot Premieres Cotes de Bordeaux 1989 (half bottle)** 15.5 C

Perfect age, perfect depth of flavour and tannic evolvement and the fruit isn't at all arthritic or lonely. It loves food and elegant conversation. A gorgeous wine.

---

**Chateau de Flaugergues Coteaux du Languedoc 1995** 14 D

---

**Chateau de Lisse, St Emilion 1989** 15 E

Cor! It's good! Perfect maturity, texture and weight of fruit. Very drinkable, dry yet fruity, classic yet not intimidating.

---

**Chateau de Lisse, St Emilion 1993 (half bottle)** 14 C

One of those halves for the hedonist whose wife and family have deserted him for the evening and in revenge he enjoys this wine all to himself – with a lamb chop strewn with garlic and herbs.

---

**Chateau de Luc Corbieres 1995** 13.5 C

---

**Chateau du Trignon Gigondas 1994** 14 E

Expensive but gets the rating in the end because the finish is lingering and fairly complex – and deliciously double-edged.

---

**Chateau du Trignon Sablet, Cotes du Rhone Villages 1995** 14 D

Not as gooey as its initial jamminess suggests. No Sablet, with its herby richness, could ever be quite that.

---

**Chateau Heroult, Bordeaux Superieur 1990** 13.5 C

Excellent value for beef-casserole eaters.

---

**Chateau l'Eveche Pomerol 1993** 15 E

---

**Chateau Labegorce, Margaux 1988** 12 G

Juicy, but a lot of loot for dry juice.

---

**Chateau Ladignac, Medoc 1990** 14 D

Delicious with roast beef – if anyone still eats it.

---

**Chateau Le Fournas Bernadotte, Haut Medoc 1989** 12.5 E

Lot of money – not a lot of excitement.

---

**Chateau Soudars, Haut Medoc 1992 (half bottle)** 13.5 B

---

**Chateau Vieux Vantenac Bordeaux, Cotes de Francs 1989** 13 C

---

**Chateauneuf-du-Pape Domaine Pontifical 1995** 13 E

With a name like this it should be the ultimate Pope's tipple.

---

**Chenas Domaine des Pierres 1995** 13 E

---

**Chinon les Garous, Couly-Dutheil 1996** 14.5 D

Classic cabernet franc raspberry, slate-dry fruit. Great chilled.

---

**Chiroubles Domaines Desmures, Duboeuf 1995** 11 D

---

**Claret Lot 278, Bordeaux 1995** 15 C

My God! Bordeaux has not just a future and a past but, with this delicious specimen, a present!

---

**Cote Rotie, Jamet 1993** 11 G

---

**Cotes du Rhone au Lys d'Or 1996** 16 B

The '96 is more exciting aromatically, more raspberryish, plumper fruitwise, spicier and more characterful on the finish.

---

**Cotes du Rhone Villages Les Lievres 1995** 14 C

Very drinkable with nary a hint of earthiness or spiky herbiness: just soft, friendly fruit.

---

**Domaine de la Baraniere, Cotes du Rhone 1994** 15.5 C

---

**Domaine de la Janasse VdP de la Principaute d'Orange 1995** 16 D

This new vintage of this syrah/merlot masterpiece is simply gorgeous: rich, deep, complex, spicy, dry, flavour-packed, with a beautiful balance of fruit and tannin.

---

**Domaine des Murettes, Minervois 1995** 15 C

---

**Fitou Les Producteurs de Paziols 1994** 14 C

---

**Fleurie Chateau des Bachelards, Duboeuf 1995** 11 E

---

**Fortant de France Syrah Vin Nouveau 1996** 14 C

Very ripe and rubbery and convincingly soft. It will appeal to many beaujolais lovers and I rate it on this basis.

---

**Gigondas Guigal 1994** 

Fails to score higher at nigh on a tenner. Too expensive and won't improve in bottle.

---

**Jacques Frelin Crozes Hermitage 1995** 12 E

---

**La Cuvee Mythique, Languedoc 1994** 16 D

One of the Midi's most fulfilling reds: characterful, dry, rich, multi-layered, assertive yet soft and polished, witty yet down to earth. It puts scores of fancy bordeaux to immediate shame.

---

**Louis Latour Pinot Noir 1994 (half bottle)** 12 C

Light, gently raspberryish. Somewhat meagre, though, and expensive for a half bottle.

---

**Mas des Bressades Cabernet Syrah VdP du Gard 1994** 14.5 D

---

**Medoc Rothschild 1994** 10 D

Austere and most unattractive.

---

**Moulin a Vent Clos de Marechaux, Duboeuf 1995** 13.5 E

---

**Pinot Noir VdP de l'Aude Louis Page 1994** 10 C

---

**Regnie Duboeuf 1995** 10 D

---

**St Amour Domaine des Pierres, Trichard 1995** 14 E

---

**St Joseph, Bernard Gripa 1995** 12.5 E

---

**St Joseph, Colombo 1994** 13.5 E

---

**Vacqueyras Vidal-Fleury 1992** 14 E

---

**VdP de l'Herault** 12 B

Very cheap and best chilled with fish.

---

## FRENCH WINE WHITE

**Beaujolais Blanc Duboeuf 1995** 12 D

---

**Big Frank's Viognier VdP d'Oc 1996** 14 C

Not as apricoty as viogniers classically are – this one has a tinge of lime.

---

**Bourgogne Blanc, Leroy 1994** 11 E

---

**Bourgogne Chardonnay Emile Trapet 1995** 12.5 C

---

**Cante Cigale Rose de Saignee, VdP de l'Herault 1996** 12.5 C

---

**Chablis Domaine Vocoret 1995** 11 E

---

**Chablis Robert Poinsot 1995** 12 D

---

**Chablis Saint Martin, Domaine Laroche 1995** 13.5 E

---

**Chardonnay Cuvee Australienne 1996** 13.5 C

The light style of chardonnay, hardly any wood or vegetality or blowsy Aussie-style richness. But at £3.99 I miss at least one of these things being there.

---

**Chardonnay Jean de Balmont, VdP du Jardin de la France 1996** 13 B

---

**Chardonnay Vin de Pays d'Oc, Ryman 1995** 16 C

One of the Pays d'Oc's tastiest and most stylish chardonnays under a fiver. The richness is controlled, balanced and in perfect harmony with the acidity – thus the overall texture is high class.

---

**Chateau d'Aqueria, Tavel Rose 1995** 13 D

Pleasant – under a plum tree in Aix in June.

---

**Chateau de Sours Rose, Bordeaux 1996** 13.5 D

More generous than many reds, it has elegance to its fruit.

---

**Chateau Haut Mazieres Blanc, Bordeaux 1993** 14 C

**Chateau la Jaubertie Blanc, Bergerac 1995** 14.5 C

Rich, well-textured, rather more flat than bergeracs normally are but this is all to the good. A plump, English-inspired wine.

**Chateau La Rame, St Croix du Mont 1993** 14 E

Lovely honeyed fruit to go with Christmas pud.

**Chateau la Touche Muscadet Sur Lie 1995** 13.5 C

**Chateau Meaume Bordeaux Rose 1996** 13.5 C

Classy and rich – yet dry.

**Domaine de Puts, VdP des Cotes de Gascogne 1995** 15 C

Cuts a beautifully clean swathe across the tongue leaving behind the residue of pineapple and a hint of spiced pear.

**Domaine de Saint-Lannes Cotes de Gascogne 1996** 14 C

The usual delicious fresh pineapple-edged, pear-tinged fruit.

**Domaine des Salices Viognier VdP d'Oc 1996** 14.5 D

A crispish viognier with an elegance and purpose which make up for its lack of richness.

**Domaine Sainte Brune Chardonnay 1995** 13.5 C

**Gewurztraminer Beblenheim, 1995** 14 D

Good but will get better over the next couple of years.

**Grand Ardeche Chardonnay, Louis Latour 1994** 14.5 E

Best vintage yet of this wine, and improving nicely in bottle. It's showing lovely richness and invigoration of fruit and wood and the finish is lingering and handsomely evolved. A classier wine than some Latour white burgundies at three and four times the price.

---

**Macon Villages, Poireaux 1995** 13.5 C

Thoroughly decent, but not quite fruity enough. Mite dull.

---

**Marc Bredif Vouvray 1993** 13 E

---

**Materne Haegelin et ses filles Pinot Blanc 1994** 14 D

Very accommodating to Chinese food, this wine. It is aromatic, robust, rich, and multi-layered.

---

**Materne Haegelin et ses filles Riesling Cru du Bollenberg 1995** 13 D

---

**Materne Haegelin et ses filles Tokay/Pinot Gris 1995** 13 E

---

**Muscat Jose Sala** 17 C

Textured, rich, beautifully scented and flavoured, this waxy, honeyed sweet wine is brilliant for the money.

---

**Pouilly Vinzelles Tastevinage 1995** 12 E

---

**Reuilly, Beurdin 1995** 13 D

---

**Sancerre Les Mouchottes Jean Dumont 1995** 12.5 D

---

**Sauternes Rothschild 1994 (half bottle)** 10 D

**Sauvignon de St-Bris, Lamblin 1995** 14 C

Classic demureness and pointedly friendly fruit. About as far as you can get from New World fruitiness without gagging, this splendidly entrenched specimen is perfect with all manner of oceanic cuisine but especially shellfish.

**Sauvignon Lot 279, Bordeaux 1996** 15.5 C

Bargain plonking! Clean and crisp with lots of pineapple/lime acidity to boost the freshness, this is a terrific wine to sip, to slurp and to sup with any fish you can think of.

**Semillon VdP de l'Agenais 1996** 15 B

Brilliant value! Crisp and nutty with a hint of minerals on the acidity and a fruity tang on the finish. A must-buy wine for slurping and supping (i.e. with food).

**St Peray Blanc, Bernard Gripa 1995** 13 E

What is one to make of a wine as forthright, individual and bloody-minded as this for nine quid? Sip it and say 'Ah! The Frogs! How austere! How civilized! How subtle and deviously delicious!'? You may, or you may feel this is overpriced for such frail shades of meaning.

**St Romain Blanc, Drouhin 1994** 10 F

**St Romain, Roland Thevenin 1995** 12 E

**Tokay Pinot Gris Ribeauville 1995** 14.5 D

Nutty, ripe, melon/lemon, hints of peach, this is one long stream of appetite-arousing pleasure for the tastebuds.

**Touraine Sauvignon, Sica les Marriers 1995** 13.5 B

Cheap, cheering, young, fresh, great with fish and chips.

**Vacheron Sancerre Rose Les Romains 1996** 10 E

---

**Vin de Pays de Vaucluse 1996** 14.5 B

Very aromatic (pear drops) with a hint of ripe pear on the fruit which is otherwise meticulous, fresh and crisp.

---

**Vouvray Jean Dumont 1995** 13 C

I'd be inclined to let this lie on its side sleeping for three to four years and, hopefully, uncork a 15/16 point wine then.

---

## GERMAN WINE WHITE

**Deidesheimer Leinhohle Kabinett Halbtrocken 1996** 12.5 D

---

**Grans Fassian Trittenheimer Altarcher Riesling Kabinett 1993** 15 D

---

**Grans Fassians Riesling 1995** 14 D

---

**Herxheimer Herrlich, Jacob Zimmermann Kabinett 1995** 11 C

---

**Kirchheimer Schwarzerde Beerenauslese, Zimmermann-Graeff, Pfalz 1994 (half bottle)** 14.5 C

Sweet but will develop for five to eight years. Drink it now with cake.

---

**Louis Guntrum Oppenheimer Kreuz Riesling Auslese 1993** 14 D

Dare to serve it as an aperitif! Risk the neighbours elevating you to the heights of wine-buffery. Sweet? This wine? Never. It's all-over fruity and very more-ish.

---

**Ruppertsberger Hofstuck Riesling Kabinett, Winzerverein 1995** 13.5 C

Pleasant aperitif.

---

**Wehlener Sonnenuhr Riesling Spatlese, Dr Loosen 1985** 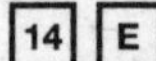

---

# ITALIAN WINE RED

**Barone Cornacchia Montepulciano d'Abruzzo 1995** 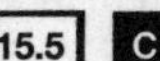

The essence of drinkable rusticity: ripe, characterful, sunny, never heavy or too dry, full of personality and sassy fruitiness.

---

**Chianti Grati, Il Cavaliere 1994** 13 C

---

**Colli di Sasso, Banfi 1995** 13.5 C

All fruit.

---

**Negroamaro de Salento, Le Trulle 1995** 14.5 C

Hints of smoke (cigar) and cherries and plums. Yet it's light and delightfully accommodating.

---

**Notarpanaro Taurino 1988** 15 C

---

**Recioto Amarone della Valpolicella, Tedeschi 1991** 13 E

Very, very attractive. The price tag, repels me, though.

---

**Sangiovese Daunia** 14 B

---

**Uva di Troia, Puglia 1995** 16 D

Has that cheeky southern Italian charm as it goes down the throat which counterpoints the rich earthiness of the fruit. A wonderful glugging bottle but also a great wine for all manner of Italian meat and vegetable dishes.

---

**Valpolicella Classico, Santepietre 1995** 14.5 C

Excellent pasta wine. Dry yet with a loose, dark cherry edge. Not your run-of-the-mill valpol by any stretch of the wallet or tastebuds.

---

**Vino Nobile di Montepulciano, Fassati 1991** 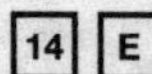

Lots of everything – including money – but it is seductively aromatic, well textured and deeply fruity. It's the sort of red Italian you feel could go straight into a risotto and produce a most compelling meal.

---

# ITALIAN WINE WHITE

**Castello di Tassarolo, Gavi 1996** 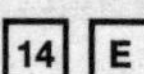

Very expensive but very elegant and finely cut. Not a big, rich wine of great depth but individual and distinctive in its own quiet but very decided manner.

---

**Chardonnay Atesino, Kym Milne 1995** 14 C

Has a creamy richness plus a decisive streak of well-ordered acidity vaguely along citric lines. Very agreeable tipple.

---

**Chardonnay del Salento Barrique, Kym Milne 1995** 16.5 D

A rich, elegant, superbly purposeful and confident wine of impressive class. Superb with scallops.

---

**Puglian Dry Muscat 1995** 14 C

Dry, restrained (not sweet and blowsily muscatty) and very delicate. Perhaps a few pennies more than it ought to be – since it is a simple aperitif (or good with scallops, curiously).

---

**Soave Classico, Santepietre 1995** 14 C

Dry, unusually so for a soave, which whilst never over-fruity is not commonly so elegant as this example.

---

**Trebbiano Daunia** 15.5 B

---

## NEW ZEALAND WINE RED

**Delegat's Cabernet Merlot 1996** 13 D

Very ripe.

---

**Linden Estate Merlot, Hawkes Bay 1995** 13 E

Expensive for the style.

---

## NEW ZEALAND WINE WHITE

**Dashwood Sauvignon, Marlborough 1996** 16 E

Dashwood's most dashing sauvignon yet. Keenly herbaceous but not overrich, concentrated gooseberry ripeness, and a decisive, balanced finish.

---

**Delegat's Chardonnay, Hawkes Bay 1996** 15.5 D

Delicious wine: stylish, bold, purposeful. The fruit is rich but not cloying, the acidity firm and delicately balanced, and the texture high-class.

---

**Linden Estate Chardonnay, Hawkes Bay 1996** 15 E

Creamy, nutty, ripe melon attack prevented from being gushing by beautiful mineral acidity. A delightful wine.

---

**Linden Estate Reserve Chardonnay 1995** 13 F

Begins like a meursault. Finishes like a Cotes de Gascogne.

---

**Linden Estate Reserve Sauvignon Blanc 1995** 13 E

Highly slurpable but not a tenner's worth of complexity.

---

**Montana Sauvignon Blanc, Marlborough 1996** 14.5 D

Good grassiness smoothly mown and well tended. Loss of impact on the finish but too individual and decently fruity to rate less.

---

**Nautilus Chardonnay, Marlborough 1994** 15.5 E

---

**Oyster Bay Chardonnay, Marlborough 1996** 14.5 E

Demure, well-fruited, and extremely delicious. Puts fresh heart into the most jaded of palates.

---

**Oyster Bay Sauvignon, Marlborough 1996** 14.5 D

Lime and pineapple complete the job of this nicely grass-edged fruit. Very attractive all round.

---

**Twin Islands Chardonnay 1995** 13 D

Rather gawky finish to the fruit.

---

**Twin Islands Sauvignon Blanc 1996** 15 D

---

**Whitecliff Sauvignon Blanc, Sacred Hill 1996** 13 D

Like a four-quid Southern French wine – not a Kiwi sauvignon.

---

## PORTUGUESE WINE RED

**Bright Brothers Estremadura 1994** 13 C

---

**Duas Quintas, Douro 1993** 15.5 D

Very individual and striking. Has a delightful tannic shroud of dryness concealing pure, rich fruit of great softness.

---

## PORTUGUESE WINE WHITE

**Joao Pires Muscat 1995** 15.5 C

---

## SOUTH AFRICAN WINE RED

**Drostdy-Hof Merlot 1995** 15 D

Rich, dry, well packed with flavour. A real merlot in all ways but one – it isn't of the leathery persuasion, more the denim.

---

**Gemsbok Cinsault/Ruby Cabernet 1996** 14 C

A thick, soupy, slightly burnt-rubbery red which is good with pasta smothered in a pungent sauce (like pesto).

---

**Kiesenhof Pinotage, Paarl 1995** 13.5 C

Lacks an element of tannicity to its soupiness and so will be vanquished by food.

---

**La Motte Millennium 1993** 14 E

Juicy at first sip, then it turns dry, tannic and rich. Perhaps a touch expensive for the length of the ride.

---

**Meerendal Pinotage 1994** 13.5 D

---

**Neil Ellis Cabernet Sauvignon 1993** 13.5 E

---

**Two Oceans Cabernet Sauvignon/Merlot 1996** 

Delicious glug with huge food-compatibility. Dry, rich and savoury.

---

## SOUTH AFRICAN WINE WHITE

**Blue Hills Chardonnay 1996** 13.5 C

Hard-to-catch fruit with a hint of lemon. Reasonably welcoming as it arrives but it departs rather brusquely. Hardly your classic chardonnay but useful pitched against rich fish dishes.

---

**Fleur du Cap Sauvignon Blanc 1995** 15 C

Taut, well-defined crispness and subtle grassiness with a nutty edge. A decent sauvignon blanc with a gently exotic edge.

---

**Kiesenhof Chenin Blanc, Paarl 1996** 13.5 C

Curious cosmetic edge.

---

**Neil Ellis Chardonnay 1995** 13.5 E

---

**Two Oceans Cape Sauvignon Blanc 1996** 14 C

Fun, fruity tippling on one hand. Hints of serious fish-friendly sauvignon crispness on the other.

---

# SPANISH WINE RED

**Berberana Gran Reserva Rioja 1987** 13 E

As good as it'll get at this age but too ripe, vanilla-ey and simplistic for such a price.

---

**Berberana Reserva Rioja 1988** 11 D

---

**Guelbenzu Evo Cabernet/Merlot, Navarra 1993** 13.5 E

---

**Guelbenzu Jardin, Navarra 1995** 15.5 C

Soft, sweet fruit of great charm married to developed tannins of class and depth give this wine structure, bite, texture and memorable depth.

---

**Guelbenzu Navarra 1994** 15.5 D

---

**Marques de Grinon Rioja 1995** 14 C

One of the most elegant riojas around.

---

**Marques de Murrieta Rioja Reserva 1992** 12.5 E

---

**Navajas Rioja 1995** 15.5 C

Light yet tobaccoey and rich-edged and delightfully drinkable. A delicious wine of quiet class.

---

**Pago de Carraovejas, Ribera del Duero 1994** 18 E

Magnificent aroma, fruit, structure, finish, flavour and so much vivid personality which never gets tiresome that you feel the tenner spent to be a bargain. The aroma of tobacco leads to richness and the final flourish of savouriness is sublime.

---

**Puerta Vieja Rioja Crianza 1992** 12 C

Disconcertingly ripe.

---

**Torres Coronas 1994** 

An excellent accompaniment to roast, herbed lamb.

---

## SPANISH WINE — WHITE

**Marques de Riscal Rueda Blanco 1995** 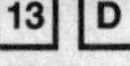

---

**Misela de Murrieta Rioja Blanco 1993** 

I'm not overkeen on these cosmetic-edged white riojas. Good with tapas, I daresay.

---

## USA WINE — RED

**Bel Arbor Merlot, California 1994** 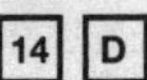

The fruit seems very soupy and ripe at first, then some lovely tannins strike and the fruit cruises home – rich and delightfully at ease.

---

**Calera Pinot Noir 1993** 

Good aroma but the fruit seems rather dry and ungiving.

---

**Clos du Val Cabernet Sauvignon, Stags Leap District 1992** 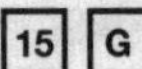

This is sinfully gluggable to the extent that it seems a message sent by Bacchic angels when of course they are only after your money. £15 is a lot but it does have beautiful fruit of lushly insistent class.

---

**Clos du Val Zinfandel 1992** 13 F

---

**Kautz-Ironstone Cabernet Franc 1994** 15.5 D

Highly polished and fruity with oodles of flavour flooding the mouth. But it's not simply a big broth of softness – it has a wicked edge to its affability. Makes it good with food.

---

**Kautz-Ironstone Merlot 1994** 13.5 D

Brilliant smell – not so sure about the finish.

---

**Kautz-Ironstone Shiraz 1993** 14 E

---

**Marietta Cellars Cabernet Sauvignon 1994** 13.5 F

Delicious chewy-biscuit texture. But the price . . . !!!

---

**Marietta Cellars Syrah 1994** 14 E

Some dry tannic palate arousal to the rich jammy fruit here. Gives the wine character.

---

**Marietta Old Vine Red Lot Eighteen NV** 13.5 E

Sweet, very drinkable, overpriced.

---

**Seghesio Old Vine Zinfandel, Sonoma 1994** 13 E

Overpriced by miles (several thousand).

---

**Seghesio Sonoma Pinot Noir 1994** 13.5 E

Impressive texture – it must be admitted. Don't like the thickness of the price tag though.

---

**Seghesio Sonoma Zinfandel 1994** 13.5 D

Touch like cough syrup.

---

**Seghesio Vivigno Toscano Sangiovese 1995** 14 E

Like a quirky chianti: aromatic, nicely earthy and yet very finely polished, complex, with a haughty fruitiness on the finish which clearly labels it very classy.

---

# USA WINE WHITE

**Beringer Fume Blanc, Napa Valley 1995** 15 D

Delicious double attack of fruit and acidity which both rain blows on the tastebuds in a well-co-ordinated assault of style and richness.

---

**Beringer Meritage White 1993** 16 E

Big chewy arboreal fruit of weight and class.

---

**Calera Chardonnay, Central Coast 1994** 16 E

Big, rich, deeply textured, buttery, and it spreads itself on the tongue like a languidly warm expanse of flesh stretching itself out to catch the sun. Indeed, this wine is so exuberantly Californian it wears a tan.

---

**Clos du Val Chardonnay, Carneros 1994** 16 F

Expensive but highly intelligent. The fruit is intellectual, witty, rich and very handsome. The harmony of wood, fruit and acidity is impressive. The ripe, almost smoky melon fruit is never overdone and is lingering and subtly nutty (brazils).

---

**Clos Du Val Le Clos Chardonnay, Napa 1995** 14 D

---

**Kautz-Ironstone Chardonnay 1995** 14.5 D

A suspicion of acidity-lack on the finish suggests this wine might not be as good as I thought it could be with boisterous fish dishes (like mussels with chillies) but it is a most delicious tippling wine.

---

**Mondavi Fume Blanc, Napa Valley 1995** 13.5 E

Somewhat sloppy on its long-term finish for a wine so highly priced and ambitious. The effect on the palate is excellent but the final effect is marred.

---

**Seghesio Sonoma Sauvignon Blanc 1995** 

A strange alien sauvignon of creamy fruit – great with food and yummy without. Has an unusual tang on the finish – like an echo of rice pudding.

---

## FORTIFIED WINE

**Blandy's 5 Year old Sercial** 15 F

Uniquely it's dry, sweet, raisiny, rich and utterly captivating, with sweetmeats of not too cloyingly honeyed a structure.

---

**Quinta do Crasto LBV 1989** 14 E

Dark, sweet, chocolatey.

---

**Taylor's LBV 1989** 14.5 E

Excellent value. Rich, dry, chewy, lingering.

---

**Taylor's Quinta de Vargellas 1984** 13.5 G

---

## SPARKLING WINE/CHAMPAGNE

**Andrew Garrett Chardonnay NV (Australia)** 

Rich and fruity, golden and delicious. At this price, it's the perfect bubbly for any season. Not dry but dry enough.

---

**Ayala Champagne NV** 13 G

**Blanquette de Limoux 1993** 15 E

Soft and intensely lovable. Like a favourite old teddy bear. Impossible to drink it without a tear rolling down the cheek.

**Bouvet Ladubay Saumur NV (France)** 14.5 E

Elegant and delightfully lemony.

**Canard-Duchene 1990 (Champagne)** 13 G

**Champagne Canard-Duchene NV** 13.5 E

This is a lot to pay for a half of bubbly. I'd prefer to spend half the sum on a full bottle of cava.

**Champagne Pommery 1990** 14.5 H

One of the most delicately delicious champagnes around. It is in the class of the finest bubblies from Marlborough, New Zealand. It is, alas, more than twice the price of them.

**De Telmont Grande Reserve Champagne NV** 14 G

**De Telmont NV (Champagne)** 13 F

Very lemony and rich.

**Devaux Grande Reserve Brut NV** 15.5 G

A genuinely delicious champagne worth its weight in copper to the value of £15 by virtue of its subtly rich fruit and nutty, lemonic finish. A complex charmer of some class and wit.

**Gloria Ferrer Brut, Sonoma County (California)** 15.5 E

You know something? I'd rather drink this than Bollinger.

**Jacquart 1990 (Champagne)** 13.5 G

Very elegant and classy if a trifle pricey.

---

**Lancelot de Hoen Cremant d'Alsace** 14 E

Elegant and very spritely on the tongue.

---

**Louis Roderer Quartet NV (California)** 14 G

Exceptionally delicious fruit. Expensive but most engaging.

---

**Moet et Chandon 1990 (Champagne)** 13.5 H

Attractive aroma and fruit but that price tag!!

---

**Oeil de Perdrix Tradition NV** 14 G

A delicate pink bubbly of elegance and restrained richness.

---

**Perrier-Jouet 1990 (Champagne)** 12 H

---

**Pommery Brut Rose NV** 13 H

Worth 13 points, even at its absurd £22, for its delicacy of approach, stealthy fruit and acid, and nutty finish. An elegant rose, if crazily priced.

---

**Pommery Brut Royal (Champagne)** 13 G

---

**Pongracz Cape Classique (South Africa)** 13.5 E

If only it were a couple of quid cheaper.

---

**Rosemount Brut (Australia)** 15 E

---

**Seppelt Pinot Noir/Chardonnay 1990** 15 E

Has more fruit than its Rheims counterpart and considerably less pounds.

---

**Shadow Creek Californian Blanc de Noirs** 14.5 E

See that cocked hat? See how sodden it is? That's the champagne this terrific bubbly has knocked there.

---

**Taittinger 1990 (Champagne)** 12 H

---

**Yaldara Reserve Brut (Australia)** 14 D

---

**Yaldara Rose NV (Australia)** 13 D

---

# ODDBINS

Did Dostoevsky have a message? Yes, and Oddbins has received it loud and clear. The message is: if you want to change the world, first change yourself. Thus, this retailer has been in the vanguard of the transformation of the hide-bound UK wine market over the past twenty-five years. Sceptics may argue that they only have 200 stores predominantly in London and the south-east so they can do things that other retailers in this book cannot do. It may be so. But it is equally the case that Oddbins has shaped and influenced what many others have done, and if there is one central element defining the Oddbins approach it is its open and adventurous buying policy. This is the retailer after all that was carrying as many as forty Chilean wines in 1992 when, with the exception of a few names, Chilean wine was scarcely more than a twinkle in the eye of most buyers. Oddbins was also in the forefront of the Australian boom which was arguably the main catalyst for the huge changes we have seen in the wine market in recent times.

What the Australians did that was different, says the Oddbins chief wine buyer Steve Daniel, was listen to what the market wanted. This open attitude and eagerness to make wines to a style which suited the retailers and ultimately their customers, has over the years spread to other wine regions, and the ability to shape the product they sell, to be involved, whether marginally or extensively, in the development of the wines is at the root of what Oddbins and its more enlightened peers now do. 'When I first started a lot of the products that people bought were from the bigger import agencies which were based in the UK,' Mr Daniel explains. 'Now a lot of people are either working directly with smaller producers or working on a more ex-cellars basis where there is more input from the winebuyers to the winemakers, the guys that count. And that really sprang up with the Australians and their open attitude to trading. At Oddbins we like to work in partnership with our producers. I certainly prefer that as a trading stance and I think at the end of the day we get better results.'

Like most modern winebuyers, Steve Daniel and his team do far more travelling than they would have done ten years ago. He is away for between four days and a week in a month, and he sees it as a vital part of his job. 'You have to keep up with what's happening,' he says. 'There are still agents involved in a lot of the process and marketeers, and with all the respect to those guys, they don't always fully understand what will work for any particular customer. So the only way to see what is available is to go out there and taste the vats so you can get that direct input. What I have found the more that I have travelled and the same with all our buyers, is that there are often little gems sitting there that the people don't know what do with. It doesn't fit into their global strategy but it might fit with ours.' Indeed, among the 1,200 wines that Oddbins lists are many of these small parcels which add so much to the retailer's range.

Travelling has allowed Steve Daniel and his team to cross-fertilise ideas from different wine regions. 'I am not a winemaker, but what I do is I travel the world and I see techniques, and styles of products that work here. We are lucky working in the UK; it's a very open market and we get to see everything that is available. What I can do is bring that to the table if you like. A winemaker out in Chile doesn't get the exposure to outside elements,' he says. 'Those guys have to make to a demand and if they don't know there is a demand there for a certain sort of product they won't make that product.'

For Steve Daniel it really is about meeting the winemakers themselves, not just about visiting the wineries or their export directors. This ability to contact the 'guy that matters' is also something that has changed about the business. 'Most of my contact in terms of the creative aspect is with the winemakers. When I first went to Chile it was very difficult to meet the winemaker. You'd meet the marketeers, and you would tell them what you wanted, they would then translate what they thought you meant some way down the line to the winemaker, and at the end of the day the communication lines get a little fuzzy. It's better for me to talk with the guys that matter. It's not trying to get rid of the agent. If there is an agent involved I am more than happy to work with them. But in terms of the product it's better to speak to the winemaker.'

It came as no surprise to me that Oddbins claims to have had some involvement in the development of 60–70 per cent of the wines it carries. The retailer even claims to have had some input into the development of Jacob's Creek when it was first being mooted for the UK market. The retailer apparently urged the producers, Orlando Wyndham, to opt for a Semillon/Chardonnay rather than a Riesling, a wise decision. Today, Oddbins buyers are constantly involved in discussions with winemakers about wine projects and improvements which can be made to existing items. These range from wines such as the Oddbins Red and Oddbins White, unusual examples of the stark staring obvious where this retailer is concerned, to examples from South America, France and South Africa. The company has been working with the same producer for Oddbins White for the past eight years and on the back of that business, the producer has been continuously investing in new equipment, another benefit of building long-term relationships in Mr Daniel's view. This year's Oddbins White, a 1996 Vin de Pays des Cotes de Gascogne, rates 13, while the Oddbins Red Chateau de Jau 1996 is a handsome rustic red with zippy ripe fruit flavours rating 15. Oddbins has also been involved in shaping the style of some of its Chilean wines, including the Vina Casablanca range and the Santa Rita Casa Real 1995.

The kinds of suggestion Steve Daniel makes to wine producers may involve leaving fruit to ripen for longer, using barrel-fermentation, taking the wine out of barrel earlier, using wild yeasts or leaving a red wine unfiltered, a particular passion of his (as it is of mine). But most of the time the discussions revolve around style. While knowledgeable about wine production, he defers to the winemakers on the technicalities. 'At the end of the day, they are the professionals, they are the winemakers,' he says.

He also forcefully rejects the idea that retailers requesting 'modern-style' wines which suit current consumers' tastes has the effect of homogenising the wine market, making wines from all over the world to a similar formula. It is not like that at Oddbins, he insists. In fact, Mr Daniel sees the diversity of geographical provenance as perhaps the most important factor in wine marketing. At a time when concept marketing, innovation and soft branding are becoming increasingly common in the wine business, Mr Daniel may even sound a little on the conservative side. It is true that he views the wine market as still being fundamentally 'product-driven' rather than 'marketing-driven', but any impression that he has an old-fashioned outlook is entirely misleading. He would no doubt advise anyone with that reaction to taste their way through the Oddbins range which would I suspect disabuse them of any such notion. Not only is he said by suppliers to have one of the best palates among the major wine buyers, he is also a proven innovator. 'I want the wines to express where they come from but I want them to be made in a modern way,' he says. 'The modern taste is for wines that are made correctly and have good fruit expression.'

This, Mr Daniel believes, should not exclude the idea of wines made in traditional ways with a strong regional character and individuality. 'Traditional style' according to Mr Daniel need not mean 'not a very well made wine. You see that in Rioja. You see some very traditional methods being used but producing a wine that absolutely fits the market because people want a taste of Rioja wine; they don't want it to taste like an Aussie wine. I don't want my wines from Chile to taste like Australian wines and I don't want my southern French wines to taste Australian.'

The Rioja is an excellent example. Oddbins was involved in the development of a new-style Garnacha called Vega Nueva, while El Portico, made by Bodegas Palacio, is also described as a traditional style of wine made in a modern way. 'If we get involved in the wines that people are producing it is to make them more in the style that they should be, to make them taste more southern French or in Rioja with the grenache to make it more like grenache, to get more of its fruit statement out. We want them to produce the best wines they can but we don't want them to produce a homogenised style because we see that as really dangerous in the long term.' I have to confess that El Portico is a glorious triumph. I wrote of it in the *Guardian*:

'El Portico Rioja 1994 is the most elegant specimen of its kind I have tasted in thirty years and though reminiscent of the old-style riojas which bargain-seekers of the 60s accurately used to compare with the Medocs of the 1940s, it also has something of the New World of winemaking about it. It is beautifully fruity, the tannins are evolved and mellow, there is a subtle tobacco-edge to the prune and blackcurrant fruit, and, best of all, there is no hint of the crass vanilla and coarse woody overtones which have disfigured many riojas for so many years. It rates 17.5 points and costs £5.75.' I consumed a bottle over three hours, lying on a sofa, as I toured the equally pungent and delicious world of Vladimir Nabokov (as represented in the fat new collection of his short stories) and it was as enjoyable a 180 minutes as I spent all year.

Short-term thrills, however, butter no parsnips with Mr Daniel. References to the 'long term' abound in any discussion with Steve and one can clearly see that this influences his and Oddbins' thinking on most things and perhaps explains why he is not a zealous advocate of some of the more radical marketing-led jiggery-pokery currently being flaunted in wine retailing circles. For instance, Oddbins does not tend to get involved in the labelling and naming of the wines. In some extreme cases, a retailer's influence in this area can lead to wines from Spain or Germany being named and packaged in a manner no different from an Australian wine. With the importance he places on regional character, it is no surprise that Mr Daniel is firmly against this. 'We don't like to get too involved in naming of products. We try and stay out of that. What we want is the wine to come from the place and be therefore very recognisable that it comes from there. We will put some input into labelling but it is not the be-all and end-all to us. What is in the bottle is the most important thing and as long as the label isn't too horrendous or horrific then we will run with it because obviously that is what the producer wants to go with. We have people, shop floor staff, who can say ignore the label and try the wine.'

Names that have been arrived at simply on the basis of maximum marketing effect are also anathema. 'It's just shock value. I don't think it's saying that much,' he says of wines with outrageous and wacky names, even the ones he thinks are very good wines. 'A South African wine should have a South African name and the producer's name should be there and if it's unpronounceable then so be it. You won't see any Chilean wines which don't sound Chilean in our range. If we do any own-label work it will sound Chilean. It won't be "Windy Hollow".'

The long-term thinking also influences how the retailer handles its suppliers. Steve Daniel has worked with the Chilean wine industry for over eight years, and was in the ground floor. He considers that they have 'grown up together'. This is a rather personal, almost sentimental view, but he considers it to be completely pragmatic. 'If a country is producing better products it makes our life easier at the end of the day. If they get more money for their products they have more money to invest and at the end of the day everybody wins. We are very long-term at Oddbins. If we are going to invest that time we want a long-term benefit.'

Building long-term relationships with suppliers pays dividends in other ways too. Even though there are more regions than ever looking to produce marketable, appealing wines, mother nature is not so market-aware. Wine, as we are always being reminded, is after all an agricultural product. Supply will always be subject to the foibles of the weather and at the moment wine, particularly quality red wine, has been in short supply. 'It's swings and roundabouts. At the moment it's definitely a seller's market and if you have been one of those buyers that just thumps the table you won't get much co-operation when there is a world shortage of quality wine. The producers will be more selective and they will work with the people who have supported them through thick and thin and have been more supportive in their attitude. When you have been in the business for ten years you see that everything is cyclical. Demand fluctuates and you go from feast to famine. And if you adopt as a buyer a far too aggressive stance you know you are going to get the same treatment from the supplier when the boot is on their foot.'

Steve Daniel suggests that the long-termism is also a distinction between supermarkets and the specialists. 'I have never worked for a supermarket but I think they view products as more of a commodity at the end of the day. And maybe their needs are different from mine. They look for continuity. I don't care about continuity. If we have an amazing product that lasts a month then I am happy and if the consumers then can't have that for another year then to me that's fine. And luckily we have the guys in the stores that can tell the customers, 'Well, you missed it this year but try this.' I am very lucky as a buyer that we have the staff that can talk to the customers, whereas a supermarket environment is more sterile and there is less interaction between the consumer and the buyer because there is no mid-point. There is no one there who can advise the customer. They have different constraints and maybe their mentality is different.'

He also makes the point that supermarket buyers can come from and go to other product areas, whereas the buyers at specialists tend to be enthusiasts. Mr Daniel himself trained and worked as a chef but soon realised that wine was his passion. Besides, being a chef was far too much like hard work he says.

Like all winebuyers, Mr Daniel bridles at the idea that the job is all about swanning around beautiful vineyards being feted by eager vignerons at every turn; he is big enough to concede that he has on balance an extremely enviable job, but for him it's more for the fundamental reason that he simply loves what he does for a living. 'It's a great job. I wouldn't change it for the world. It's my ideal job. It's my hobby as well as my line of work. The wine industry is full of people like that. We are in the industry not to make a lot of money, but because we are interested in it, and that motivates people. Certainly with Oddbins that is why the people are so motivated because they are in a job that they want to be in.'

Whenever one discusses Oddbins, the conversation sooner or later comes around to the staff, whether in the buying team or in the stores themselves: Mr Daniel has made it clear that having knowledgeable and enthusiastic staff on hand in the stores allows the retailer to worry less about fancy labels and tom-fool names of wines and to concentrate as much as possible on the liquid in the bottle, providing as diverse a range of wines with great local character and personality as it possibly can.

It is not every retailer that can afford to have this attitude. Oddbins is in something of a privileged position. 'If I was in a different seat, I would say that the label is the most important thing and the wines have to stand out on the shelf,' says Steve Daniel. 'But I work for Oddbins and that isn't really our main concern in life because we have 1,200 wines. How can they all stand out on the shelf? They can't but hopefully what is in the bottle will speak for itself when the person gets it home. And we have got guys in the stores to help customers make that choice.'

It is ironic that the retailer which has arguably done most to advance the wine market in terms of the range of wine available to the consumer should have a rather downbeat and almost conservative view on some marketing innovations, but it is perhaps not that surprising. In a way, it says something about Oddbins and the consumers who shop there. Steve Daniel maintains his customers will be less concerned about making an impression on friends with a peculiarly named or outlandishly labelled wine. It may even be that buying a wine at Oddbins in the first place is a sufficient statement. 'I would rather they were bringing something to a dinner party because it is an interesting wine,' Steve Daniel says. 'I would rather they went to a dinner party with a wine with a very innocuous label that causes no comment until the bottle's open and they taste the wine inside and then they "wow!"'

This is the epitome of Oddbins thinking. The chain has been cleverly marketed, there is no doubt of that, but there has always been the prevailing sense that it does not have to try too hard. Steve Daniel does not disagree with this and feels that it has a lot to do with taking the long-term view. 'Well, I think we have done our work over the years and what the customers expect from us are good-quality wines, different wines and staff that can talk to them about it. People will try our recommendations because they have not been disappointed before.'

Perhaps Mr Daniel's sceptical view of some of the purely marketing-led aspects of the modern wine market has much to do with the retailer's view of itself. 'I am very keen that Oddbins is not seen as a marketing concept because we are not, and we never have been. We are a culture and it's just evolved and I think that is what the customer respects. The best marketing is when you enhance something that had intrinsic value to begin with,' he says. Amen to that.

(I feel it best to end this litany here. I shall not repeat Mr Daniel's views of certain other wine retailers who have attempted to copy, ineptly, Oddbins shop layouts and approach or ape, crassly, the originality of the presentation of its wine lists. But then imitation, it may be some comfort for him to know, is the homage mediocrity forever pays to talent.)

ODDBINS
31-32 Weir Road
Wimbledon
London
SW19 8UG
Tel 0181 944 4400
Fax 0181 944 4411

**SEE STOP PRESS SECTION AT END OF BOOK FOR LAST-MINUTE ADDITIONS TO THIS RETAILER'S RANGE.**

# ARGENTINIAN WINE RED

**Balbi Vineyards Malbec 1995** 13 C

---

**Norton Barbera, Mendoza 1996** 14.5 C

A better barbera at a lot less money than certain Italians produce. And it's both food-friendly and very gluggable.

---

**Norton Cabernet Sauvignon 1996** 15.5 C

Oh! What texture and richness of tone here!

---

**Norton Malbec 1995** 14 C

Juiciest of the four Norton reds.

---

**Norton Merlot 1995** 15 C

Lovely dry, fruity finish.

---

**Norton Sangiovese 1995** 14 C

Nothing like chianti – it's lighter, richer, smoother and totally without coarseness.

---

**Valentin Bianchi Asti Vineyard Malbec Limited Release, Mendoza 1991** 14 E

Curiously delicious curiosity: soft, soupy, very ripe.

---

**Valle de Vistalba Barbera, Mendoza 1996** 13.5 C

Simple fruity stuff.

---

**Valle de Vistalba Cabernet Sauvignon, Mendoza 1995** 15 C

Approachable but has characteristic back-bite.

---

## ARGENTINIAN WINE — WHITE

**Norton Torrontes 1996** 13.5 C

Pleasant tipple – aperitif style or good with shellfish.

---

## AUSTRALIAN WINE — RED

**Chateau Reynella Basket Pressed Cabernet Merlot, McLaren Vale 1994** 16 E

The texture is superb, the flavour ripe and deep and concentrated, the finish long and rich. An expensive treat.

---

**Chateau Reynella Basket Pressed Shiraz, McLaren Vale 1994** 14.5 E

Juicy edge to the soft richness.

---

**Coldstream Hills Reserve Cabernet Sauvignon, Yarra Valley 1994** 13.5 G

Classic cabernet at an inflated price.

---

**Coldstream Hills Reserve Pinot Noir, Yarra Valley 1996** 14 G

Not quite La Tache but it hits the spot in every other way. For pinot freaks only, though.

---

**D'Arenberg d'Arry's Original Shiraz Grenache, 1994** 14 D

Very soft and juicy. Hugely drinkable.

---

**D'Arenberg Old Vine Shiraz, McLaren Vale 1995** 13.5 D

Sheer beef stock. Like a health drink.

---

**D'Arenberg The Custodian Grenache, McLaren Vale 1995** 15 E

Lovely rich flourish on what is normally a superficial grape. Terrific class here. All the same, the '96 will probably be coming into store by the time this book appears and at time of writing I haven't had a chance to try that vintage.

---

**Glenloth Private Bin 108** 13.5 C

Sloppy stuff but hugely drinkable for beginners.

---

**Jamiesons Run Pinot Noir, Yarra Valley 1995** 11 E

---

**Leasingham Classic Clare Cabernet Sauvignon, Clare Valley 1994** 15 G

Gorgeous! But is it worth sixteen quid? Just about, but Chile is going to make Aussies look pretty stupid – any day now.

---

**Leasingham Classic Clare Shiraz, Clare Valley 1994** 14 G

It's delicious and rich but I must protest at the price hike. It's obscene.

---

**Lindemans Bin 45 Cabernet Sauvignon 1995** 13 D

I suppose one can imagine toying with a glass, but the wine tries to be liked so unimaginatively, it's embarrassing. I prefer more character in wine, as in people – especially at this price.

---

**Norman Bin C106 Cabernet Sauvignon, 1995** 13.5 D

Very juicy, very soft, very eager to please.

---

**Normans Chais Clarendon Cabernet Sauvignon, McLaren Vale 1995** 14 E

Juicy stuff!

---

**Normans Chais Clarendon Shiraz, McLaren Vale 1995** 16 E

Savoury, rich, concentrated, not soppy, deep, beautifully textured.

---

**Penfolds Bin 2 Shiraz/Mourvedre 1995** 15.5 D

Rich, dry, stylish, this has fluidity of fruit yet tannic firmness of tone.

---

**Penfolds Bin 407 Cabernet Sauvignon 1993** 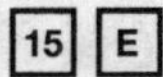

Ripe fruit, sound tannins, richness and flavour. A sedate yet invigorating cabernet of style and elegance.

---

**Penfolds Rawson's Retreat Bin 35 1995**  

Respectable rather than raunchy.

---

**Peter Lehmann Cabernet Sauvignon, Barossa 1995** 16 E

One of the better Aussie cabernets for it has lovely rich tannins beautifully amalgamated with the fruit.

---

**Peter Lehmann Clancy's, Barossa Valley 1995** 13 E

A marinade for tired tongues.

---

**Peter Lehmann Shiraz, Barossa 1995** 14 D

Very soft and tidal. It'll disappear under rich food.

---

**Peter Lehmann Vine Vale Grenache, Barossa 1996** 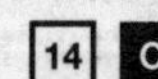

Linctus-textured, soft as syrup.

---

**Riddoch Coonawarra Cabernet Shiraz 1995** 13 D

Where's my tannin? I need my tannin!

---

**Robertson's Well Cabernet Sauvignon, Coonawarra 1993** 12 E

Over the hill.

---

**Rothbury Estate Shiraz 1994** 13 D

---

**Rouge Homme Richardsons Red Block, Coonawarra 1994** 14 E

Curious lush rich finish on dryly undertoned fruit. Delicious. Limited availability, however.

---

**Saltram Mamre Brook Cabernet Sauvignon/ Shiraz 1994** 13.5 D

---

**Saltram Stoneyfell Metala Shiraz Cabernet, S Australia 1994** 13.5 D

---

**Sandalford Margaret River Shiraz 1995** 14 E

Shiraz in its accommodating mode.

---

**Tim Gramp Grenache 1994** 15 E

Fine Wine shops only.

---

**Wirra Wirra R S W Shiraz 1994** 14 E

---

**Yarra Valley Hills Cabernet Sauvignon, Log Creek Victoria 1995** 12 F

---

**Yarra Valley Hills Pinot Noir, Yarra Valley 1996** 13 F

Fades on the finish. But good . . . until then.

---

# AUSTRALIAN WINE WHITE

**Ballingal Estate Chardonnay 1996** 

Brilliant old-style Aussie chardonnay – but with finesse and class.

---

**Campbells Old Rutherglen Muscat** 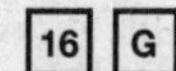

Expensive but a superbly rich and highly flavoured wine for rich puddings, fruit cakes and Christmas pudding. Fine Wine Shops only.

---

**Campbells Rutherglen Liqueur Muscat (half bottle)** 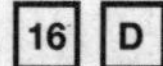

Superb depth of raisiny richness and sweetness. A wondrous accompaniment to rich cake.

---

**Coldstream Hills Reserve Chardonnay, Yarra Valley 1996** 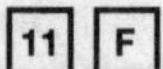

Only half as good, if that, as the Sandalford wonder (qv). So by rights it ought to rate 8.25. But let's be charitable . . .

---

**D'Arenberg McLaren Vale Noble Riesling 1992 (half bottle)** 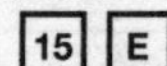

Limited availability.

---

**D'Arenberg The Olive Grove Chardonnay, McLaren Vale 1996** 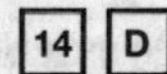

Not as rampantly oily as its name might suggest, but still a bucketful of richness for the tastebuds.

---

**Deakin Estate Alfred Chardonnay, Victoria 1996** 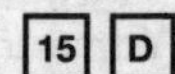

Swirly with rich ripe fruit flavours interlaced with acidity. Real depth of couth fruit here.

---

**Edwards & Chaffey Chardonnay Unfiltered 1994** 17 E

I can pay this Aussie cheerfully no higher tribute than to remark how exquisitely Californian it is. Fine Wine Shops only.

---

**Green Point Chardonnay, Yarra Valley 1995** 13.5 E

---

**Hill Smith 'Air-Strip Block' Sauvignon Blanc, Eden Valley 1996** 15 E

The air-strip needs mowing. Plenty of grassy richness here.

---

**Jamieson's Run Chardonnay, Coonawarra 1995** 14.5 E

Restraint all round (oily, rich, dry) but on the finish a certain flourish gives it true class.

---

**Katnook Estate Sauvignon Blanc, Coonawarra 1996** 15 E

Very classy and fine. Has nuts and a gentle herbaceous acidity undertoning the ripe fruit.

---

**Killawarra Dry White** 15 B

Fantastic value here! A deliciously well-fruited, elegant wine with a clean but incisive finish.

---

**Lenswood Chardonnay, Knappstein 1993** 14 E

---

**Lenswood Vineyards Sauvignon Blanc 1996** 15 E

The rich, ripe end of the sauvignon spectrum.

---

**Lindemans Bin 65 Chardonnay 1996** 15.5 C

---

**Lindemans Cawarra Unoaked Chardonnay 1996** 13 C

---

**Normans Bin C207 Chardonnay 1996** 15.5 C

Oh yes! Great with Thai food or just a blue mood – this wine will lift both.

---

**Penfolds Old Vine Semillon, Barossa 1996** 14.5 D

Terrific roast-chicken wine.

---

**Penfolds Rawsons Retreat Bin 21 Semillon/Chardonnay/Colombard 1996** 15 C

Richly textured, warmly fruity (some complexity on the finish where the acidity is most pertinent), this is an excellent vintage for this wine.

---

**Penfolds The Valley Chardonnay 1995** 15 D

Packed with flavour which never intrudes rudely – only graciously.

---

**Penfolds Trial Bin Adelaide Hills Chardonnay 1995** 13 F

Lot of money only to be expended by those who like sticking their noses into trial bins.

---

**Petaluma Chardonnay, Piccadilly Valley 1994** 13 F

---

**Sandalford Margaret River Chardonnay 1995** 16.5 E

A wonderfully delicate yet paradoxically very rich chardonnay of charm, class and huge style. Great finesse, sheer gorgeous fruit.

---

**W W Chardonnay, McLaren Vale 1996** 13.5 C

---

**W W Semillon, McLaren Vale 1996** 13 C

Touch reluctant on the finish.

---

**Yarra Valley Hills Chardonnay, Victoria 1996** 16 E

Big plump texture which leaves an impression behind on the tongue as if thickly buttered bread with melon jam had just been idling there. A wonderfully creamy, opulently textured wine.

---

**Yarra Valley Hills Riesling, Victoria 1996** 14.5 D

Lovely sherbety bite on the finish. Wonderful fish and shellfish wine.

---

**Yarra Valley Hills Sauvignon Blanc, Victoria 1996** 15 E

One of those flavoursome sauvignons at the rich, vibrantly coloured end of the spectrum. Good seafood wine.

---

## BULGARIAN WINE RED

**Stowells of Chelsea Bulgarian Red (3-litre box)** 11 B

Vague hints of Bulgaria. Price has been adjusted to show equivalent per bottle.

---

## CHILEAN WINE RED

**Carmen Reserve Petite Syrah, Maipo 1995** 16 D

If you want a more sweetly fruity version of the dry northern Rhone's style, this wine is essential tippling.

---

**Carta Vieja Antigua Cabernet Sauvignon, Maule 1994** 14.5 C

Compelling richness and texture.

---

**Carta Vieja Cabernet Sauvignon, Maule 1995** 16 C

Runs free with rich dry fruit which is compelling – especially at the price.

---

**Casa Lapostolle Cuvee Alexandre Merlot, Rapel 1995** 17 E

A conjuring trick, surely. How can grapes be so bewitched as to yield such textured richness? Is Chile another planet?

---

**Casa Porta Cabernet Sauvignon 1996** 16 C

The rich fruit has a black, mysterious, almost charcoal edge to it (tannins). It's lovely.

---

**Concha y Toro 'Explorer' Bouschet, Maule 1996** 13.5 C

To be explored only by the unadventurous.

---

**Concha y Toro Explorer Cabernet/Syrah, Maipo 1996** 17 C

Makes you limp with pleasure. World-class texture, balance, depth and length and . . . price. Fabulous stuff!

---

**Concha y Toro Unfiltered Aspiran Bouschet, Rapel 1995** 14 C

Sweet juicy fun. Try it on grandpa (who hates red wine).

---

**Cono Sur Selection Reserve Cabernet Sauvignon, Chimbarongo 1995** 15.5 D

Has that dazzling double-act of ripe, soft fruit *and* character. You can do almost anything with a wine like this. Will it bring the dead back to life?

---

**Cono Sur Selection Reserve Pinot Noir, Chimbarongo 1995** 15 D

More drinkable than any amount of Cote d'Or wretches.

---

**Errazuriz Cabernet Sauvignon 1996** 16.5 D

Utter balm! Sheer textured brilliance from nose to throat and beyond (i.e. the soupy richness of the wine lingers in the mind).

---

**Errazuriz Cabernet Sauvignon Reserve 1995** 15 E

Has a curious reluctance on the finish to complete the job it started of crushing the tastebuds.

---

**Errazuriz Merlot 1996** 17 D

Totally delicious: textured, dry, multi-layered, gently leathery and enticingly aromatic, rich yet not forbidding, stylish, very classy and overwhelmingly terrific value for money.

---

**Errazuriz Reserva Merlot, Aconcagua 1996** 16 E

Great, soupy throughput of rich, deep, gently leathery flavours.

---

**Isla Negra Tinto 1995** 15.5 C

Such magnificent blue-mood-crushing texture! You cannot feel down after downing this wine.

---

**La Palma Merlot 1996** 15 C

Ripe and opulent in the mouth like inhaling a pearl. A delicious gem of a wine, wildly soft and accommodating, it is one long draught of fruit.

---

**Los Vascos Cabernet Sauvignon 1994** 15.5 C

---

**Luis Felipe Edwards 'Pupilla' Cabernet Sauvignon, Colchagua 1996** 16 C

Must be tasted to be believed at this price. Dark chocolate fruit with an edge of dry cassis.

---

**Santa Rita Reserva Merlot 1995** 

The texture, fruit, balance and lingering leathery finish are world class. Concentrated, deep, fine and the flavour goes on forever.

---

**Villa Montes Cabernet Sauvignon, Curico 1996** 

C

It's the softly robed fruit which makes it so delicious: it wears this soft towelling robe so well.

---

**Villa Montes Malbec, Colchagua 1996** 

Everything in the right proportions here: fruit, acidity and texture. It's almost smug – but it can afford to be.

---

**Vina Casablanca Cabernet Sauvignon, Santa Isabel 1995** 

Sheer blackcurrant juice. Like dry Ribena from nose to throat – at first. But give it two to three hours' airing and concentrated cassis emerges.

---

**Vina Casablanca El Bosquet Cabernet Sauvignon, Maipo 1995** 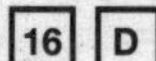


So elegant and velvety, picked out by hints of cassis to the fruit, you can't quite credit it. Wonderful stuff.

---

**Vina Casablanca Santa Isabel Cabernet Sauvignon 1996** 

In texture, richness, ripeness, balance and sheer deliciousness of fruit this is a great cabernet of sublime drinkability and style. It has guts yet finesse, flavour yet ineffability, utter class in every drop from nose to throat. An experience evoking sheer joy.

---

**Vina Casablanca Santa Isabel Merlot, Casablanca 1996** 14.5 

The elegance makes you want to weep. (Actually, no. Not you – wine growers in Bordeaux.)

---

# CHILEAN WINE WHITE

**Andes Peaks Casablanca Chardonnay 1996** 15 C

Delicious classy glugging.

---

**Andes Peaks Sauvignon Blanc 1996** 15 C

Interesting grassy edge to the ripe, rich fruit. Terrific combination of fruit and acid, great fish partner.

---

**Caliboro Blanco 1996** 14 B

---

**Carmen Reserve Chardonnay 1995** 15.5 D

Rich and buttery. Lacks acid for long-term drinking, so needs food – rich, creamy-sauced fish.

---

**Carta Vieja Chardonnay, Maule 1996** 13.5 C

Rather a spritzy chardy.

---

**Carta Vieja Sauvignon Blanc, Maule 1996** 14 C

Rich and almost creamy but the crispness pulls it back from the soft option.

---

**Casa Lapostolle Sauvignon Blanc, Rapel 1996** 17 C

Quite wondrous texture! It's like finely wrought velvet. The fruit is very fragrant, rich and very individual. Fabulous wine for the money.

---

**Casa Porta Chardonnay 1996** 15.5 C

Delicate, decisive, decidedly Chilean. It has elegance and real style, never overstated, thanks to the richness of fruit, never flashy, to be beautifully counterpoised by the acidity.

---

**Concha y Toro Casablanca Sauvignon Blanc 1996** 14 C

Has a soft finish.

---

**Cono Sur Chardonnay Reserve 1996** 

What a smashing wine! It has depth, richness, staying power, balance, high-quality fruit and tons of style. This style is buttery melon with a nutty undertone. Mouth-watering? Every sip, every smell, every dribble down the throat and the sense demand a further glass. Stoppered with a plastic cork, what's more – so every bottle should be in the condition described above.

---

**Errazuriz Chardonnay, La Escutura Estate 1996** 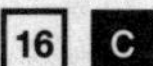

Very elegant and richly flavoured by the sun of Chile. It brightens up your day in one sip.

---

**Errazuriz Reserve Chardonnay 1996** 14 E

Somewhat flat on the finish but up to then it's fat, fat, fat . . .

---

**Errazuriz Sauvignon Blanc, La Escultura Estate 1996** 

The '97 vintage may have replaced it by now but at time of writing (September) it hasn't been available to taste.

---

**Errazuriz Wild Ferment Casablanca Chardonnay 1996** 16 E

A collector's item for the tongue. The wine washes over like buttered, spiced, ripe smoky melon . . .

---

**La Palma Chardonnay, Rapel 1996** 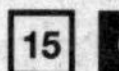

Soft, rich with a polished edge to the rolling fruity finish.

---

**Santa Carolina Chardonnay, Lontue 1996**

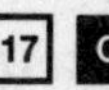


Rich, textured, ripe – yet very elegant and food-friendly. Wonderful with coriander-spiced rice and fish.

---

**Santa Carolina Dry White, Maule 1996**

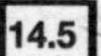


Brilliant value. Not complex but real hints of class here.

---

**Santa Carolina Reserva de Familia Chardonnay, Maipo 1995**

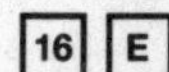


Expensive but exceedingly superior. The fruit is rich, nutty, balanced, flavoursome, warm, never cloying or muddy, and with masses of class.

---

**Villard Casablanca Vineyard Chardonnay, Aconcagua 1995**

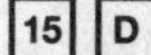


Odd wood and fruit aroma and fruit which becomes relaxed and brilliant with food.

---

**Villard Reserve Barrel Fermented Chardonnay, Casablanca Valley 1996**

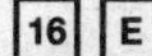


Cream, wood, nuts, ripe ogen melon – they're all there in superb array. A richly exciting wine.

---

**Vina Casablanca Barrel Fermented Chardonnay, Casablanca 1996**

Incredible length to this wine. Its glorious fruit persists like a welcome guest with a fund of delicious anecdotes.

---

**Vina Casablanca Chardonnay, Santa Isabel 1995**

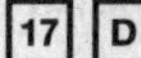


The texture of this wine is like dry melon infused with balsam. Glorious fruity feel on the tastebuds – uniquely Chilean.

---

**Vina Casablanca Lontue Valley Sauvignon Blanc, Curico 1996** 14 C

**Vina Porta Chardonnay 1995** 14 D

## ENGLISH WINE WHITE

**Denbies Late Harvest 1995 (half bottle)** 14 D

**Denbies Pinot Blanc 1995** 12 C

**Nutbourne Vineyards Sussex Reserve 1995** 13 D

A delicate, energetic wine of averagely pleasing fruit but above-averagely upsetting price tag.

**Valley Vineyards 'Regatta' 1995** 12.5 D

Almost sweet on the finish, but it's a dry wine conceptually. High price for such run-of-the-mill fruit. Sentimentally, it may get support but six quid is still six quid.

**Yellowhammer Blanc 1995** 12.5 C

## FRENCH WINE RED

**Banyuls Les Clos de Paulilles 1993** 16.5 E

Sweet, pruney, honeyed, blackcurrant-and-raspberry-and-plum-scented, this is a terrific wine for fruit cake. Fine Wine Shops only.

**Chateau de Lascaux, Coteaux du Languedoc 1995** 14 C

Soft and inviting. Most civilized rustic tippling.

**Chateau de Mousquet Bordeaux Superieur 1995** 13.5 D

Lay it down for a couple of years to let the tannins soften.

---

**Chateau de Musset, Montagne St Emilion 1994** 14 E

Real class here with that edge of cigar-box fustiness coddled by attendant tannins.

---

**Chateau de Nages Reserve du Chateau, Costieres de Nimes 1996** 16.5 C

Great-value fruit here. Rich, herby, flavour-packed, softly tannic, very positively structured. Terrific!

---

**Chateau Les Chalets Hosteing 1995** 13.5 D

---

**Chateau Lousteauneuf, 1995** 14 D

---

**Chateau Parenchere, Cuvee Raphael Gazaniol 1994** 14 E

Rich and ready (having improved somewhat in bottle since last year) and excellent with roast and grilled meats.

---

**Chinon Domaine de la Perriere 1996** 15.5 D

Cherries and dry pencil ends (the sharp end) combine to create an unusually food-friendly red of great versatility. Can be drunk chilled with fish. Brilliant stuff!

---

**Clos Sainte Anne Premieres Cotes de Bordeaux 1994** 14.5 E

Classy style of immediate claretability.

---

**Cotes du Rhone Cepage Syrah, Lionnet 1995** 14 E

Curious juicy fruit with a dry, tannic edge.

---

**Cotes du Rhone Guigal 1994** 15 D

Still one of the best basic red Rhones around. But why does it have to be seven quid?

---

**Crozes Hermitage, Domaine de Thalabert, Jaboulet 1994** 14 F

---

**Crozes Hermitage 'Meysonniers', Chapoutier 1994** 14 E

---

**Cuvee de Grignon VdP de l'Aude 1996** 15 B

Very light and cheering. A wonderful welcome-home-from-work glug.

---

**Domaine de Mas Carlot, Costieres de Nimes 1995** 17 C

Complex, rich, ripe, smoky, chewy, characterful and extremely individual. Wonderful fruit.

---

**James Herrick Cuvee Simone VdP d'Oc 1995** 16 C

Getting on a bit but good until Christmas 1997 when its superb structure and rich fruit will begin to wilt under the tannins. I simply cannot understand Oddbins customers permitting this under-a-fiver beauty to stay on the shelf for so long. A vivid wine of great class.

---

**La Baume Philippe de Baudin Cabernet Sauvignon VdP d'Oc 1994** 15 C

The tannins are fast running delicious riot with this wine and the fruit has got drier, angrier, less lush and the result is a concentrated cabernet of some class and style.

---

**La Baume Syrah Grenache 1995** 15 

---

**Le Secret VdP de Vaucluse 1996** 14 B

Simple fruity fun!

---

**Mas Cal Demoura, Coteaux du Languedoc 1994** 16.5 D

So dry and deliciously rustic it brings tears to your eyes. But the '95 will be coming in any minute, and I haven't had the chance to taste the new vintage yet . . .

---

**Mas Saint-Vincent, Coteaux du Languedoc 1995** 17 C

Forget Chateauneuf! Buy this. Great gobbets of tannin-shrouded fruit of dryness yet very rich, thyme-scented depth. Magical elixir! Like a blood transfusion. Only at Oddbins.

---

**Metairie du Bois Syrah VdP d'Oc 1996** 14 C

The fruit runs away with the tastebuds.

---

**Oddbins Red Chateau de Jau 1996** 15 C

A good honest red with freshly ripened fruit and only vague hints of the farmyard.

---

**Parallel '45' Cotes du Rhone 1995** 14.5 D

Raisins and almonds greet the nose and raw fruit the palate. This fruit is young and raw but of great potential – tannin and acidity in harmony – and the wine will age beautifully. Year 2000 . . . 16? 16.5?

---

**Pouilly Fume, Domaine Henry Pelle 1996** 14 E

Hmm . . . it has a lot of charm and style . . . and if I seem to hesitate it's because I wonder if its agreeable subtleties aren't *too* subtle.

---

**Stowells of Chelsea Vin de Pays du Gard (3-litre box)** 13.5 B

A good fruity party wine. The occasional glass is perfect before settling down to a session of bingo. Price has been adjusted to show equivalent per bottle.

---

**Wild Pig, VdP des Cevennes 1995** 15 B

A clean, simple glug, hinting at Rhone's earthy dryness, for a dead simple price.

---

# FRENCH WINE WHITE

**Chateau de la Chartreuse, Sauternes 1990** 

Superb waxy fruit and sweetness which is complex, vivid and very fine. Half bottles available for about half the price.

---

**Chateau de la Genaiserie Coteaux du Layon, Yves Soulez 1996** 15 D

Lovely honeyed fruit with incisive and complex acidity. Will age brilliantly for many years. But try it now as a uniquely different aperitif.

---

**Clos du Chateau Bourgogne, Domaine du Chateau de Puligny-Montrachet 1995** 12 E

Lot of money for this fruit. Chile's half the price and twice as delicious.

---

**Condrieu Les Chaillets, Cuilleron 1996** 13 G

I cannot rate it higher at £20. It has a hugely enticing aroma and some reasonable fruit, but it doesn't finish with great emphasis. Perhaps needs five years more to develop.

---

**Coteaux de Giennois, Balland-Chapuis 1995** 14 D

Crisp, clean, very French (touch standoffish fruit-wise). Excellent with shellfish.

---

**Coteaux du Layon Saint Lambert Cuvee Nectar, Domaine Sauveroy 1995** 13.5 G

Magnificent fruit! Give it a decade and it will be sublime.

---

**Cotes de Nuits Villages, Domaine du Chateau de Puligny-Montrachet 1995** 12.5 F

---

**Cuvee de Grignon Blanc, VdP de l'Aude 1996** 14.5 B

Good crisp intentions not fully realized but amply fruity and well turned out.

---

**Domaine de Duisse Molleux 'Cuvee de Diane', Pacherenc du Vic-Bilh 1995** 13 E

Not heavy enough for pud, nor heady enough for fruit. An aperitif? Not yet. Give it a year in bottle.

---

**Domaine Garras VdP des Cotes de Gascogne 1996** 13 C

Lemon – hint of pineapple – a simple Gascon.

---

**Domaine St Hilaire Chardonnay VdP d'Oc 1996** 15 C

Rich, nutty, subtle (yet ripe and inviting), this is a deliciously satisfying bottle.

---

**Gewurztraminer, Hugel 1995** 12 E

Face-powder fruit.

---

**Gewurztraminer Tradition, Hugel 1995** 12 F

I'm sorry to say I don't find any of these Hugel wines worth the money. They struggle.

---

**James Herrick Chardonnay, VdP d'Oc 1995** 15 C

---

**La Baume Philippe de Baudin Chardonnay VdP d'Oc 1995** 14.5 C

**La Dame de Maucaillou, Bordeaux Blanc 1995** 15 C

Delicious – calm melony fruit with a crisp undertone. Classy stuff.

**Le Plan de Jean Vouvray Molleux, Domaine des Aubuisieres 1995** 14 E

Unusual aperitif but wait seven to ten years! It'll be a 17/18 pointer!

**Le Secret Blanc VdP de Vaucluse 1996** 14 B

Has an aroma that might have come from a Turkish brothel, the fruit is friendly and soft and the finish is ho-hum. But for cheap tippling it's a good glug.

**Macon Davaye, Domaine de Deux Roches 1996** 15 D

Rich! Ready! White Burgundy! £6.99! (There really is no more to be said.)

**Menetou Salon 'Clos Ratier', Domaine Henry Pelle 1996** 13.5 D

It tries, only echoically, to be the crisp clean sauvignon of yesteryear but the muddiness of the finish clouds the fruit.

**Metairie du Bois Sauvignon Blanc VdP d'Oc 1996** 14.5 C

I'd rather drink it than any amount of sancerres at twice the price.

**Michel Lynch Blanc, Bordeaux 1995** 12.5 D

**Montagny Premier Cru Les Coeres, Domaine Maurice Bertrand 1995** 14 E

Expensive but its plump vegetality is unique – and it's terrific with food.

---

**Muscat, Mann 1995** 15 E

---

**Oddbins White VdP des Cotes de Gascogne 1996** 13 C

---

**Philippe de Baudin La Baume Sauvignon Blanc VdP d'Oc 1996** 14 C

Has some classic mineral hints.

---

**Pinot Blanc, Mann 1995** 13.5 D

---

**Pouilly Fuisse Hors Classe, Domaine Ferret 1994** 13 G

Exceedingly drinkable for a fiver. Trouble is, it's four times that sum.

---

**Pouilly Fuisse Tete de Cru, Domaine Ferret 1994** 13.5 G

I should rate it 14 in all fairness. But. Malcolm, it's £19! Nineteen quid! Yes, it's drinkable but is it so complex and vibrant to rate such a price tag? No way.

---

**Pouilly-Fuisse Cuvee Prestige, Lassarat 1995** 12.5 G

Fifteen quid! My life!

---

**Pouilly Fume Sur Lie 'Comte de Berge', Jean-Claude Dageneau 1996** 14.5 E

Has richness and vigour, a big palate – walloping flavour and a lovely lemonic edge to the finish. Very stylish.

---

**Puligny Montrachet Louis Carillon 1995** 13.5 G

A delicious wine – at £4.99 not £17.99.

---

**Riesling, Hugel 1993** 13 E

Some classic riesling touches but the finish is soppy.

---

**Riesling Tradition, Hugel 1990** 11 F

Sloppy finish (again!).

---

**Saint Veran Les Chailloux, Domaine des Deux Roches 1995** 14 E

---

**Sancerre, Domaine de Rossignol 1996** 15 E

A lovely sancerre! Haven't said that for donkey's!! It's rich, crisp, beautifully textured and acidically elegant. But . . . drink it before '97 is out.

---

**Sancerre La Croix au Garde, Domaine Henri Pelle 1996** 13 E

Expensive and hasn't the elegance or the finesse of the Rossignol (q.v.)

---

**St Aubin 1er Cru 'En Remilly', Domaine du Chateau de Puligny-Montrachet 1995** 13 F

---

**St Romain, Domaine du Chateau de Puligny-Montrachet 1995** 12 F

---

**St Veran Cuvee Prestige, Lassarat 1995** 13 E

A touch expensive for the simplicity of the style.

---

**Stowells of Chelsea Vin de Pays du Tarn (3-litre box)** 14 B

Crisp and clean as it starts work then it waves goodbye with a pleasant fruity lilt. Good to glug, good with grub. Price has been adjusted to show equivalent per bottle.

---

**Tokay Pinot Gris Vieilles Vignes, Mann 1995** 17 E

Expensive but worth every farthing. The fruit is rich, deep, lengthy and energetic on the tongue and the acidity is intensely interwoven and fine. A beautifully textured wine. Will improve for four to five years.

---

**Tradition 1639, Hugel 1996** 12 D

Muddy and ill-defined on the finish.

---

**Vin d'Alsace Pinot Blanc Martin Schaetzel 1994** 14 D

---

**Vouvray 'Girardieres' Demi Sec, Domaine des Aubuisieres 1996** 15 D

A wonderfully different aperitif wine of textured class, richness, waxy/honeyed/peach and rose petal fruitiness. Has a future in a cellar but also in a glass – now.

---

**Vouvray 'Les Chairs Salees', Domaine des Aubuisieres 1996** 14 D

Lovely hints of flowers of honey held back from sweetness by acidity. But it's very young. I'd give it four to five years to blossom fully.

---

## GERMAN WINE WHITE

**Bechtheimer Hasensprung Huxelrebe Spatlese, Wittmann, Rheinhessen 1996** 13.5 D

A deliciously different aperitif which in seven years will rate considerably more.

---

**Burrweiler Schlossgarten Riesling Kabinett Halbtrocken, Messmer 1996** 13 D

Will develop, but I wonder if its half-dry status isn't too dry to make the wine blossom interestingly.

---

**Gaubischofsheimer Herrnberg Riesling Kabinett, Schulz Werner 1996** 13 C

I'd be inclined to pop it away somewhere dark and cool for five to six years. It'll be tremendous then.

---

**Hochheimer Herrenberg Riesling Kabinett, Kunstler 1995** 12 E

---

**Hochheimer Holle Riesling Spatlese, Kunstler 1995** 13 E

---

**Muller Thurgau, Messmer 1996** 12 C

Touch sweet and monodimensional.

---

**Ockfener Bockstein Riesling Kabinett, Kesselstatt 1994** 13 D

---

**Von Buhl Armand Riesling Kabinett, Pfalz 1996** 12.5 E

Love to try it again in five or six years' time!

---

**Von Buhl Forster Jesuitengarten Riesling Spatlese 1996** 14 E

Buy it! But don't drink it! Reserve this sublime treat for 2008 when it will be a 17-point wine, maybe even more. The acidity will preserve it.

---

**Von Buhl Riesling Kabinett Trocken, Pfalz 1996** 12 D

---

**Westhofener Aulerde Bacchus Kabinett, Wittmann, Rheinhessen 1995** 12 D

---

**Westhofener Kirchspiel Scheurebe Kabinett, Wittman, Rheinhessen 1996** 12 D

Energetic wine which needs time to rate more highly. In three years it could be a 16-pointer.

---

## ITALIAN WINE RED

**Bricco Zanone Barbera d'Asti 1995** 14 C

Good basic glugger with a hint of mystery.

---

**Duca di Castelmonte 'Cent'are', Rosso di Sicilia 1994** 15.5 C

Brilliant drinking here. Novel ripeness to the edge of the fruit, it's regal, cherry-rich yet fresh, and it's hugely quaffable.

---

**Due Aquile** 14 B

---

**Notarpanaro Rosso del Salento, Taurino 1990** 14.5 D

Ripe, figgy, curranty – needs rich food.

---

**Primitivo del Salento, Le Trulle 1994** 15 C

---

**Santa Barbara Brindisi Rosso 1993** 14 C

---

**Torre Veneto Torre del Falco, Murgia Rosso 1995** 14 D

Primarily a food wine. Great with anything from game to greasy sausages.

---

**Trabucco Rosso, Campomarino 1994** 14 C

**Uva di Troia di Puglia, Cantele 1993** 13 D

## ITALIAN WINE WHITE

**Chardonnay del Salento Barrique, Kym Milne 1995** 16.5 D

A rich, elegant, superbly purposeful and confident wine of impressive class. Superb with scallops.

**Dindarello Moscato Veneto, Maculan 1995 (half bottle)** 16 D

Exquisite sweet wine which is brilliant with fresh fruit. Utterly hedonistic experience.

**Fuedi di San Gregano Falanghina, Sannio Beneventano 1996** 14 D

Curious rich fruit but it makes a delicious change from chardonnay.

**Grecanico Pellegrino 1995 (Sicily)** 14 C

Clean, fresh, very crisp and endearing to the palate.

**Il Vignola Grechetto, Umbria 1996** 14 C

Has a sort of controlled rusticity with a veneer of urban sophistication. Delicious.

**Torcolato, Maculan 1995** 16.5 G

Nuts, honey, pineapples, melons, pears, limes – is there a fruit not represented here? A world-class dessert wine which will age for a decade – and then some.

**Zagaro Catarrattoo, Sicilia 1996** 14.5 C

Deliciously different tipple with a hint of creamy fruit to the soft melon.

---

## NEW ZEALAND WINE WHITE

**Dashwood Sauvignon Blanc, Marlborough 1996** 16 E

If you can still find the odd bottle of it, this is Dashwood's most dashing sauvignon yet. Keenly herbaceous but not overrich, concentrated gooseberry ripeness, and a decisive, balanced finish. By the time this book appears, though, the '97 will probably be in most stores (not tasted at time of writing).

---

**Grove Mill Sauvignon Blanc, Marlborough 1996** 15.5 D

Energy, bite, flavour (fruit and nuts), lots of personality and it's very easy to sip or glug. The herbaceous character is subtle and very easy to love.

---

**Jackson Estate Sauvignon Blanc 1996** 15.5 E

A grandly complex wine running a gamut of nutty citricity to lemonic, almost lime-like, but subtle melon-ness. It has developed astonishingly quickly in bottle and has therefore a capriciousness and wilfulness of its own making. A truly individual wine. Might be running low on stock by Christmas '97, catch it if you can.

---

**McDonald Church Road Reserve Chardonnay, Hawkes Bay 1995** 17 F

Seems to me there's no need to spend £40 on a fabled meursault when this extraordinary specimen speaks such exquisite French. Ravishing fruit here.

---

**Montana Church Road Chardonnay, Hawkes Bay 1995** 15 E

Good up front, very good (rich and balanced) and lovely melon/wood flavour in the mouth.

---

**Montana Reserve Barrique Fermented Chardonnay, Marlborough 1996** 14 E

Expensive for a piece of wood.

---

**Montana Reserve Vineyard Selection Sauvignon Blanc, Marlborough 1996** 15.5 E

Unusually rich, nutty, ripe yet dry sauvignon of immense nubility – where, that is, scallop or lobster or salmon is at the altar.

---

**Montana Sauvignon Blanc 1996** 14.5 D

Ripe, grassy, lean yet muscular, this is an archetypal Marlborough sauvignon of quiet class. The '97 might be replacing it as this book comes out, though, and as yet (September) I haven't been able to taste it.

---

**Selaks Sauvignon Blanc 1996** 15.5 D

The '96s from Marlborough seem more complex acidically and this is an excellent example. It is absurdly delicious.

---

**Stowells of Chelsea New Zealand Sauvignon Blanc (3-litre box)** 13.5 C

Price has been adjusted to show equivalent per bottle.

---

**Villa Maria Cellar Selection Chardonnay, Gisborne 1995** 14 E

---

**Villa Maria Private Bin Chardonnay 1996** 13.5 D

---

**Villa Maria Private Bin Gewurztraminer, Gisborne 1996** 13.5 C

Good with Thai food and will improve in bottle over the next year.

---

**Villa Maria Private Bin Sauvignon Blanc, Marlborough 1996** 15 D

Very high-class act, this. On the top ripe, rich fruit with huge restraint so you sense its presence rather than wallow in it. The acidity is whiplash-crisp and biting.

---

**Villa Maria Reserve Riesling 1996** 12 E

Very fruity, almost off-dry, with an impactful aroma of ripe pear. Good acidity, though, but this needs time to assert itself. 12 points now at this price, but in three to four years' time maybe 16. *Maybe.*

---

## PORTUGUESE WINE RED

**Quinta do Crasto, Douro 1995** 15 D

Rich, juicy, plump, with a dry finish. Extremely drinkable.

---

**Quinta do Crasto Reserve, Douro 1994** 13.5 E

Almost sweet on the finish – very ripe figs here.

---

## SOUTH AFRICAN WINE RED

**Beyerskloof Pinotage 1996** 13.5 C

Not as richly compelling as previous vintages.

---

**Boschkloof Merlot, Stellenbosch 1996** 13 D

Very quiet and cosy.

---

**Clos Malverne Devonet Cabernet Merlot 1996** 16 C

Rich yet in the sippin' style of fruit which accompanies curling up in an armchair with a saucy book.

---

**Clos Malverne Pinotage 1996** 16 D

Wonderfully invigorating and enticing bouquet of chestnuts roasting and cedar wood-smoke. The fruit is less complex and juicier than anticipated but still impressive. Will age interestingly for two years.

---

**Coree's Kraal Cabernet Sauvignon, Western Cape 1994** 13.5 D

---

**Fairview Tower Red, Paarl 1995** 14 D

Very ripe and well flavoured with the plummy fruit looked after by firm tannins.

---

**Fairview Zinfandel Cinsault 1996** 15.5 D

Try and catch any last remaining bottles of this. It has a tobacco-scented richness but not overripeness of gluggability. Fruity rather than downright dry, but the texture is soft. The hint of chutzpah – a Fairview characteristic – is subtly detectable. It's the finish which supplies the cheek: warm, erotic, spicy. It is excellent with grilled and roast vegetables and meats.

---

**Genus Shiraz 1996** 14.5 C

A rubbery shiraz of great depth and ripeness. Has a savoury finish. It needs food to really dazzle.

---

**Jacana Cabernet Sauvignon/Shiraz/Merlot, Stellenbosch 1996** 14 D

Rubbery and supple on the tastebuds. Stretches the vocabulary as much as the tongue. (I'm lost for words.)

---

**Jacana Pinotage, Stellenbosch 1995** 16.5 D

One of the pinotage tribe which is deliciously anxious to please with its upfront fruit and richness. Soft, ripe, aromatic and keen.

---

**John Faure Cabernet Shiraz 1996** 13.5 C

Light and fizzing with youth.

---

**Landskroon Pinotage Reserve, Paarl 1996** 13.5 D

Pinotage as a fruit drink. Could be given, beneficially, to invalids.

---

**Landskroon Shiraz, Paarl 1996** 13 D

Lighter-styled shiraz.

---

**Louisvale Cabernet Sauvignon/Merlot, Stellenbosch 1995** 15 E

Expensive but what the heck? How often do you taste such quirky flavours?

---

**Louisvale LV Cabernet Sauvignon, Western Cape 1996** 14 D

Has stalky richness and brambly fruitiness, nicely amalgamated with tannins and the result is flavour, depth and vibrancy.

---

**Louisvale Red, Stellenbosch 1996** 13 D

Swings a mean punch but only really connects on the finish.

---

**Savanha Shiraz, Western Cape 1996** 13.5 

---

**Sentinel Cabernet Sauvignon, Stellenbosch 1996** 15.5 C

Very gluggable but has sufficient depth, richness and some decent tannins, to go well with food.

---

**Sentinel Shiraz 1996** 15 D

---

**Stellenzicht Cabernet Sauvignon 1995** 14 D

Curious friendliness of approach mitigated (and saved from over-jamminess) by its tannins.

---

**Stellenzicht Merlot/Cabernet Franc, Stellenbosch 1994 and 1995** 14.5 D

The '95 rates 14 points. Not a lot to choose from here except there is a touch more depth in the '94. A very friendly, easy-going wine either way.

---

**Swartland Reserve Pinotage 1996** 15.5 D

Smoky richness and a touch of spice. Lovely wine of real style and individuality.

---

**Veenwouden, Coastal Region 1994** 15 F

Expensive, like its merlot sister, but so one-of-a-kind upfront drinkable, it's irresistible.

---

**Veenwouden Merlot, Paarl 1994** 16 F

A real treat. So likeable you have to down the bottle, as the ripe fruit drowns your tastebuds. Rich, ripe, comfortably one of the finest Cape merlots.

---

**Vergelegen Cabernet Sauvignon, Stellenbosch 1995** 16.5 D

Truly a delicious cabernet of smoothness, flavour, texture and polish.

---

**Vergelegen Merlot, Stellenbosch 1994** 16.5 E

Full of incisively rich, almost rampant fruit which finishes dry and very polished.

---

**Wildekrans Caresse Marine 1996** 13 C

---

**Wildekrans Pinotage, Western Cape 1996** 15 E

Packed with flavour and ripe blackcurrants – tight as a kiln jar.

---

## SOUTH AFRICAN WINE WHITE

**Bouchard Finlayson Sauvignon 1996** 13 D

Getting like sancerre – in price.

---

**Chavant Louisvale Wooded Chardonnay 1995** 14.5 D

The wood here evens out the richness of the fruit, adding finesse yet also personality and real style. An excellent wine for refined fish and shellfish dishes.

---

**Chavant Unwooded Louisvale Chardonnay 1996** 13 D

Has some richness but it seems to me a come-on rather than the real thing. A deep meaningful relationship is not possible with this flinty bottle.

---

**Collingbourne Cape White** 14 B

Astonishing price. Okay so it's not hugely fruity or complex but it's very drinkable, charming and well balanced.

---

**Eikendal Chardonnay, Stellenbosch 1996** 15 D

There is little doubt in my mind that anyone partnering a wine of this class with any kind of oceanic tidbit is obeying a law of nature. Wonderful rich stuff.

---

**Glen Carlou Chardonnay, Paarl 1996** 15 E

If you find yourself invited to dinner by someone who serves this wonderfully rich wine, marry her/him. S/he is unique.

---

**Haute Provence Vineyards Chardonnay 1996** 14 D

Richness all the way through with a nutty finish.

---

**Haute Provence Vineyards Sauvignon Blanc 1996** 12 D

---

**Jacana Chardonnay, Stellenbosch 1996** 15.5 D

Rich and creamy, lingering and deep, outrageously seductive company.

---

**Jacana Sauvignon Blanc, Stellenbosch 1996** 14 C

Very unusually textured and fruited sauvignon of individuality, flavour and controlled ripeness.

---

**John Faure Chenin Blanc, Paarl 1996** 12 C

Somewhat coarse as a tipple. But with a fish stew it might *just* pass.

---

**Louisvale Chardonnay, Stellenbosch 1996** 15.5 E

Ditto what I said about the Glen Carlou Chardonnay. Scrumptious stuff. Aisle drink it any day, any hour.

---

**Scholzenhof Ken Forrester Barrel Reserve Chenin Blanc, Stellenbosch 1996** 14 D

Very individual, highly personalized chenin of depth and flavour. Wonderful wine for prawns, squid, etcetera.

---

**Sentinel Chardonnay 1996** 14.5 D

---

**Springfield Chardonnay, Robertson 1996** 14.5 C

Serious introduction to the fruit (creamy and hints of wood) and a lingering finish. A serious, well-priced chardonnay of character.

---

**Stellenzicht Chardonnay 1996** 16 D

The wine is warm and aromatic – with deliciously inviting wood undertones which the fruit has firmly in control. The smoky vanilla edge is subtle yet incisive.

---

**Stellenzicht Gewurztraminer 1996** 13.5 D

Quirky aperitif: talcum powder sprinkled on rose petals.

---

**Stellenzicht Pinot Gris, Stellenbosch 1996** 12 C

A little awkward as it clogs rather than refreshes the throat.

---

**Swartland Reserve Chenin Blanc 1996** 13 C

---

**Van Loveren Colombar/Sauvignon Blanc 1996** 13.5 C

---

**Vergelegen Chardonnay 1995** 16 D

A wooded wonder: rich, deep, purposeful, hugely flavoured yet not inelegant and terrifically quaffable. One sip and you feel everything's all right with the world.

---

**Vergelegen Reserve Chardonnay 1995** 14 E

---

**Villiera Estate Blue Ridge Sauvignon Blanc 1996** 16 D

Lovely creamy richness perfectly offset by a crisp, fruity undertone.

---

**Wildekrans Caresse Marine 1996** 14 C

Caresse Marine is not the littoral harlot of some steamy epic but a wine. Incredibly, it is tasty, fruity, elegant and with rich flourish on the finish.

---

**Wildekrans Sauvignon Blanc 1996** 13.5 C

Thoroughly decent. Do with more ooooomphhhh . . .

---

## SPANISH WINE RED

**El Portico Rioja, Bodegas Palacio 1994** 17.5 D

The most elegant rioja I've tasted in thirty years. At the price, it's a steal. It is beautifully fruity, not one whit of vanilla or dank wood, just beautifully evolved tannins and subtle tobacco-edged prune and blackcurrant fruit of cosy drinking concentration. A lovely wine. A new start for rioja!!

---

**Orobio Tempranillo, Alaveses 1996** 15.5 C

Touch of shoe leather gives the soft fruit great character – and charm.

---

**Palacio de la Vega Crianza, Navarra 1994** 16.5 C

Oh! What gorgeous texture and flavour here! It's a sublimely well-priced wine of class, vigour and richness.

---

**Palacio de la Vega Merlot, Navarra 1994** 15 D

Rich, dry yet soft, and with a hint of soft leather on the finish.

---

**Vega Sindoa Tempranillo, Navarra 1995** 14 C

---

**Veganueva Garnacha 1996** 15.5 C

Every beaujolais should be but isn't like this: fresh, fruity, lovely natural clean fruit and great chilled.

---

**Vinas del Vero Cabernet Sauvignon, Somontano 1995** 15 C

Great cabernet value. Has a hint of ripe cassis to some very alert acidity, supple tannins, and it's all packed together beautifully.

---

**Vinas del Vero Pinot Noir, Somontano 1994** 12 

---

# SPANISH WINE WHITE

**Albacora Sauvignon Blanc, Duero 1996** 13 C

Curious fruit – difficult to classify.

---

**Burgans Albarino 1996** 13.5 D

Interesting – but six quid is a mite difficult to swallow.

---

**Marino White, Berberana** 13.5 

---

**Rioja Cosme Blanco, Bodegas Palacio 1995** 13.5 D

---

**Santara Chardonnay 1996** 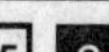

One of the tastiest and best-value chardonnays around.

---

**Vega Sindoa Chardonnay, Navarra 1996** 14 D

Great with food. Has lovely wood presence and some rich melon/lemon fruit.

---

**Vinas del Vero Barrel Fermented Chardonnay, Somontano 1995** 16 D

This is a wine! Elegantly wooded, finely textured, delicious from nose to throat, it enjoys fish, chicken, vegetables and soups. It is also, with its aromatic, creamy fruit, very pleasant to sip whilst listening to sexual overtures. Or Bach's.

---

# USA WINE RED

**Chateau de Baun Pinot Noir, Russian River Valley 1994** 13 D

**Chateau de Baun Rouge 1993** 14 C

Not at all bad. But strictly for the pinot freak – who will like a distant hum of long-dead grouse.

**Franciscan Oakville Zinfandel 1994** 14 E

**Havenscourt Barbera, California** 13 C

Very juicy.

**Havenscourt Zinfandel, California** 14.5 C

Juicy and ripe but hints of spice, tannins, and depth. Great quaffing wine and good with food.

**Marrieta Old Vine Red Lot 19, Geyserville** 13.5 E

Goodness, it's juicy, forwardly soppy.

**Rocking Horse Lamborn Vineyard Zinfandel, Horwell Mountain 1994** 12 G

Hits back on the finish but the fruit before this picks itself up off the floor.

**Sterling Redwood Trail Cabernet Sauvignon 1994** 13.5 C

**Sterling Vineyards Cabernet Sauvignon, Napa 1994** 13.5 D

**Sterling Vineyards Winery Lake Pinot Noir, Carneros 1995** 14 E

Infinitely better than most high-priced dross from Burgundy.

---

**Villa Mount Eden Zinfandel Cellar Select 1994** 14 D

Turn syrah lover into zin zealot with this bottle.

---

## USA WINE — WHITE

**Bonny Doon Framboise (half bottle)** 16 D

Wonderful concentrated fruit. Incredible crushed cassis aroma and flavour. Pour it over ice-cream or use it as an aperitif addition to dry white or sparkling wine.

---

**Chateau de Baun Symphony, Russian River Valley 1994** 12 

Smells like a Turkish delight and almost tastes like one.

---

**Echo Ridge Fume Blanc 1995** 13.5 

---

**Fetzer Bonterra Chardonnay 1995** 14.5 E

Lovely musk of melon aroma, rich and inviting, which leads to unhurried fruit of charm and poise, finishing the melony fruit with vague hints of pineapple and firmer hints of lemon. A fine, well-textured wine.

---

**Landmark Damaris Chardonnay 1994** 16 G

Drink it in five years and it'll blow any white Burgundy at three times the price out of the water and rate maybe 18/19 points. Right now, it's soft and seductive but its real charms are all hidden. Fine Wine shops only.

---

**Landmark Overlook Chardonnay, 1995** 16.5 F

What a treat: woody, balanced, beautifully ripe, rich fruit in perfect form, and a deep lingering finish. Quite delicious. Expensive but very fine.

---

**Mariquita 1994** 13.5 C

---

**McDowell Grenache Rose 1995** 12 D

---

**VIlla Mount Eden Chardonnay, Cellar Select 1994** 15 D

Lovely texture here.

---

# FORTIFIED WINE

**Quinta do Crasto LBV 1991** 16 E

One of the best LBVs around. Lovely figgy fruit and velvet texture. Good for several years yet.

---

# SPARKLING WINE/CHAMPAGNE

**Casa del Valle Brut (Chile)** 16.5 D

Ignore the crass label. Concentrate on the classic fruit inside the bottle. Brilliant value.

---

**Casa del Valle Demi Sec (Chile)** 12 E

---

**Champagne Alfred Gratien NV** 13 G

An elegant hint-of-lemon bubbly which is rashly overpriced.

---

**Champagne Pommery 1990** 14.5 H

One of the most delicately delicious champagnes around. It is in the class of the finest bubblies from Marlborough, New Zealand. It is, alas, more than twice the price of them.

---

**Deakin Estate Brut (Australia)** 13.5 D

Fruity fruit. Very flashily labelled. Touch of flash on the fruit, too.

---

**Deutz Marlborough Cuvee (New Zealand)** 15.5 E

As elegant as any on the market.

---

**Graham Beck Blanc de Blancs (South Africa)** 13 E

---

**Gratien & Meyer Saumur Cuvee Flamme Brut NV (France)** 12 E

Curious soapy finish.

---

**Lindauer Special Reserve (New Zealand)** 15.5 E

Has finesse and flavour and classic style. Good price for the quality of the fruit.

---

**Seaview Brut** 14 D

---

**Seppelt Great Western Brut** 15 C

---

**Shadow Creek Californian Blanc de Noirs** 14.5 E

See that cocked hat? See how sodden it is? That's the champagne this terrific bubbly has knocked there.

---

# SPAR

Wine buying, like British business in general it seems to me, is a more creative business than it used to be. Whereas buyers were once simply briefed to find wines to fill all the relevant price brackets, the popularisation of wine and the revolution in its marketing mean today's wine buyer is developing new wines, dreaming up innovative marketing concepts and creating original and eye-catching packaging. Such creative freedom can lead to wine buyers going into innovation over-kill, their imaginations running risibly riotous to the detriment of loyal customers' prejudices and thus, ultimately, sales. The risk of this happening at Spar, however, is minimal for a variety of solid reasons.

Spar's wine buyer and departmental supremo, Liz Aked, knows she has to keep her feet firmly on the ground, not least because the 2,031 licensed retailers belonging to this franchise group are not actually obliged to buy any of the wines she sources. They can stick two fingers up to any, or indeed every, wine on her list. But in spite of this fierce independence, the caution bred by it does not lead to a lack of imagination or a degree of originality. What she has achieved in terms of improving and broadening the Spar range in the four years since her arrival from Asda, bears eloquent witness to the fact that Ms Aked is not only no mean judge of wine but one who can keep her wilder creative juices firmly in check yet still enjoy herself.

She believes the wine buyer's prime responsibilities are commercial rather than creative. 'A wine buyer is a curious animal,' she begins. No argument there. 'You have to have a commercial brain and you've got to be able to understand the technicalities of wine production. But you have to understand the marketing side of it and be able to promote, and you have to have a good palate as well. That is a mixture of business, art and science.' But surely with new concepts to devise and distant new vineyards and regions to discover, the wine buyer's job is rather . . . well, romantic? 'I don't think it's romantic,' says Ms Aked, feet not so much on the ground at this point as nailed to it. 'I think if I had a romantic view of wine then I would purchase lots of bottles I couldn't sell.' (Curious view of romance but, the more you think about it, a decidedly feminine and intelligently defining view too.)

Spar's wine sales are up 24 per cent so far this year, continuing a fairly healthy upward trend, according to Ms Aked, so one can fairly deduce that she is indeed buying things which she can sell to the wholesalers who deal with all those independently minded grocers. Around half of the 200 wines in the range are Spar brands sourced specifically for the retailer. And some recent additions among them suggest that Ms Aked is playing down her creative capabilities. New this year is a range of Chilean wines, produced and bottled for Spar in the Maipo Valley by the Chilean producer, Canepa. At £4.49 a bottle, these four wines – comprising the perennial fab four of the grape world – Chardonnay, Sauvignon Blanc, Cabernet Sauvignon and Merlot – are decent value for money. The rich and elegant Cabernet Sauvignon scores 15 points, while the Merlot rated 14. The whites fared equally well in tasting. I found the Chardonnay was a classy wine with interesting pineapple and lemon flavours. I have had no qualms about awarding it 15 points. The Sauvignon Blanc, clean, fresh and strident with a lemony finish, walked away with 14.5 points.

Not a disappointing flavour in the range. But then the labels created for these wines also catch the eye, giving a decided impression of quality with pizzazz. The labels feature works of art owned by the Canepa family, so it wasn't any problem cajoling the producer into considering the labels right for the job. While Liz Aked naturally feels the liquid has to come first – it is after all the quality of the wine which will determine if customers come back for more – she does appreciate that packaging is vital if a wine retailer is to be successful. The evidence is everywhere throughout Spar's range. The wines have not only been transformed in the bottle, but in general the wines are far more visually appealing. 'You have to be able to package a wine successfully if it is to sell. It is the single most important part of getting consumers to pick it up off the shelf in the first place,' Liz Aked points out. (Darn. I was hoping that wine guides like this one might play a part. Shall I retire now?)

The collaboration with Canepa – now in the second vintage – is a perfect example of the new forms of relationship that exist between today's suppliers and today's retail buyers. As is quite customary nowadays, Liz Aked has had a hand in the blending and selection of the wines. Another Spar offering which has been specially commissioned by Ms Aked is the Italian Rondolle range, produced in Puglia under the direction of that tireless oenologist with wings, Mr Kim Milne. The flying winemaker is very much a product of, and in some cases a catalyst for, the wine revolution of the last few years. The most successful of them are renowned and versatile winemakers with sufficient acumen and chutzpah to pop up on demand all over the world. Many of them are Australian, incidentally, reflecting the itinerant tendencies of the Australians as a tribe. The thought occurs that while Ms Aked believes her job necessitates keeping her feet on the ground, Kim Milne's job description conversely prescribes he remain perpetually airborne. Given the near deification of some flying winemakers by the wine-buying fraternity, perhaps unassisted flight will be their next trick.

Liz Aked, however, does not subscribe to the current idolisation of the flying winemaker, not least because the idea of such a concept means, she believes, very little to her customers. 'The public have no idea what a flying winemaker is,' she says. She points out that many of the wines made this way are homogenous in style, lack personality and fail 'to say something about the place they come from'. But, she adds: 'Kim is fine. I can work with him. But there are others I can't work with and wouldn't want to work with.'

In fact, it was not Spar which brought Kim Milne into the Rondolle project, though the retailer has worked with him directly in other regions. The winery in Puglia was already involved with the ubiquitous Aussie when it was approached by Spar. Ms Aked's confidence in Kim Milne is more than justified by the Rondolle wines. There is certainly nothing homogenous about the style since the local Bombino grape variety is used along with the Chardonnay – a variety which has more foreign stickers on its suitcase than any other. However. I found this year's Rondolle Bianco to be somewhat grudging, in stark contrast to its red Cabernet/Negroamaro stablemate which gushed with flavour and richness and was very very eager to please.

Let us hope that Spar's latest Italian innovation, the Pasta Red and Pasta White, have as much to say for themselves. So new are these wines that the retailer is yet to send me samples but I do know that they will retail for £3.99 for a 1-litre bottle and should be in the shops in September. The idea is not new, Tesco has a so-called Great with Pasta/Chicken/Fish/Etc. of similarly titled, food-matching wines, and Victoria Wine has Ravioli Red. Ms Aked's approach will not, then, break virgin territory. It could not be otherwise. 'Spar does not tend to pioneer,' says Ms Aked. 'I would say that Spar tends to follow the market.' She believes that her job involves more pioneering than it would have done five years ago, but she has to be more circumspect than her counterparts at, say, Tesco and Sainsbury's. 'I can't take as great a risk but I can provide something that is unique, interesting and specific. You have to bear in mind at the end of the day that I am working for 2,000 retailers and they have to sell the product.'

Arguably Spar's most successful supplier collaboration in the last year or so has been with the Graham Beck Winery in Robertson, South Africa, on its South African Classic Red and

Classic White. Both of these sell for £3.99 and the white is perhaps a bit on the pricey side. Neither wine this year, in fact, is quite up to the fruit of last year's but this range has undoubtedly gone down well with Spar customers. Its success has led to other projects in collaboration with Graham Beck, with two further wines in the pipeline. 'This year they have picked blocks of Chardonnay specifically to make me a Chardonnay to a brief,' says Ms Aked, who also spoke fervently of a Pinot Noir/Chardonnay sparkling wine, laid down eighteen months ago, which will be introduced as a Spar exclusive line in the middle of next year.

It is the close rapport and spirit of partnership, says Ms Aked, that has spawned these other wines. The strong implication here is that if a retailer adopts an over-aggressive approach with a supplier, they can ultimately lose out when wine is in shorter supply or something special comes along. 'Sometimes I do need to get the last squeeze from a supplier,' she admits, 'but if I do that I know that when it comes to anything special they are going to produce, I won't be in line for it.'

Furthermore, particularly in South Africa, Ms Aked was quick to acknowledge that there are ethical factors to consider. 'I would like to think that we as a wine department would not exploit any supplier anywhere in the world and I would consider many forms of rhetoric about partnerships to be empty words,' she says.

Travelling to a region personally, a buyer is without doubt in a better position to judge how a supplier treats its workforce, and Ms Aked says that in somewhere like South Africa a supplier's labour practices would be taken into consideration. 'These guys are not the cheapest I could have bought from but I am not prepared to sell anything cheaper at the expense of exploitation,' she says. 'I am sure their practices are not perfect but from what I have seen they are fair and equitable and a darn sight fairer than many.'

She was anxious not to be seen to be scoring public relations points with these comments, and one gained the impression that Liz Aked and her employers really do take these considerations extremely seriously, possibly because rather than being part of a large conglomerate, Spar is essentially an association of small shopkeepers. 'Without getting too political about it,' she adds choosing her words carefully, 'I think that is the sort of attitude that Spar has across the world because we are the small retailer against the multiples.'

Noble ideals, but Spar is in so many ways a one-off that the claim does have the ring of truth about it. As for Ms Aked, she too is one-off. Running her own show, she is resolute and fairly forceful and at the same time completely approachable, a rare combination. And while she may downplay the creative side of her job, she said that it was enormously fulfilling, with projects like the South African and Chilean collaborations providing the most satisfaction. She asserts that the job is 95 per cent commercial and only 5 per cent creative but is quick to concede that buying anything else would not be nearly so much fun. When asked how she would react if offered the job of buying biros, with a concomitant promotion and salary rise, she quietly retorted, 'They would be told to sod off,' and one got the distinct impression, as one does with quite literally everything else she says, that she means it.

SPAR LANDMARK
32-40 Headstone Drive
Harrow
Middlesex
HA3 5QT
Tel 0181 863 5511
Fax 0181 863 0603

## AUSTRALIAN WINE RED

**Four Winds Red** 12 C

Struggles. One of the winds is going in the wrong direction.

---

**Hardys Bankside Shiraz 1995** 14 D

Classy stuff – has oodles of flavour but it doesn't sag in the middle like some Aussies. It has some weight, some tannin, some character to last the course (meat or veg or cheese).

---

**Lindemans Cawarra Shiraz Cabernet 1996**  C

Soupy richness and flavour make it highly drinkable.

---

## AUSTRALIAN WINE WHITE

**Four Winds White** 12 C

Doesn't altogether blow me over. Touch of honey on the finish is a mite crude.

---

**Lindemans Bin 65 Chardonnay 1996** 15.5 C

Elegant, purposeful, balanced, finely wrought and handsomely textured. A text-book Aussie chardonnay.

---

**Lindemans Cawarra Semillon/Riesling 1996** 13.5 B

Somewhat flattish on the finish to rate higher. Needs food to shine.

---

## BULGARIAN WINE — RED

**Bulgarian Country Red, Russe, Spar** 14 B

---

**Korten Region Cabernet Sauvignon 1992** 13 B

Ripe, lacking in acidity and tannins, but very fruity – and curiously foppish for a Bulgar.

---

## BULGARIAN WINE — WHITE

**Bulgarian Country White, Slaviantzi, Spar** 14 B

---

## CHILEAN WINE — RED

**Canepa Cabernet Sauvignon 1995** 15 C

Lovely richness, style, depth and drinkability. Really elegant shape to the wine. Has wit.

---

**Canepa Merlot 1996** 14 C

Good rich attack of soft ripe fruit. Touch untypical on the finish where the leathery edge seems to falter, but the texture wins it its points.

---

**La Fortuna Malbec 1996** 15 

Softer and less tannic than previous vintages, this is still a lovely wine – rich, very dry, characterful and gently rustic. It has already improved since I first tasted it in November 1996 and will continue to do so over the next twenty months and rate maybe 16 points or more in time.

---

## CHILEAN WINE — WHITE

**Canepa Chardonnay 1996** 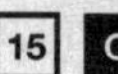


Softly encroaches on the tongue, then strikes rich, pineappley and lemony on the throat. An excellent wine of some class.

---

**Canepa Sauvignon Blanc 1996** 

C

As zippy a label as the wine in the bottle – strident, clean, fresh and crisp, touch of melon/lemon fruit on the finish and it turns more citric as it goes down.

---

## FRENCH WINE — RED

**Chateau Bories-Azeau, Corbieres 1996** 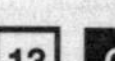


Somehow, I feel there is huge potential in the fruit from this vineyard but it isn't being realized.

---

**Claret 1995** 

C

Brilliant easy-drinking claret, great in the big, sexy magnum size (at around £7.25) which has serious cabernet character and style.

---

**Coteaux du Languedoc** 

Attractive when drunk with a plate of roast vegetables strewn with herbs covered in melted cheese.

---

**Cotes de Catalanes Rouge NV** 

Excellent food wine – has depth, richness and texture. Surprisingly, the softness and velvety quality of the fruit dominate what little rusticity it has.

---

**Fitou NV** 13.5 C

Somewhat expensive, at four quid, for it is essentially simple and fruity but it does have some ripely interwoven, well-wrought texture to it.

---

**Gemini Merlot 1995** 14 C

Interesting double attack of rich ripe fruit with dry characterful tannins. Good stuff.

---

**Le Rossignol Cotes du Ventoux 1995** 13 B

Ripe and cherryish at first, then dry and brusque on the finish.

---

**Lussac St Emilion 1995** 14 D

Classy, soft, perfectly textured and stylish on the lingering, rich finish.

---

**Merlot, VdP d'Oc Cuxac, Spar** 12.5 B

---

**Oaked Merlot, VdP d'Oc** 13 C

Touch pricey for the home-spun style, but eminently drinkable.

---

**Syrah VdP d'Oc** 14.5 C

---

**Tuileries du Bosc Cotes de St Mont 1994** 15.5 C

The perfect southern French red: priced right and fruited right. It's dry, herby, flavourful, great with robust food.

---

**VdP de la Cite de Carcassonne 1996, Spar** 13 B

Fresh and cherry/plum ripe with faint, very faint echoes of earthy rusticity.

---

**Vignerons des Pieve, Cuvee San Michele Pinot Noir** 12 C

I strongly suspect it tastes more delicious in Corsica, where it's made, than in England.

---

**Vin de Pays de l'Aude Rouge NV** 10 B

---

## FRENCH WINE WHITE

**Chablis 1995** 13 E

Decent enough except when one's eye alights on the price tag.

---

**Chardonnay, VdP d'Oc 1995** 12 C

Bit of a dull dog.

---

**Chardonnay VdP d'Oc, Oak Aged 1995** 14 C

An attractively balanced wine. The wood is chaste and thus the fruit unsullied. The richness is stylish.

---

**Cotes de Catalanes Blanc NV** 8 B

I suppose I might, being a softie, offer a glass to a thirsty dog.

---

**Gemini Sauvignon Blanc 1994** 13.5 C

Seems lean and grassy as it commences but then turns fat and rich. Curious feat but a worthy one.

---

**James Herrick Chardonnay VdP d'Oc 1996** 14.5 C

More lemonic than previous vintages and less like the Old World style – but it will, I feel, pull itself round more richly over the next nine months.

---

**Muscadet, Spar** 14 B

A good solid fresh muscadet at the right price, it won't last much beyond the end of January 1998. So slurp early!

---

**Muscat de St Jean de Minervois (half bottle)** 15 B

Rich, honeyed, beautifully waxy and great value. Brilliant with fruit or blue cheese.

---

**Oaked Chardonnay VdP d'Oc 1996** 15 C

Rich and tasty, elegant yet ripe, smoochy yet serious.

---

**Rose d'Anjou, Spar** 11 B

---

**Rose de Syrah VdP d'Oc 1996, Spar** 12 B

Light, hints of richness, touch cosmetic.

---

**VdP de la Cite de Carcassonne 1996, Spar** 15 B

Simply terrific value: flavourful yet crisp, soft yet zippy, textured yet easy to get down.

---

**VdP des Cotes Catalanes, Spar** 13 B

---

**Vouvray Donatien Bahuaud 1995** 11 C

Somewhat raw and indecisive – as yet. It might grow up and the dryness be less uncertain of the fruit. But I wonder?

---

## GERMAN WINE WHITE

**Grans Fassian Piesporter Goldtropfchen Riesling 1992** 16 D

Tasted for the second time in July 1997 (after eleven months), this wine was still up to snuff. A dilemma: do you drink it now and risk your guests' derision at the honeyed edge? Or do you wait and let the superb petrol and mineral tones develop? Drink now! A plague on your guests' heads!

---

## HUNGARIAN WINE RED

**Danube Hungarian Country Red, Spar** 12 B

---

**Misty Mountain Merlot** 11 B

Doesn't make my heart flutter.

---

## HUNGARIAN WINE WHITE

**Danube Hungarian Country White, Spar** 13 B

---

**Misty Mountain Chardonnay, Spar** 14 B

Stylish, on the lemonic side, good-value sipping and fish eating.

---

## ITALIAN WINE RED

**Ariento Sangiovese del Rubicon** 12 B

Touch like ketchup in its fruity clottedness.

---

**Chianti 1995** 11 C

Simple as a gulp of fruit juice – with earth.

---

**Montepulciano d'Abruzzo Cantina Tollo 1995** 12 C

You can't loathe it. Equally, you won't walk over hot coals to acquire it.

---

**Rondolle Negroamero/Cabernet, Spar** 13.5 C

Soft, full of flavour and richness and very, very eager to be loved.

---

**Sicilian Red Table Wine, Spar** 15 B

This is the sort of soft, rich, simple fruit I love, even chilled as a welcome-home-from-work bottle.

---

**Valpolicella, Spar** 12 B

---

## ITALIAN WINE WHITE

**Rondolle Bianco, Spar** 10 C

Is Ron on the dolle through lack of opportunity or laziness? Either way, this wine doesn't work to please greatly.

---

**Sicilian White Table Wine, Spar**  

Cheeky chappie: nutty and clean with a hint of soft melon. A refreshing glug as well as a good fish wine.

---

**Trebbiano d'Abruzzo 1995, Spar** 11 

A touch on the muddy side.

---

## MORAVIAN WINE RED

**Moravian Vineyards Czech Red Wine** 11 

Dull.

---

## MORAVIAN WINE — WHITE

**Moravian Vineyards Czech White Wine** 12 C

Interesting chewy finish which clogs rather than excites the throat.

---

## PORTUGUESE WINE — RED

**Dona Elena Portuguese Red, Spar** 13 B

A bit of a young thug. Has no manners, little grace and it's soft and soppy at heart.

---

**Sogrape Vinho de Monte Altenejo 1993** 13 D

Good fruit but at six quid, I want more thrills on my tastebuds.

---

## PORTUGUESE WINE — WHITE

**Dona Elena Portuguese White, Spar** 13.5 

Cheap and almost cheerful. Not an exuberant wine.

---

**Vinho Verde NV** 10 

---

## SOUTH AFRICAN WINE — RED

**Paarl Heights Red 1995** 14.5 C

---

**South African Classic Red** 12 C

They used to shoot reds in South Africa – lock 'em up certainly. This one would benefit from a short spell of character-building incarceration.

---

**Table Mountain Pinot Noir** 13.5 C

Cherryish, dry, earthy and good with food. An unusually old-fangled pinot.

---

## SOUTH AFRICAN WINE WHITE

**South African Classic White** 13.5 C

Touch pricey at £3.99. Should be £3.39 it seems to me. The fruit's okay but a touch ho-hum on the finish.

---

**Table Mountain Chenin Blanc** 13.5 B

Comes from the small obscure Cape wine area of Goudini – pronounced with an H. This wine isn't magic but it is nutty and fresh.

---

## SPANISH WINE RED

**Albor Campo Viejo Rioja 1996** 15 C

Catch it while it's young. The '96 is vigorous and rich, deep and stylish.

---

**Albor Rioja 1995** 13.5 C

---

**Campo Rojo Carinena** 14 B

Cheap enough for real cherry-ripeness yet dry food-friendliness.

---

**Rioja La Catedral NV** 12 C

Bullies the palate a little. It should be more deft.

---

**Valdepenas, Spar** 14.5 B

---

**Valencia Soft Red NV** 11 B

---

## SPANISH WINE WHITE

**Campo Verde Carinena** 14 B

It somehow reminds me of the last time I changed a nappy: soft towelling, talc, a young rubbery bum, and coos. Yes, I like this wine.

---

**Valencia Dry White NV** 13 B  

Party wine.

---

## USA WINE RED

**Fir Tree Ridge** 12.5 C 

I'd like it more if it wasn't four quid.

---

## USA WINE WHITE

**Fir Tree Ridge** 13.5 C 

Has some warmth and sun but I wish it also had some citric acidity to finish off with more aplomb.

---

# FORTIFIED WINE

**Old Cellar LBV Port 1990, Spar** 15 E

One of the best-value ports around: rich, cloying, deep and delicious. Brilliant with Christmas pud or cake.

---

# SPARKLING WINE/CHAMPAGNE

**Marquis de Preval Champagne, NV** 13 F

A lemony champagne which I prefer to certain more famous so-called 'grand' marques.

---

**Seppelt Great Western Brut**  

---

# THRESHER

Thresher is a giant octopus. With over 1,500 stores this retailer casts an enormous and complex shadow, and not only in the UK. Its buying policy makes it extremely active and involved in many wine-producing regions. Not only able to buy on a large scale, Thresher has become one of the prime movers in having wines developed specially to suit its own requirements. For an explanation of how Thresher buys its wines, I turned to the ebullient David Howse. Responsible for running Thresher's PR, David is charged with expressing the retailer's official word on such matters. It is a job which he enjoys with unabashed relish and the energy with which he throws himself into his task is inspiring if rather exhausting to behold. But the pages of correspondence I have received detailing Thresher's buying philosophy have been most illuminating.

'We have the benefit of being quite a large purchaser of wine,' he starts modestly. But then nice but resonant understatement rather than ripe braggadocio is Mr Howse's style. Thresher, in truth, has huge buying power, as it needs to source wines for its Thresher Wine Shops, Wine Rack, Bottoms Up, The Drinks Cabin general off-licences and Hutton's convenience stores. The company is currently piloting another concept, Booze Barn, a 10,000 sq ft retail warehouse at Staples Corner in north-west London. All in all the company serves some 3.5 million customers per week and last year sold 53 million bottles of wine (this is less than half that of Tesco or Sainsbury, as a matter of interest). Mr Howse continues: 'This means that for the volume lines, say under £5 and £6, we can very often take a whole batch rather than a part of the production. This then allows a lot of it to be made specifically for us. When I had a quick look at the range I reckoned that about half of what we sell has either been made at our request or blended to our specifications. By this I don't just mean "ranges" like King's Canyon from California, Winelands from South Africa, Southlands from France, Las Colinas from Chile or Corizon from Argentina but also other wines which, although sold by our competitors under the same label from the same producer, are in the bottle in our shops to our specification. A good example of this is our basic Alsace varietals from Caves Vinicoles de Turckheim. These are stocked by many other retailers but ours have been made with more reserve wines to up the quality after a blending trip by Lucy.'

'Lucy' refers to Lucy Warner, one of Thresher's large team of buyers, who has responsibility for certain French regions, Eastern Europe and South Africa. Like all the Thresher buyers, Ms Warner spends a massive amount of time in these regions of production because of Thresher's close involvement with the producers in the creation and development of the wines. This contrasts sharply with how business would have been done in the 1970s. 'In those days the way we bought wine was different,' Mr Howse explains. 'We didn't get involved in the wine itself really. It was before the age of wine enlightenment and we all went to worship at the great and well-known areas and took what they gave us (gratefully too). This means that, unless you were going somewhere as a Jolly, there was little point in sending a buyer. There was nothing for them to become involved in. Most of the travelling was done by agents. Now we work as a partnership – experts in the consumer working hand in glove with the experts in winemaking.'

Although the idea of commissioning wines is seen as a new trend in the wine market, Kim Tidy (a senior member of Thresher's wine-buying department) pointed out that some of the Thresher projects have now been going for many years. One of the earliest commissions, he remembers, was for Domaine du Tariquet which dates back to 1982. Kim Tidy still reckons this to be one of the most successful projects the retailer has initiated. The idea was simply to make a competitively priced dry white wine from the South of France; it has been one of the company's best-selling bottles ever since. A Domaine du Tariquet Sauvignon Blanc is now in the pipeline incidentally. Another big seller for Thresher has been the Tollana range, made to a specific brief by the giant Southcorp wine company in Australia (and better known as Penfolds). It began with four wines and now the range extends to more than ten. 'Put simply,' says Mr Tidy, 'Tollana is a brand. It is the fourth or fifth biggest wine brand in this country and it is only sold in our stores.'

The idea of partnership is central to these and many other wines and the result is that a major proportion of Thresher's bottles come from wine companies and flying winemakers with whom it has a close and continuing relationship. 'The more I look, the more I realise that more and more of our wines come from producers with whom we have a relationship,' David Howse continues. 'It is a function of post-revolution wine buying. Another function of the revolution is that we don't just have relationships with producers from areas. As important to us are the flyers such as Ryman, Boudinaud, Lurton and Milne, people who can go the world over on our behalf and create exciting, brilliantly made new wines. We don't ask these people to go to, say, Germany or Chile or California and make us an Australian lookalike. That's rather missing the glorious point about wine. Neither do we tell them how to make the wine. We know our customers. That is our area of expertise. They know how to make bloody wonderful wine. That is their area of expertise. Then they add the local character to their winemaking skills, often in collaboration with local winemakers. That's what we believe our customers want.'

But as David Howse points out, the retailer needs to guide the winemakers on the style of the wine. 'It doesn't matter how brilliant a winemaker is. If he doesn't have consumers to buy and drink his wine there is diddly-squat point in him or her making any. Winemaking may be the perfect blend of science and art – controlling a natural process and yet being at one with nature at the same time – but the end result is a consumer product and always has been.'

There is, in all this, a fine line to draw. While Thresher does not want to tell the winemakers how to make the wines, it does work closely with them to determine the style of the wine and ensure that it fits with what Thresher consumers expect. 'We work with the producers before the grapes are even harvested, sometimes before the vines are even planted. We suggest directions that they should go. We give them the fiscal security to experiment and innovate by commissioning ranges of wine. But as I have said before, we are knowledgeable about the market . . . not oenology. We don't tell them how to make it or ask them to make impressions of a wine from another country. It would be as daft as hiring a great chef and then telling him what ingredients to use and how to cook them.'

As previously revealed, the vast amount of travelling the Thresher wine buyers have to do to maintain these close links is not regarded as a Jolly by the buying team. Ms Warner, who was reckoned to have travelled around 23,000 miles last year on buying business, and Kim Tidy who clocked up some 55,000 miles, bridle at the idea that this is a perk of the job. However, neither looks on it as a chore either. It is simply part of the job. It goes with the territory and it is hard work. There is almost a hint of irascibility in Kim Tidy's voice when he explains yet again that his job is not about being wined and dined in beautiful locations, amassing a personal collection of fine wines in the process. He explains that when he meets people for the first time at dinner parties he tries to avoid telling them what he does because he knows what questions will follow. 'People are always asking me about my cellar and I say I don't have one. It's one of those misconceptions,' he says. 'You have a cellar full of wine, that you have long lunches and are being entertained a lot and also when you go abroad you may be in the winery until 10:00, then you are on the beach or skiing. The first question you get is "Oh, you must do a lot of travelling, where have you been to?" As if it is all play and no work.'

Mr Tidy likens his reticent attitude towards divulging what he does to that of a doctor in a similar situation. He once, he recounts, met such an individual at a dinner party and found they both shared a preference to keeping quiet about their lines of work. Whereas Mr Tidy finds himself quizzed covetously on his sumptuous lifestyle, the doctor generally found that dinner guests would divest articles of clothing to reveal festering carbuncles or angry rashes and say, 'I've had this for a couple of weeks. How long have I got?'

Lucy Warner takes a slightly different view, but agrees that it is annoying if people have the preconception that the life is all fun and no work. 'It's something I love,' says Ms Warner (and thanks for the postcard, Lucy, you sent me from Cape Town this summer. I loved getting it). 'If people are interested in what you do, then it's brilliant because it's nice to talk about enjoying your job because a lot of people don't enjoy their jobs. But the real buggeration is when you feel you have to justify what you are doing.' As a wine writer who goes to dinner parties or luncheons where guests often sigh and stare longingly into space when the nature of my employment comes into the conversation, I understand the problem. But then I'm not a wine buyer. In France, I always describe myself, when asked, as *un parasite du vin.*

One of the most recent collaborations Lucy Warner has been working on provides an excellent example of the kind of wines Thresher is keen to create. Arniston Bay is a South African wine and Thresher has been instrumental in the development of both the wine and its packaging. 'It's the first flange bottle to come out of South Africa,' Ms Warner explained. A flange bottle has a lip at the top. 'We wanted to have a new bottle shape, new labelling and something completely different.' Interestingly, the wine itself has created much interest back in South Africa because it has been so successful. Apparently, South African consumers also want to get their hands on some. Unfortunately for the natives of its homeland it is sold only in Thresher Wine Shops. It is quirky, spicy, creamy, delicious and well worth its 15-point rating.

Arniston Bay illustrates that the retailer's involvement in packaging and label design is every bit as crucial as the specifications it may give with regard to taste. Two other recent introductions which exhibit the same innovative approach to packaging are the Original Zin Primitivo del Salento 1995 and the Original Sin Chardonnay del Salento 1996, two Italian wines made for the retailer by Kim Milne. They are very respectable tipples, ranking 13 and 14 points respectively, but what makes these fun wines stand out are the names, the blue bottles, the distinctive labelling and the use of crown capsules rather than traditional corks. The fruit inside, not hugely thrilling at present, will, I have a feeling, improve in future vintages once the vines catch up with the nattiness of the presentation. Slow wits, vines.

Establishing a close rapport with the winemakers has the main benefit of producing wines tailored to modern tastes, but there are also other marketing pluses such as bringing the winemakers into contact with sales staff. 'From the shops' point of view they absolutely love having a tasting held by a winemaker,' says Lucy Warner. 'If we have brand days when we have the winemakers there to talk to the staff you can see the difference in the enthusiasm in the staff. It's incredible.'

In essence, the difference in the way Thresher conducts its business today compared with how a retailer would have bought wine twenty years ago is that the person making the wine is effectively now so much closer to the final consumer, with the retail buyers forming the bridge. Of course even though retailing is a much more sophisticated business today, the impetus for this change did not come just from the retailers. Most buyers agree that it was the dynamic, market-led strategy of the Australian wine producers which was the main lever of change. Today, however, apart from what Kim Tidy refers to as a few 'bastions of indifference', wine producers the world over are keen to work in partnership with retailers to produce the wines they and their customers demand. I can only congratulate Thresher for its blend of size with unstuffiness. It's the best way for the high street retailer to keep the supermarkets on their toes.

THRESHER
Sefton House
42 Church Road
Welwyn Garden City
Herts
AL8 6PJ
Tel 01707 328244
Fax 01707 371398

**SEE STOP PRESS SECTION AT END OF BOOK FOR LAST-MINUTE ADDITIONS TO THIS RETAILER'S RANGE.**

## ARGENTINIAN WINE RED

**Corazon Bonarda, Mendoza 1996** 15 C

A delightfully roguish red with dry-edged softness and richness and a good characterful personality.

---

**Corazon Tempranilla, Mendoza 1996** 14.5 C

Chocolate and cream, tannin, and blackcurrant and plums – jammy, clotted, rampant.

---

**La Rural Malbec 1996** 15 C

In spite of its brassy beer-labelling appearance, the wine inside is more respectably clothed in velvet-textured deep scarlet. Has a real flourish in the finish.

---

**Libertad Sangiovese Malbec 1996** 13 

Nice plump texture and soft fruit.

---

## ARGENTINIAN WINE WHITE

**Corazon Chardonnay Chenin, Mendoza 1996** 

Well priced and fruited. Good with food, good with mood.

---

**Corazon Chenin Blanc, Mendoza 1996** 15.5 C

Charming balance of elements, richness and flavour, depth and style.

---

**Etchart Torrontes Cafayate 1996** 15.5 

Spicy, warm, giving and immensely well-dispositioned to create a feeling of everything's-all-right-with-the-world.

---

**La Rural Mendoza Pinot Blanc/Chardonnay 1996** 15 C

Rich, smoky-melon fruit with a hint of grapefruit on the acidity. Great for fish dishes.

---

## AUSTRALIAN WINE RED

**Chapel Hill Coonawarra Cabernet Sauvignon, McLaren Vale 1993** 15 E

---

**Chapel Hill McLaren Vale Shiraz 1995** 14 E

Immediately all-embracing of the tastebuds if not so tender on the pocket. Not at Thresher Wine Shops.

---

**Chapel Hill The Vicar (Cabernet Sauvignon/ Shiraz) 1994** 13.5 F

Figgy, slightly minty, very hot-blooded red which suggests, as it opens on the nose, subtlety and complexity. However, it's more straightforward as a piece of fruit on the tastebuds where it is rich and soupy. Not at Thresher Wine Shops.

---

**Hartenberg Cabernet Sauvignon/Shiraz, Stellenbosch 1995** 13 D

Like worsted in texture. I suppose you could ask someone in Savile Row to cut it for you. Wine Rack only.

---

**Heritage Cabernet/Malbec, Barossa 1992** 16 E

Combines an unusual (in an Aussie) blend of elegant, earthy, ripe immediacy with a subtle carpet of rich tannins which are soft and integrated.

---

**Leasingham Domaine Cabernet Sauvignon/ Malbec, Clare Valley 1994** 15.5 E

Classy, rich, balanced and with enough versatility and arrangement of elements to even go with food. Not at all branches.

---

**Nanya Estate Malbec/Ruby Cabernet, South Australia 1996** 14 C

Some richness and ripeness and an easy-going personality.

---

**Penfolds Kalimna Shiraz Bin 28 1994** 14 E

Expensive but very impressively fruity and fine. Dry and flavourful.

---

**Red Cliffs Coonawarrra Cabernet Sauvignon 1996** 14.5 C

Approachable and juicy but with great rich style due to acidity and tannins in cahoots.

---

**Riddoch Coonawarra Cabernet Shiraz 1993** 13 E

---

**Riddoch Coonawarra Shiraz 1993** 13.5 E

Delicious but rather wimpish on the finish.

---

**Rosemount Estate Cabernet Sauvignon 1995** 14 D

Stylish and drinkable but a touch expensive.

---

**Rosemount Grenache Shiraz 1996** 13 D

The conventional breakdown of this wine is simple: soft fruit swimming with juice and a light spicy edge to the finish. Overall, I find the style characterless and sloppy – and it is straining so hard to be liked it seems forced. It is a fair whack of dosh, and frankly while I admire drinkability in a young wine I would like backbone – otherwise it flops all over the tongue and disappears without trace with food. What wood there is clouds the definition of the fruit, and the tannin is too low. Come on, Oz, grow up!

---

**Rosemount Merlot 1995** 13.5 E

Classy stuff which isn't soft and soppy, rather supple and authoritative. But it costs.

---

**Rosemount Shiraz 1995** 13.5 D

Very soft and drinkable but you can pay £4 for wines which fit this bill.

---

**Samuels Bay Pinot Noir, Eden Valley 1996** 13 E

Rather light and sweet on the finish. Not at Thresher Wine Shops.

---

**Samuels Bay Grenache, Barossa 1996** 13.5 E

Good chilled. Indeed, I suspect it's the only way to get through it. Not at Thresher Wine Shops.

---

**Samuels Bay Malbec, Padthaway 1995** 13 E

All rich soup. Every drop. Even the tannins are cowed by the richness of the fruit. Needs food. Not at Thresher Wine Shops.

---

**St Hallett Blackwell Shiraz, Barossa 1994** 14 E

Dry-edged, rich, has some character and deftness, but it's also as good to sip as it is to glug with food. Not at Thresher Wine Shops.

---

**St Hallett Shiraz, Barossa 1994** 13.5 E

Soft and very rich.

---

**Tatachilla Grenache Mataro 1996** 15.5 C

Spicy, rich, vibrant but slyly classy with clout. A bit more bite and more savoury classiness than most under-a-fiver Aussie reds. Even so, too robust food will frazzle it. Stick to the plainer roasts.

---

**The Franc, Cabernet Franc, Tim Knappstein Clare Valley 1994** 16 D

Better than many a Chinon! Has real richness and fruit and it'll really go with food not run a mile as many a soppy Aussie red does. Not at all branches.

---

**Tim Adams The Fergus, Clare Valley 1995** 

Mint, coriander, cassis, leather – it's all there in this impressively aromatic, fruity wine. Good texture and richness, drinkability and food-compatibility. Not at Thresher Wine Shops.

---

**Tollana Red, S E Australia NV**  

Not as exciting or textured as previously.

---

## AUSTRALIAN WINE — WHITE

**Amberley Margaret River Semillon 1995** 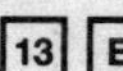

Yes, it's delicious. Yes, it has elegance and style. But, like the centre-forward with but a single leg, it has problems convincing the crowd of the ability, at a tenner, to score on the ground.

---

**Bridgewater Mill Riesling, Clare Valley 1994** 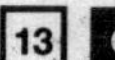

---

**Chapel Hill Eden Valley Riesling 1995** 

Seems to lap the tastebuds like energized waves of well-flavoured fruit. Not at Thresher Wine Shops.

---

**David Traeger Verdelho, Victoria 1996** 15.5 E

Makes a refreshing and richly quirky change from chardonnay. Not at Thresher Wine Shops.

---

**Heritage Semillon, Barossa Valley 1993** 15.5 E

---

**Jacobs Creek Chardonnay 1996**

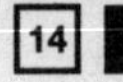


It still rates well – in spite of sailing perilously close to a fiver.

---

**Katnook Estate Coonawarra Sauvignon Blanc 1996**

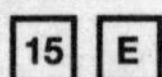


Hints of rich grass and crushed flowers. Needs food – fancy fish dishes, salads, poultry, mild Thai. Not at Thresher Wine Shops.

---

**Lindemans Bin 65 Chardonnay 1996**

Delicious combination of butter, hazelnuts and melon undercut by a perfectly weighted uptide of acidity.

---

**Penfolds Barossa Valley Semillon Chardonnay 1996** 15 D

Great! And it's decently priced.

---

**Penfolds Bin 202 South Australian Riesling 1996** 14.5 C

Interesting softish fruit with a crisp pineapple tang. Will develop well in bottle over the next year.

---

**Penfolds Rawsons Retreat Bin 21 Semillon/Chardonnay/Colombard 1996** 15 C

Richly textured, warmly fruity (some complexity on the finish where the acidity is most pertinent), this is an excellent vintage for this wine.

---

**Primo Estate Colombard, Adelaide Plains 1996** 13 D

Expensive – even if the fruit wears big rings on its fingers (i.e. flashes its fruit a bit). Not at Thresher Wine Shops.

---

**Red Cliffs Estate Chardonnay 1995** 15 C

---

**Red Cliffs Estate Colombard Chardonnay 1995** 14 C

Dry, good acid character.

---

**Red Cliffs Estate Riesling/Traminer, Victoria 1996** 14 C

Great with Chinese and Thai food.

---

**Riddoch Coonawarra Chardonnay 1994** 15 D

Great oleaginous texture, good with scallops and rich seafood.

---

**Rosemount Estate Chardonnay 1996** 15.5 D

Opulence vinified. Rather grandly fruity, proud and rich.

---

**Samuels Bay Riesling 1994** 14.5 D

Delicious soft, spicy fruit. Brilliant seafood wine.

---

**Samuels Bay Sauvignon Blanc, Barossa Valley 1996** 13.5 D

This is tasty and highly drinkable but not offering the complexity expected of a seven-quid wine.

---

**Samuels Bay Unoaked Chardonnay, S E Australia 1995** 15.5 D

Wonderful wine for salmon, scallops, etcetera. Has a smoked cream edge.

---

**The Willows Vineyard Semillon, Barossa Valley 1995** 16 E

It even smells thick! Can texture have an aroma? This wine's can. It's so rich you could weatherproof the average semi from one bottle.

---

**Tim Adams Semillon 1995** 12 E

Not quite convincing at eight quid, even though it's £1 less than at Tesco (and correspondingly rated higher). Try me at £3.49 and I might be more enthusiastic.

---

**Tollana Chardonnay 1996** 14 C 

Rich and full-edged. Not elegant or classic but good with food.

---

**Tollana Dry White, South Australia 1996** 12 C

---

**Tollana Oak-matured Chardonnay 1996** 14 C 

Rich and buttery with a lovely shroud of finely honed acidity.

---

# BULGARIAN WINE RED

**Bulgarian Country Red Cabernet/Cinsault** 13 B

---

**Bulgarian Vintage Premier Merlot, Iambol Region 1994** 14 B

---

**Domaine Boyar Cabernet Sauvignon Plovdiv 1991** 14 C

---

**Domaine Boyar Vintage Blend Cabernet/ Merlot 1994** 16 B

Magnificent value here. Superb depth of dry chewiness overlaid with a medley of fruit flavours, rich and bold, warm and deep.

---

**Domaine Boyar Vintage Blend Merlot & Pamid 1994** 14 B

**Iambol Cabernet Sauvignon 1995** 14 B

**Iambol Special Reserve Cabernet Sauvignon 1993** 15 C

Lovely concentrated fruit here.

**Iambol Vintage Premiere Cabernet Sauvignon 1994** 14 B

**Reserve Cabernet Sauvignon Sliven 1990** 16 C

Aroma and fruit begin as dry and richly fruity and a touch exotic, then the throat is moved to recognize cedarwood undertones which are reminiscent of an ancient musty Medoc.

**Svischtov Cabernet Sauvignon, Controliran 1987** 18 C

Like a minor Bordeaux deity at the height of its powers in a vintage generally regarded as poor. This is a highly aromatic, dry, perfected wine of great, old fruit and complex depth. Absurdly good value for the money. Wine Rack and Bottoms Up only.

**Twin Peaks Oak Aged Cabernet Sauvignon 1991** 15 C

## BULGARIAN WINE WHITE

**Chardonnay Reserve Khan Krum 1994** 13 C

Good with mild chicken dishes.

**Targovischte Barrel-fermented Chardonnay 1995** 15 C

Bags of personality and flavour without being too soppy or over-enthusiastic.

---

**Yantra Valley Bulgarian Dry 1994** 12.5 B

---

## CHILEAN WINE RED

**Caballo Loco No 1, Valdivieso NV** 13.5 E

Decent enough but not a tenner's worth. Wine Rack only.

---

**Concha y Toro 'Casillero del Diablo' Cabernet Sauvignon, Maipo Valley 1995** 15.5 C

One of the most elegant cabs you can hail. Takes your tastebuds for a very comfortable trip.

---

**Cono Sur 20 Barrel Pinot Noir, Rapel Valley 1995** 14 E

Starts excitingly, finishes by hitting the post. But the fruit's better than many a £30 Cotes de Beaune.

---

**Errazuriz Cabernet Sauvignon Reserva 1995** 15 E

Touches of chocolate and coffee on the blackcurrant fruit, a hint of leather, and well-developed tannins. Seductively put-together wine. Not at Thresher Wine Shops.

---

**Isla Negra Cabernet Sauvignon, Rapel Valley 1996** 16 C

Lovely texture and flavour which rolls like a rich brook over the tongue, down the gullet, and doesn't, at £4.99, trouble the pocket. Not at Thresher Wine Shops.

---

**Las Colinas Chilean Red** 15 B

**Las Colinas Merlot 1996** 14.5 C

Hints of jamminess stopped from going over the edge by the texture. Great flavour.

**Santa Carolina Malbec 1993** 13.5 C

**Santa Ines Legado de Armida Reserve, Maipo Valley 1996** 13.5 D

Very rich and ripe – a touch too so. Wine Rack only.

**Valdivieso Malbec 1996** 17.5 C

Wonderful wine! Quite wonderful! The texture is the softest velvet, the fruit is exquisite plum and blackberry, the balance is poised. Not at Thresher Wine Shops.

**Valdivieso Merlot, Lontue 1996** 16.5 C

A delicious merlot, no mistake, which begins juicy and ripe and then turns seriously complex and clinging. Huge array of flavours: spiced damsons predominate. Not at Thresher Wine Shops.

**Wine Rack 'Own Label' Merlot/Cabernet, Maipo 1995** 14 C

Very soupy and clinging, but very good with food. It's a hot and happy wine – in small doses. Wine Rack only.

## CHILEAN WINE WHITE

**Concha y Toro 'Casillero del Diablo' Chardonnay 1996** 17 C

So full and deep you can dive into it from the top board. Scrumptious stuff.

**Errazuriz 'La Escutura Estate' Chardonnay, Casablanca Valley 1996** 16 D

Very elegant and richly flavoured by the sun of Chile. It brightens up your day in one sip.

---

**Isla Negra Chardonnay 1996** 14 C

Classy stuff – great fish wine. Not at Thresher Wine Shops.

---

**Las Colinas Sauvignon Blanc 1996** 15 C

---

**Santa Carolina Chenin Blanc 1995** 16.5 C

Oh my God! Loire winegrowers, cash in your pensions now! The Chileans, having shown France how to grow chardonnay, sauvignon, merlot, pinot noir and cabernet, are now, with this chenin blanc, invading your territory. Not since Caesar has Gaul faced so impressive an adversary.

---

**Santa Carolina Gran Reserva Chardonnay Cinca Estrellas 1995** 17 E

Take a glass of this wine, fry some squid and a little chilli and garlic, throw coriander over the stuff when it's on the plate – eat, sip . . . are you in heaven? Certainly knocking on the gates.

---

**Santa Rita Reserva Chardonnay, Maipo Valley 1995** 17 D

One of those wines which brings instant elevation to the black mood you returned home with. One swill of this wonderfully rich, soft, invigorating, fresh, hugely quaffable, immensely classy, utterly ambrosial stuff – and you relax. Not at Thresher Wine Shops.

---

**Trio Chardonnay, Concha y Toro 1996** 15.5 C

Lovely cosy fruit: warm, classy, rich.

---

**Wine Rack 'Own Label' Chardonnay, Lontue 1996** 14 C

Rich? Very, but it's restrained by the acidity. The balance, therefore, is good with a nod in favour of the deep fruit. Wine Rack only.

---

## ENGLISH WINE — WHITE

**Heritage Fume 1994** 11 C

---

## FRENCH WINE — RED

**Cahors Chateau le Poujol 1994** 13 D

---

**Chateau Bonnet Bordeaux 1993** 13.5 D

---

**Chateau Cap de Faugeres Cotes de Castillon 1992** 14 E

Soft, tobaccoey, perfectly mature.

---

**Chateau Coucheroy Pessac-Leognan, Graves 1994** 14 D

Opulent, dry, very rich, well suited to roast meats.

---

**Chateau d'Aiguilhe Cotes de Castillon 1993** 13 E

Rather muted for the money. Wine Rack/Bottom Up only.

---

**Chateau de Francs, Cote de Francs 1993** 13.5 E

---

**Chateau de la Riviere, Fronsac 1992** 14 C

---

**Chateau de Lastours, Corbieres 1993** 14.5 D

Smooth, rich, ready to soothe the sorest throat. Wine Rack only.

---

**Chateau de Laurens Faugeres 1995** 16 C

Delicious, tobaccoey fruit – soft, gently rich, elegant, smooth. An instantly likeable mouthful.

---

**Chateau du Grand Prebois, Cotes du Rhone 1994** 15.5 D

Great stuff! Loads of character, rich fruit, and lovely generosity.

---

**Chateau Lamarche 'Lutet', Bordeaux Superieure 1993** 13.5 D

Wine Rack/Bottoms Up only.

---

**Chateau Mercier Cotes de Bourg 1995** 14 D

Those tannins! Drink it in AD 2001 (with lamb).

---

**Chateau Mercier Cotes de Bourg (Oak-aged) 1995** 15 E

Takes the fillings out of your mouth and replaces them with cheroot-edged, blackcurrant fruit of rich concentration. Hugely dry wine.

---

**Chateau Puy Bardens Cuvee Prestige, Premieres Cotes de Bordeaux 1994** 13 D

---

**Chateau Rose d'Orion Montagne, St Emilion 1995** 14 D

Brilliantly assertive tannins. Great to keep for the Millennium.

---

**Chateau St Esteve Tradition Cotes du Rhone 1995** 14 D

Classy and very dry.

---

**Chateau Suau, Premieres Cotes de Bordeaux (Oaked) 1995** 13.5 D

The wood adds something: 50p.

---

**Chateau Suau, Premieres Cotes de Bordeaux (Unoaked) 1995** 13 D

All fruit, no wood. Well, at least it forcibly demonstrates why claret needs wood.

---

**Chateauneuf du Pape Les Oliviers 1995** 13 E

Touch too soft and highly polished.

---

**Claret Regional Classics NV** 12 C

---

**Cotes de Ventoux La Mission 1996** 13 B

Touch light on the teeth.

---

**Domaine de Montine, Coteaux du Tricastin 1995** 13.5 C

Light, Cotes du Rhone style.

---

**Domaine des Moulins Cotes du Rhone 1995** 14 C

---

**Domaine Font de Michelle Chateauneuf-du-Pape 1992** 14 F

---

**Domaine Ste Eulalie, Minervois 1994** 16 C

Gorgeous herby fruit of great warmth and food compatibility. Rustic but sophisticated.

---

**Fitou Special Reserve** 14 C

---

**La Ramillade Rasteau, Cotes du Rhone 1995** 16 E

Aroma of the hillsides (thyme and earth), rich fruit, dry finish, great tannins. Brilliant food wine.

---

**Lurton Oak Aged Claret 1992** 15 D

---

**Mas de Daumas Gassac 1993** 14 E

---

**Morgon Duboeuf 1996** 13.5 D

Thresher select their own cuvees at Duboeuf – so this is a unique specimen. And it has a lot more muscle than most. The aroma is spineless but not the fruit.

---

**Soleil d'Or Shiraz/Cabernet, VdP d'Oc 1995** 16.5 C

Fabulous stuff! Knocks Aussies into last year, let alone last week. A wine as vibrant as its label. Brilliant, brisk, dry, rich, bruising.

---

**Southlands Cabernet Sauvignon 1995** 13.5 C

---

**Southlands Merlot VdP d'Oc 1995** 13 C

---

**Southlands Syrah 1995** 12.5 C

---

**SPARKS Merlot VdP d'Oc 1996** 13.5 D

Somewhat coarse of finish.

---

**Terroire de Tuchan, Fitou 1993** 13 E

---

**Torgan Valley 'Old Vines' Carignan, VdP du Torgan 1996** 14 B

Has echoes of a rich life once lived but the fresh approach of the acidity gives it vigour and bite.

---

# FRENCH WINE — WHITE

**Blanc de Blancs Dry, Donatien Bahuaud** 15 B

Dry, crisp, well-flavoured, refreshing, pert and purposeful. Emphatically drinkable.

---

**Blanc de Blancs Medium Dry, Donatien Bahuaud** 12 B

---

**Chablis 1er Cru Fourchaume, Chateau de Maligny Jean Durup 1994** 13 F

Elegant, classy, expensive.

---

**Chablis Premier Cru Cote de Lechet, Defaix 1991** 13 G

---

**Chablis Vieilles Vignes Domaine Defaix 1994** 12.5 E

---

**Chateau Bonnet Entre Deux Mers 1993** 12 C

---

**Chateau Bonnet Entre Deux Mers Oak Aged 1992** 11 E

---

**Clos de la Fine Muscadet Sur Lie, Cotes de Grandlieu 1995** 13.5 C

---

**Cuvee de l'Arjolle Rose, VdP des Cotes de Thongues 1996** 13 C

Expensive but deliciously inconsequential on a warm day.

---

**Domaine de Tariquet VdP des Cotes de Gascogne 1996** 15 C

One of the more delicate Gascogne wee beasties – but still has that lovely rippling fruit on the finish.

---

**Domaine Virginie Cabernet Sauvignon Rose, VdP d'Oc 1996** 14 C

Has the charm of a new-bloomed rose.

---

**Fat Bastard Chardonnay VdP d'Oc 1996** 

I went out and bought a few bottles of this wine after I'd tasted it. Its lemon edge and subtle melon richness were perfect for a fish dish I planned to cook. N.B. if a wine writer spends his own money he *really* likes a wine.

---

**Figaro White, VdP du Gers 1996** 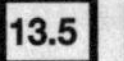 B

Pretty – nice lemon touch on the finish.

---

**Gewurztraminer, Turckheim 1996** 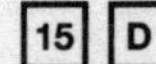

Chinese food for this beauty.

---

**James Herrick Chardonnay VdP d'Oc 1996**  C

New World restrained by Old World coyness. A chardonnay of subtlety and crisp fruit which is always nicely understated.

---

**Laperouse VdP d'Oc White 1995** 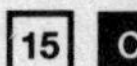

Has lovely depth to it, nuttily edged and refined, but there's also a delicious crisp, cos lettuce freshness.

---

**Muscadet Cotes de Grand Lieu Sur Lie 1995**  C

Hmm . . .

---

**Pinot Blanc Turckheim 1995** 13 

---

**Pinot Blanc Zind Humbrecht 1994** 14.5 E

---

**Pinot Gris Turckheim 1995** 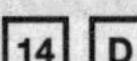

Lovely apricot-tinged fruit to go with Thai food dishes.

---

**Reserve Gewurztraminer, Turckheim 1994** 14.5 D

**Riesling Gueberschwihr Zind Humbrecht 1994** 12 F

**Riesling Herrenweg Zind Humbrecht 1993** 16 F

A genuinely exciting riesling which sends shivers up the spine. Even so, I would still be patient and let it develop into a 20-pointer in the year AD 2002.

**Sancerre La Cresle de la Porte 1996** 11 E

Like seeing an octogenarian football hooligan.

**Soleil d'Or Chardonnay VdP Isle de Beaute 1996** 13 C

Label is cheering, the fruit is clean – good with shellfish.

**Southlands Chardonnay 1995** 13 C

**Southlands Sauvignon Blanc 1995** 13.5 C

**SPARKS Chardonnay VdP d'Oc 1996** 13 D

The sparks trot, rather than fly.

**Vin de Pays du Gers Au Loubet 1996** 14 B

Fresh hints of soft fruit and garden spade, with a crisp finish. Good-value tippling.

**WR/001/96 Chardonnay VdP d'Oc 1996** 16 D

Deliciously playful, lemonic and elegantly fruity. Preferable to any number of meursaults at five times the price. Wine Rack stores only.

# GERMAN WINE — WHITE

**Bereich Bernkastel, Regional Classics 1996** — 12 C

**Bereich Nierstein, Regional Classics 1996** — 13 C

Makes a reasonable aperitif in hot weather.

**Bretzenheimer Vogelsang Riesling Spatlese, Schloss Plettenberg, Nahe 1994** — 13 E

**Dr Loosen Riesling Kabinett 1995** — 16 D

Exquisite angularity of shape – it's as perfectly proportioned fruitwise and acidically as young Moselles can be and it has the sleek grace of a strolling panther.

**Hock, Regional Classics** — 10 B

**Niersteiner Langenbach Gutes Domtal 1995** — 13.5 C

Has hints of genuine class.

**Niersteiner Pettenthal Scheurebe, Weingut Rappenhoff, Rheinhessen 1994** — 13 D

**Niersteiner Spiegelberg Silvaner 1994** — 13 C

**Piesporter Michelsberg, Regional Classics 1995** — 11 C

**Ruppertsberger Linsenbusch Riesling Spatlese, Winzervergin Hoheburg, Rheinpfalz 1993** — 15 D

**Solus Langenbach, Rheinhessen 1995** 14.5 C

Interesting, how it's developed. Good fruit, off-dry, saved from sweetness by the acidity. Great food wine.

---

**Wormser Liebfraumorgen Kabinett 1994** 14 C

---

## HUNGARIAN WINE RED

**Butlers Blend Red 1995** 11 B

---

## HUNGARIAN WINE WHITE

**Butlers Blend Hungarian Country Wine** 13.5 B

A mildly appetite-encouraging tipple.

---

**Cool Ridge Barrel Aged Chardonnay, Nagyrede 1994** 15 C

---

**Cool Ridge Barrel Fermented Chardonnay 1994** 16 C

Very elegant, gently woody, firmly fruity and beautifully balanced. A very stylish, classy wine.

---

**Cool Ridge Chardonnay, Unoaked, Nagyrede 1995** 14 C

---

**Disznoko Tokaji Furmint 1993** 12 C

---

**Gyongyos Chardonnay 1995** 13.5 C

---

**Sauvignon Blanc Gyongyos Estate 1995** 14 C

---

# ITALIAN WINE RED

**Alasia Dolcetto d'Asti 1994** 13 C

---

**Barolo Ceretto 'Zonchera' 1992** 13 G

Simply not worth seventeen quid. But it is nicely dry and fruity (figgy, slightly wood-spicy). Wine Rack only.

---

**Le Trulle Primitivo del Salento 1996** 13.5 C

The New World meets the Old World and the winner is . . . me and you. Ripe, fresh, rustic but zippy, this wine.

---

**Newlands Rosso** 14 B

---

**Original Zin Primitivo del Salento 1995**  14 C

The tannin on the finish receives a fresh, appley touch (acidity) and this rather militates against the initial impact. But it's great fun, this wine, in name and nature.

---

**Ricasoli Sangiovese Formulae 1995**  13.5 E

Intensely likeable fruit at, say, £3.99. But at four quid more it makes you think a bit. Not at Thresher Wine Shops.

---

**Rosso di Puglia Campione**  13.5 C

Light and drinkable and decently priced. Exciting? Alas not.

---

**Valpolicella Classico Superiore, Zenato 1993** 15 C

Possibly the most drinkable valpol you will encounter. Quite delicious.

---

**Zanna Montepulciano d'Abruzzo, Illuminati Vecchio 1991** 14 E

Expensive but sufficiently impressively dry, characterful and fruity. An excellent food wine. Wine Rack only.

---

## ITALIAN WINE WHITE

**Alasia Cortese del Piemonte 1994** 13 C

---

**Alasia Muscate Sec 1994** 11 C

---

**Chardonnay del Salento Vigneto di Caramia 1996** 16 D

One of the classiest southern Italian chardonnays around: rich, giving, textured, ripe but not rampant, it's silky and quite delicious. Not at Thresher Wine Shops.

---

**Chardonnay Trentino, Concilio Vini 1996** 14 C

Very firmly fleshed and rich. Terrific flavour. Not at Thresher Wine Shops.

---

**Marche Trebbiano, Moncaro 1996** 14.5 B

Great-value tippling here: a well-flavoured, fresh white of some wit.

---

**Newlands Bianco** 13 B

---

**Original Sin Chardonnay del Salento 1996** 13 C

Charming name but not so brilliantly fruity – for the money. Not at Thresher Wine Shops.

---

**Orvieto Classico Antinori Abbocatto 1994** 12 D

---

**Planeta Chardonnay, VdT di Sicilia 1995** 15 F

You may think twelve quid a lot for a Sicilian white – but not, I think, if it is in the class of a first-rate Californian chardonnay. This is one lovely long-legged beauty of a bottle. Wine Rack only.

---

**Soave Classico Superiore, Pieropan 1995** 14 E

Eight quid for a soave? Think of the noughts in lira!!! However, it is delicious and smugly elegant. Wine Rack only.

---

**Soave, Regional Classics 1993** 12 

---

## NEW ZEALAND WINE RED

**Church Road Cabernet Sauvignon/Merlot, Hawkes Bay 1994** 16 E

Lovely rich, textured fruit of depth, balance, flavour and real class.

---

**Martinborough Vineyard Pinot Noir 1995** 12 F

This has improved a little in bottle and would be a nice wine at £4. Not at £13.

---

**Montana Cabernet Sauvignon/Merlot 1995** 14.5 D

Grass meets wet earth, but the result, though interesting, is not exactly paydirt. A dry, vegetal wine which needs food.

---

**Palliser Estate Pinot Noir 1994** 13 F

Lot of money, which you spend up front and only get up-front fruit in return.

---

## NEW ZEALAND WINE — WHITE

**Azure Bay Sauvignon Blanc/Semillon 1996** 10 C

I like little about this wine: fruit, price, label, and silly tart's boudoir bottle.

---

**Church Road Montana Chardonnay, Hawkes Bay 1995** 15 E

Deep, rich, full of beautifully integrated wood and fruit, and very, very classy.

---

**Church Road Reserve Chardonnay, Hawkes Bay 1994** 14.5 F

Very expensive but chewy fruit of depth and richness.

---

**Cooks Chardonnay, Gisborne 1996** 13.5 C

Disappointing lack of focus.

---

**Hunters Sauvignon Chardonnay, Spring Creek Vineyard 1995** 13 E

---

**Kapua Springs Dry White, Gisborne 1996** 13.5 C

Lilts along – like a Scott Joplin rag played on a harmonica.

---

**Kapua Springs Medium Dry White, Gisborne 1996** 12 C

---

**Montana Sauvignon Blanc 1996** 14.5 D

---

**Montana Timara Chardonnay Semillon 1995** 13.5 C

---

**Nobilo White Cloud 1996** 13 C

---

**Ormond Estate Chardonnay 1995** 13 E

---

**Palliser Estate Chardonnay 1995** 15.5 E

Gorgeous fruit, off-puttingly priced but undeniably full of finesse, guile, personality and some degree of wit.

---

**Palliser Estate Sauvignon Blanc 1996** 14 E

Ten quid, but luxurious fruit of length, elegance and classic Kiwi disdain.

---

**Stoneleigh Chardonnay, Marlborough 1995** 14.5 D

Very elegant, expensively cut and fruited.

---

**Te Kairanga Barrel Aged Sauvignon Blanc 1996** 12 E

Terribly expensive, terribly. Breaks my heart, prices like this.

---

**Villa Maria Lightly Oaked Chardonnay, Marlborough 1995** 15 D

Delicate deliciousness.

---

**Villa Maria Private Bin Sauvignon Blanc 1996** 15 D

Delicate grassy notes to the richly restrained fruit. Elegantly and finely cut.

---

**Villa Maria Reserve Sauvignon Blanc, Marlborough 1996** 13.5 E

Nervy, rich, very temperamental on the tongue but interesting (mildly).

---

## PORTUGUESE WINE RED

**Alandra Esporao 1996** 13 C

---

**Bright Brothers Douro Red 1995** 14.5 C

**Cabernet Sauvignon Esporao 1993** 13.5 C

**Espiga Red, Estremadura 1995** 13 C

Jammy as a jar of the stuff you spread on toast.

**Esporao Reserva 1990** 15 D

**Fiuza Cabernet Sauvignon, Peter Bright, Ribatejo 1994** 17 C

Lovely dry fruit with an excitingly textured complexity and richness. A serious wine of manners and aplomb.

**Monte Velho Red, 1995** 14 C

Brilliant soft fruit but with enough oomph to go with spicy sausages.

**Ramada 1994** 13.5 B

## PORTUGUESE WINE WHITE

**Bright Brothers Estremadura 1994** 13.5 C

**J.P. Branco** 14 B

## SOUTH AFRICAN WINE RED

**Bellingham Pinotage 1994** 14.5 C

**Delheim Cabernet Sauvignon 1994** 14.5 D

**Delheim Pinotage 1995** 14 D

**Halves to Hogsheads Chapter One Zinfandel/Cabernet Sauvignon, Stellenbosch 1996** 14 C

Immensely drinkable and soft with a hint, just a hint, mind, of wild richness. Bottoms Up only.

**KWV Cabernet Sauvignon 1993** 13.5 C

You won't believe cabernet can be made this puppyish and all-over-your-tongue friendly.

**KWV Pinotage 1993** 13 C

**KWV Roodeberg 1993** 12.5 C

**Sinnya Red, Robertson Valley 1996** 12.5 C

Very juicy and overripe.

**Villiera Cabernet Sauvignon 1994** 15 D

**Villiera Merlot 1994** 13.5 E

**Warwick Pinotage 1995** 16.5 E

Drink it. Then smile at your dentist – it's a wine pit-dark, pit-deep, and pit-full of rich pleasures.

**Winelands Cabernet Sauvignon/Cabernet Franc 1995** 14 C

**Winelands Cinsault/Tinta Barocca 1996** 14 C

Fabulous tobacco aroma, light and plummy thereafter.

**Winelands Premium Shiraz/Cabernet 1995** 15.5 C

## SOUTH AFRICAN WINE WHITE

**Arniston Bay Chenin Blanc/Chardonnay, Western Cape 1996** 

A lovely warm-hearted yet refreshing white wine with a peculiar cosmetic charm. Quirky, spicy, creamy, delicious. Thresher Wine Shops only.

---

**Bellingham Sauvignon, Franschoek 1996** 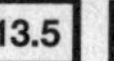 

Has some hints of lawn-mowers – infrequently used ones.

---

**De Wetshof Chardonnay d'Honneur 1995** 

---

**Delheim Chardonnay 1996** 

Not bad. Pricey.

---

**Delheim 'New Release' Chenin Blanc, Stellenbosch 1996** 

Has a lovely touch of the steel edge on the deep-flavoured fruit. Makes it a conversational chenin of marked style. Wine Rack only.

---

**Glen Carlou 'Devereux' Chenin Blanc/Chardonnay, Paarl 1996** 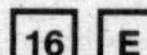

Individual, quirky, very lingeringly delicious and even dares to throw in a hint of white chocolate on the fruit. An addictively delightful sipping wine. Wine Rack only.

---

**Halves to Hogsheads Chapter Three Madeba Chardonnay, Robertson 1996**  

One of those shrug-of-the-shoulder chardonnays: not rich, not lemonic, not typical. You take it or leave it. I'll take it – but with grilled mackerel. Bottoms Up only.

---

**Halves to Hogsheads Chapter Two Sauvignon Blanc/Chenin Blanc/Chardonnay, Paarl 1996** 14.5 C

Interesting combination of the flinty sauvignon with the fruity chenin. An accessible marriage of opposites. Bottoms Up only.

---

**Hamilton Russell Chardonnay 1995** 14 E

---

**KWV Chenin Blanc 1996** 14 C

Doesn't overwork to create its effect. The subtle pear/pineapple fruit has a creamy edge. An amusing wine.

---

**KWV Sauvignon Blanc 1996** 10 C

---

**Lesca Chardonnay, Danie de Wet 1995** 16 D

The master of the lemonic style weaves his magic fruitiness. Wine Rack only.

---

**Stellenbosch Dry White 1996** 14 C

---

**Stellenvale Chardonnay 1994** 15 C

---

**Thelema Chardonnay 1994** 16 E

Not cheap but . . . Wine Rack only.

---

**Thelema Sauvignon Blanc 1995** 15.5 E

---

**Villiera Blanc Fume 1995** 15.5 D

---

**Villiera Estate Chardonnay, Paarl 1996** 16.5 E

Demure yet determined, passionately formed yet quietly spoken, rich yet not ostentatious, full of flavour yet not fancy, it's one long elegant mouthful of creamy fruit. Wine Rack only.

---

**Villiera Estate Chenin Blanc, Paarl 1996** 15.5 C

One of the Cape's most accomplished chenins. Rich yet balanced, ripe yet refreshing, full yet possesses finesse.

---

**Villiera Gewurztraminer 1996** 15 D

Seems rather cheeky to me. There are lots of Alsatians who will find this wine worrying. Bottoms Up only.

---

**Winelands Bush Vine Chenin Blanc 1996** 14 C

A simple aperitif tipple for those living in elegant homes with chintz curtains and pile carpets.

---

**Winelands Chenin Blanc 1996** 13.5 C

Drinkable – but a touch pricey for the style.

---

**Winelands Sauvignon Blanc 1996** 13.5 C

Decent enough. Decency – the theme of New Labour. Could this be the wine for them?

---

## SPANISH WINE RED

**Agramont Tempranillo/Cabernet Sauvignon, Navarra 1994** 16 C

Plump, soft, ripe, gorgeously fruity and forward yet never soppy – this is a terrific glug with or without food.

---

**Albor Rioja 1995** 13.5 C

---

**Baron de Ley Rioja Reserva 1991** 15 E

Expensive but a ripely fruity wine with great classiness. Oodles of flavour.

---

**Campo Viejo Reserva Rioja 1991** 13 D

---

**Casa Rural Tinto NV** 13 B

Rather inexpressive and has little character – but it is pleasant, inoffensive and cheap.

---

**Conde de Valdemar Rioja Crianza 1994** 14 D

Beastly elegance and litheness. Should be put down – the throat.

---

**Conde de Valdemar Rioja Reserva 1992** 14 E

Greater refinement here than its cousin above. Smoother and a touch more polished.

---

**Copa Real Plata** 14.5 C

---

**Copa Real Tinto** 14 B

---

**Don Darias** 14 B

---

**Marques de Grinon Dominio de Valdepusa Cabernet Sauvignon 1993** 18.5 E

Magnificent sensuality of texture, depth, complexity and thrilling fruit. Has a lingering flavour which is truly exciting and bold. Why can't Bordeaux produce cabernets like this under a tenner? Wine Rack and Bottoms Up only.

---

**Marques de Grinon Rioja 1995** 14 C

One of the most elegant riojas around.

---

**Martinez Bujanda Rioja Gran Reserva 1990** 15 F

One of the smoothest riojas I've tasted in years, to begin with. To end with, it's *too* darned smooth and smug. It's attractively aromatic and balanced, but I couldn't finish the bottle.

---

**Martinez Hujanda Garnacha Reserva 1990** 10 F

Hugely overpriced. At £3.49 I'd buy everything about it.

---

**Monte Ory Tempranillo/Cabernet Sauvignon, Navarra 1993** 14 C

**Remonte Navarra Crianza Cabernet Sauvignon 1992** 15.5 C

**Santara Dry Red Conca de Barbera 1995** 14 B

**Torres Sangredetoro 1993** 13 C

**Valdemar Tinto, Rioja 1996** 14 C

Cigar ash and dry blackcurrants. Good weapon in the fight against robust meat dishes.

**Valduero Ribera del Duero Crianza 1992** 15 D

**Valencia Red** 13 B

Party wine – not a conservative party. Wine Shops only.

**Vina Albali Reserva, Valdepenas 1989** 13.5 C

Enjoyable with ham dishes.

**Vina Amezola Rioja Crianza 1991** 13 D

**Vina del Recuerdo, Navarra 1994** 13 C

Bangers-and-mash party wine. Good tannins here.

## SPANISH WINE WHITE

**Copa Real Bianco** 11 B

**Moscatel de Valencia** 15 C

Sweetly honeyed and perfect with pud.

**Santara Dry White Conca de Barbera 1995** 14 B

**Torres Vina Sol, Penedes 1996** 13 C

Simple and crisp.

## USA WINE RED

**Columbia Crest Cote de Columbia Grenache 1995** 8 C

Possibly the worst red wine on this retailer's rich shelves. It is appallingly pretentious as a label and as an example of liquefied grenache I would rather sip cough syrup in purgatory.

**E & J Gallo Turning Leaf Cabernet Sauvignon 1994** 13.5 D

**E & J Gallo Turning Leaf Zinfandel 1994** 12 D

## USA WINE WHITE

**E & J Gallo Turning Leaf Chardonnay 1994** 14 D

**Kings Canyon 'Black Label' (Oak Aged) Chardonnay, California 1994** 15 C

Lovely woody smoothness and textured fruit.

**Prosperity White, Santa Ynez Valley 1994** 14 C

## FORTIFIED WINE

**Charter LBV Port 1987** 14.5 E

## SPARKLING WINE/CHAMPAGNE

**Angas Brut** 16 D

Simply great value for money: stylish, subtly fruity, classically dry yet not austere.

**Angas Brut Rose (Australia)** 15.5 D

**Asti Martini (Italy)** 10 D

Sweet granny's brew.

**Asti, Regional Classics (Italy)** 12 C

**Castelblanch Cava Extra Brut** 13 C

**Castellblanch Extra Brut (Spain)** 13 D

**Cordon Negro Freixenet Brut 1993 (Spain)** 16 D

Great price for such boldness of style and subtle flavour. Has finesse and class.

**Cordon Negro Freixenet Medium Dry (Spain)** 14.5 D

**Croser Brut 1994 (Australia)** 13.5 F

I'd be inclined to lay it down for the Millennium.

**Deutz Marlborough Cuvee (New Zealand)** 15.5 E

**Drappier Carte d'Or Brut** 12 G

---

**Green Point Vineyards Brut 1994** 12.5 F

---

**Jean de Praisac Brut** 13 F

---

**Le Mesnil Grand Cru, Blanc de Blancs 1990** 15 G

The most convincing case for spending twenty quid on a bottle of champagne on this retailer's shelves.

---

**Lindauer Brut** 13.5 D

---

**Lindauer Brut Rose** 14 D

---

**Lindauer Special Reserve** 15.5 E

One of the most elegant bubblies around. Fresh, gently fruity, very poised, deliciously incisive.

---

**Moscato Sweet Spumante, Regional Classics (Italy)** 12.5 C

---

**Mumm Cuvee Napa Brut (California)** 15 E

Lovely lemony finesse – preferable to scores of champagnes.

---

**Mumm Cuvee Napa Rose (California)** 14 E

Lovely rosy-cheeked fruit of style and flavour.

---

**Pol Roger Champagne White Foil** 11 H

---

**Pol Roger Vintage 1988** 12 H

£30? I should coco.

---

**Seaview Pinot Noir/Chardonnay 1994** 15 E

Terrific champagne reputation crusher.

---

**Seppelt Great Western Brut**  

**Yalumba Pinot Noir Chardonnay Brut** 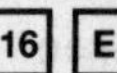

Quite delicious. Perhaps a touch soft to seduce or convince the classicist but its quality and style, to me at least, sing out.

**Streetplonk 1998**

# UNWINS

Times they are a-changing at Unwins? I should say so. It's not every year that I contemplate one complete entry in this book swallowing another one – whole. But that's what Unwins, to the surprise of many of us, has gone and done. Davisons, as a listed *Streetplonk* retailer and wine chain, is no longer. Unwins has gobbled it up.

Now this is usually the point in this book where I explain that I don't really understand *exactly* what makes this retailer tick. Well, I still don't know exactly. But I have discerned of late that this retailer is beginning to assume a shape I feel I might just recognise and relate to more strongly. This may or may not make the retailer easier to fathom in the future, but the changes are interesting in themselves, not least because they relate precisely to the area of product innovation I have been discussing throughout this book.

At present, Unwins does less of the bespoke form of sourcing wines than most of its peers. It lists nine different wines in which it has had some involvement including a couple of new varietal ranges: Volcanic Hills from Hungary and Stockman's Bridge from Australia. However, as part of its renewed approach, the company is intending to place far more emphasis on these kinds of products. 'We are definitely moving forward,' says Bill Rolfe, a senior member of Unwins' six-strong all-male wine buying team. 'There is more emphasis being placed on the way we source our wines, the way we market our wines. We have put a great deal of importance on what the market wants.'

It is as though this rather comfy retailer (the image I've had of it evokes the image of a somewhat corpulent *Daily Telegraph* reader snoozing in a deckchair) has finally woken up to the changes in the world of wine (and its current image, for me, summons up a more athletic type, still perhaps a *Telegraph* man but fonder of the Sunday edition, waxing his cricket bat). To be fair, the range at Unwins has always been surprisingly interesting considering that the retailer has generally had a far more reserved view of the market than many of the other chains. 'A few years ago it was a totally different arena. It was a lot slower-paced, there weren't so many fashions and fads. Now the whole world has opened up.'

Broadly speaking Unwins is looking to improve its credentials as a wine merchant. Unlike some of the retail entrants in this book, Unwins really is a traditional off-licence chain. Its stores are in the type of location where this format works best and, when it was considering its options for its strategic review, it ruled out the idea of converting some of them into an Unwins Cellars style of format. The chain now numbers some 385 stores following the acquisition of Davisons and they will all remain under one identity, Unwins. Some stores, such as its outlet in Sawbridgworth for instance, have the potential to become specialist wine stores and it is this potential that the company want to be able to fulfil wherever possible. 'We're not wine shops, we're off-licences, but there is a definite focus on improving our wine range and the customers are going to start seeing the benefits.'

The work has in fact already begun. In the last twelve months, the retailer has added some 150 new wines to its range. To meet the new demands, the buying team has doubled its strength. Last year there were only two other buyers alongside Mr Rolfe and purchasing director Gerald Duff. 'We are going to travel more to influence the winemakers. We have plans to do more visiting, more talking with winemakers,' says Bill Rolfe. ' You have to identify areas where you need to focus and tailor and spend your time doing that. That's the idea of having more people with their own areas. The brief to the wine buyer was too broad. Now, with six of us, there is more opportunity to focus and specialise.'

In addition to commissioning more products directly from suppliers or through key agents, the company also wants to expand its range of one-off parcels. 'We have identified a customer need to buy "parcels" of wine to stimulate interest in our ever more knowledgeable customers and are progressing this policy at present which will increase our importation direct from wine regions,' says Bill Rolfe. 'We are doing an awful lot more than we were doing a year ago, by restructuring the buying responsibilities, by being more proactive on the marketing front, so there will be an all-round new approach from Unwins.' (That curious word proactive again. I wonder how it strikes a native French or German speaker seen for the first time in print?)

However, Unwins is still likely to progress at its own pace whatever its adoption of trendy marketing wordspeak. This is 'a family-owned, independent company', it is proud to say (meaning not publicly quoted – so it's a small family which owns its shares rather than a large family of anonymous shareholders). While it is clearly intent on updating itself to a degree, Bill Rolfe says Unwins will nevertheless remain true to its basic values. The location of its stores means that Unwins outlets can be described as neighbourhood stores, but when Bill Rolfe says, 'We are in a different trading environment from some of our competitors. We are in communities,' I think it means more than just that. Bill Rolfe and Unwins believe there is still a place for moral values in business. Unwins, for instance, has certain rules about 'alcoholic carbonates' – alcopops to you and me – and which ones it is prepared to put on its shelves. By a similar though not identical token, it is unlikely to be listing Fat Bastard Chardonnay (Fullers q.v.), not because the marketing is too modern but because it might cause offence to some customers (whether these might be the obese boozers or the ones born out of wedlock, I didn't discover). As I have said before, I have difficulty in guessing exactly who the Unwins customers are, what they are like, and how they view the world. Bill Rolfe will only go as far as to reveal that it's a very broad range of people, though actually rather more upmarket than sometimes wine writers (including me) might imagine, and they require 'a broad range of products'. In order to design wines to suit this retailer's 'broad range' of customers, will the winemakers be given a rundown, a secret document, on exactly who the Unwins customer is? I very much doubt it. I would be greatly interested to have sight of such information if it remotely existed but I don't believe matters will proceed along such ordered, logical lines. Why? Because I reckon Unwins has no more precise idea of who its customers are than I do.

UNWINS WINE GROUP LIMITED
Birchwood House
Victoria Road
Dartford
Kent
DA1 5AJ
Tel 01322 272711
Fax 01322 294469

# AUSTRALIAN WINE RED

**Berri Estates Cabernet Sauvignon 1994** 14 D

---

**Best's Bin 0 Great Western Shiraz 1993** 15 E

---

**Best's Great Western Cabernet Sauvignon 1992** 14 E

---

**Brown Brothers Tarrango, Victoria 1996** 13.5 C

Sweet and ripe.

---

**Caversham Cabernet/Shiraz 1995** 13.5 E

Expensive for the style – even if it is highly drinkable.

---

**Ironstone Cabernet/Shiraz 1994** 15 D

Richness, flavour, depth, excellent balance of fruit and tannins, and a terrific soft punch of hedgerow flavour on the finish. Delicious.

---

**Maglieri Shiraz, McLaren Vale 1994** 13.5 E

Sheer bloody gravy.

---

**Orlando St Hugo Cabernet Sauvignon Coonawarra 1990** 16 F

Expensive but extremely fine. Minty, dry, deep, very classy.

---

**Penfolds Rawson's Retreat Bin 35 Cabernet Sauvignon Shiraz 1995** 13.5 C

Usual decent turnout.

---

**Stockman's Bridge Shiraz/Cabernet Sauvignon** 12.5 C

I'm surprised Penfolds can't turn out a smarter fruited specimen for Unwins than this – especially at a fiver.

---

**Tyrrell's Old Winery Pinot Noir 1995** 12 D

---

**Tyrrell's Vat 8 Shiraz/Cabernet Coonawarra 1993** 11 G

---

**Wakefield Cabernet Sauvignon, Clare Valley 1994** 15 D

Brilliant choice of spicy rich red for turkey with all the trimmings. Like balm in texture.

---

**Wynn's Cabernet Sauvignon Coonawarra 1993** 15 E

---

## AUSTRALIAN WINE WHITE

**Brown Brothers Chenin Blanc, Victoria 1996** 14.5 C

Almost a honeyed finish to the fruit which is a far cry from the towel-dry fruit of chenin blanc sec. Great with oriental food.

---

**Goundrey Unwooded Chardonnay, Mount Barker 1995** 16 E

Ravishingly delicious. Pure fruit, fresh and fine.

---

**Ironstone Semillon/Chardonnay 1996** 16 D

Ooh! What a succulently fruity beast of richness, flavour and great depth yet amazingly cheeky freshness. Starts off like smoky melon and pineapple and finishes with a hint of creme brulee. But this is not all custard, this wine. It is palate-arousing and very vibrant.

---

**Lindemans Botrytis Riesling, Coonawarra 1994 (half bottle)** 15.5 D

This wine and dessert like panna cotta, creme brulee or simply fresh strawberries are a delight.

---

**Maglieri Cellar Reserve Riesling 1994** 13 C

Seems to charm but rather rude and off-hand on the finish.

---

**Maglieri Semillon 1994** 14 D

---

**Penfolds Rawson's Retreat Bin 21 Semillon/Chardonnay/Colombard 1996** 

Richly textured, warmly fruity (some complexity on the finish where the acidity is most pertinent), this is an excellent vintage for this wine.

---

**Rothbury Estate Chardonnay 1996** 15.5 D

Rich and willing to go the whole way: from aroma to back of the gullet. Has a deep, sunburned charm.

---

**Saltram Mamre Brook Chardonnay 1995** 14.5 D

One of the more successfully rich and happy Australian chardonnays, although at the price the weight of fruit and the degree of complexity are too slight for comfort. That said, this is a highly drinkable wine, make no mistake. This is delicious, if not sensational in its plot.

---

**St Huberts Chardonnay, Yarra Valley 1993** 13 E

---

**Tyrrell's Old Winery Semillon 1994** 13.5 D

Plumply textured, expensively conceived wine striving for a

level of classiness it still doesn't quite reach, a year after first tasting.

**Tyrrell's Vat 47 Pinot Chardonnay 1995** 13 F

## AUSTRIAN WINE — WHITE

**Eiswein Neusidlersee Burgenland 1992 (half bottle)** 14 E

**Gruner Veltliner Weinviertel Region Estate Bottled, 1995** 12 C

## BULGARIAN WINE — RED

**Domaine Boyar Country Wine Cabernet Sauvignon/Merlot, Pomorie Region** 13 B

**Domaine Boyar Mavrud Reserve, Assenovgrad 1991** 13.5 B

Good with food.

**The Bulgarian Vintners Cabernet Sauvignon Reserve, Rousse 1990** 13.5 C

Touch on the dull side as it ages and boringly reminisces about a glorious youth.

## BULGARIAN WINE — WHITE

**Chardonnay Reserve Rousse Region 1993** 13.5 C

**Country Wine Muskat & Ugni Blanc, Slaviantzi Region** 14 B

A deliciously simple aperitif tipple. Tastes of crushed grapes!

---

## CHILEAN WINE RED

**Canepa Cabernet Sauvignon Maipo Valley 1995** 13.5 C

Rich and purposeful. Perhaps it's fading a little on the finish since I first tasted it.

---

**Domaine Oriental Clos Centenaire Merlot, Maule Valley 1996**

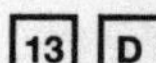


Somewhat sweet on the finish.

---

**Undurraga Merlot 1995**

Not tasting so well as it was last year. Seems rather mild and unadventurous.

---

**Undurraga Pinot Noir 1995**

Creditable texture, rather classy, but the finish is somewhat toothless.

---

## CHILEAN WINE WHITE

**Canepa Sauvignon Blanc Sagrada Familia 1996**

C

This has improved immeasurably in bottle over the last ten months. It now delivers great flavour, great fruit, great balance and real purpose at a great price. Delicious.

---

**Domaine Oriental Clos Centenaire Chardonnay, Maule Valley 1996** 13.5 D

Not as elegant as other Chilean chardonnays but it does have a sticky richness of texture which might adhere nicely to food.

---

**Undurraga Chardonnay Reserva 1995** 14 D

Good frontal attack of aroma (very opulent). Finish needs smartening up. But very classy in ambition.

---

**Undurraga Chardonnay Santa Anna, Colchagua Valley 1996** 14 C

Not as unflinchingly rich and potent as other Chilean chardonnays for the same money but there is goodness of heart here.

---

## ENGLISH WINE — WHITE

**Denbies Chardonnay 1993** 12.5 C

---

**Lamberhurst Sovereign Medium Dry** 10 B

---

**Three Choirs Estate Premium 1993** 14 C

---

## FRENCH WINE — RED

**Beaujolais Villages E Loron 1994** 10 D

---

**Bergerac Comtesse Catherine 1996** 13.5 C

A rustic peasant bursting out of his velvet bodkin. He passes muster disguised by food.

---

**Bourgueil Les Barroirs, Couly-Dutheil 1995** 13.5 D

I'd be inclined to charity here: leave this wine for three years more before drinking. A 15/16 pointer may emerge.

---

**Burgundy Pinot Noir Albert Bichot 1995** 10 D

I could be wrong. But I'll say it anyway: this is the feeblest red burgundy, without being undrinkable, I've tasted in years.

---

**Chateau Biquet, Mauregard 1995** 14 C

This is a solid partner for roasts and grills. It has some plumpness to the fruit but also a dry, rugged edge.

---

**Chateau Courteau Mauregard, Bordeaux 1996** 14 C

Everyday drinking claret. Not grand but far from ugly either.

---

**Chateau de Dracy 'Baron de Charette' Pinot Noir Bourgogne 1994** 11 E

---

**Chateau du Perier Medoc 1992** 12 E

---

**Chateau du Pin St Martial Borie-Manoux, Bordeaux 1995** 12 C

Somewhat bereft of wit as it says, simply, 'farewell'.

---

**Chateau Ducla, Yvon Mau 1995** 12 D

---

**Chateau Grand Lartique St Emilion Grand Cru 1992** 13.5 E

---

**Chinon Les Gravieres, Couly-Dutheil 1996** 14 D

Classic young Chinon: pure raspberry essence drunk over charcoal. Great chilled. Terrific with fish, meat and any mood.

---

**Claret Yvon Mau 1996** 13 C

Fireworky edge to the fruit. Needs food.

---

**Domaine de l'Estagnol Minervois** 12 B

**Domaine des Caunettes Hautes Cabardes 1993** 14 C

Nice maturity to the wine, touch cranky and austere perhaps but soft as it initially grips the palate and a sympathetic partner for rich foods.

**Domaine St Andre Cabernet Sauvignon VdP d'Oc** 12.5 B

Bit too fruit-juicy for me. Has little cabernet character or bite but what it does have is soft drinkability.

**Fitou Chateau de Segure 1993** 14 D

**Fitou Les Producteurs du Mont Tauch 1994** 13.5 C

**Fitou Les Producteurs du Mont Tauch 1995** 13 C

Some cherry-edge to fruit and tannin. So with food it's on its best behaviour.

**J P Chenet Syrah Carte Noir 1994** 11 C

**Rivesaltes Vintage Les Producteurs Reunis 1994 (50cl)** 15 C

**Vacqueyras Domaine de la Soleiade 1995** 15.5 C

Smells like the inside of a warm gymshoe but the fruit, tannin and acidity are electrifyingly rich and alert. Terrific stuff.

# FRENCH WINE — WHITE

**Bergerac Comtesse Catherine 1996** 14 B

Dry, crisp, very clean and on the elegant side of fruity. Good to glug or for oceanic plates.

---

**Blanc de Blancs Yvon Mau** 12 B

Sound rather than exciting.

---

**Bordeaux Sauvignon Yvon Mau 1996** 13.5 C

---

**Burgundy Chardonnay Albert Bichot 1996** 11 D

---

**Buzet 'Renaissance', Les Vignerons de Buzet 1995** 12 C

---

**Chablis Olivier Tricon 1996** 11 D

---

**Chateau de Montpatey Marquis d'Espies Chardonnay Bourgogne 1994** 13.5 E

---

**Chateau Ducla Entre Deux Mers 1996** 14 C

Good with shellfish. Austere without.

---

**Chateau Saint-Seurin Mauregard Bordeaux 1995** 14 C

Has that final flinty, mineral-edged touch on the fruit which makes a solid bet for the money.

---

**Domaine Colin Rosier Chardonnay, Vin de Pays d'Oc** 10 C

---

**Domaine de Plessis-Glain Muscadet de Sevre et Maine Sur Lie, J P Petard 1996** 12 C

---

**Domaine Lanine Cotes du Gascogne 1995** 14 C

**Domaine Sainte Agathe Barrel Fermented Chardonnay d'Oc 1995** 13 C

Curiously toffee-nosed wine. Probably at its best with chicken dishes.

**Gewurztraminer Cuvee des Seigneurs de Ribeaupierre Trimbach 1990** 12.5 G

**J P Chenet Chardonnay Carte Noir 1995** 10 C

**VdP d'Oc Syrah Rose** 12 C

## GERMAN WINE WHITE

**Liebfraumilch Muller 1996** 10 B

This is the sort of wine which makes you wonder what goes into it besides grapes: sweet old Oxfam knitwear, perhaps?

**Mainzer Domherr Kabinett Muller 1995** 10 C

## GREEK WINE WHITE

**Retsina of Attica 'Kourtaki'** 13 B

Essentially a Greek food wine where. like the elephantine yob who turns out to be poetry on a football pitch, it belongs and comes alive.

**Samos Vin Doux Naturel, Kourtakis NV** 13.5 C

## HUNGARIAN WINE RED

**Volcanic Hills Cabernet Franc, Villany Region 1996**

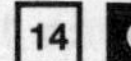


In the class of Chinon or Bourgueil – but cheekier on the finish.

---

## HUNGARIAN WINE WHITE

**Volcanic Hills Leanyka Mor Region 1996**

Vibrant, individual, only gently volcanic on the tongue, very refreshing and pert. A great aperitif to slurp.

---

**Volcanic Hills Sauvignon Blanc Tok Region 1996**

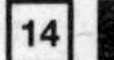


Has crisp mineral-edged fruit of great keenness and appetite – arousing incisiveness.

---

## ITALIAN WINE RED

**Canaletto Veduta Rosso VdT Puglia 1994**

Cherries, ripe and, oddly, dry.

---

**Montepulciano d'Abruzzo Miglianico 1996**

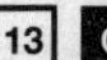


Touch dull. No more than a touch . . . it impresses you with its worthiness but dullness.

---

**Villa Selva Chianti 1995**

Light? My dear – light isn't the word for it.

---

## ITALIAN WINE — WHITE

**Frascati Superiore Selezione, Tullio San Marco 1996** 13.5 D

An elegant frascati of polish and some style.

---

**Frascati Superiore, Tullio San Marco 1996** 11 C

---

**Gavi Antario 1996** 13 D

Expensive.

---

## MEXICAN WINE — RED

**L A Cetto Cabernet Sauvignon 1993** 15 C

Now this has its touch of sweet fruitiness well melded with the dry tannins and acidity so it's all in tasty tone.

---

## NEW ZEALAND WINE — RED

**Cooks Hawkes Bay Cabernet Sauvignon/ Merlot 1995** 12 C

Doesn't exactly register on the Richter scale.

---

## NEW ZEALAND WINE — WHITE

**Cooks Chardonnay, Gisborne Valley 1996** 13.5 C

Disappointing lack of focus.

---

**Matua Sauvignon Blanc, Marlborough 1995** 13.5 E

**Selaks Chardonnay, Marlborough 1996** 13 D

Too expensive for the style.

**Villa Maria Private Bin Chardonnay 1995** 13.5 D

Highly drinkable but too highly priced.

**Villa Maria Reserve Sauvignon Blanc 1996** 13.5 E

Nervy, rich, very temperamental on the tongue but interesting (mildly).

**Waimanu Dry White Muller Thurgau/ Sauvignon Blanc 1996** 13.5 C

Tries hard but has not put in the effort to make more impact this term. Position in class: towards the bottom.

## PORTUGUESE WINE RED

**Alta Mesa Estremadura 1995** 15.5 B

Brilliant quaffing: soft, slightly rich and flavourful and exceedingly friendly.

**Garrafeira Reserva Particular, A Bernardino 1987** 13 D

Needs food. Or heat it up in a saucepan and pour it over the roast.

**Palha-Canas, Estremadura 1996** 14 D

Hugely fruity and sweet on the finish but has some gentle complexity. An unintimidating wine of effortless drinkability.

**Quinta da Boa Vista Portada, Estremadura 1995** 13.5 C

Almost sweet on the finish. Excellent with curries.

---

**Terras de Xisto Alentejo 1995** 13 C

Getting a bit past it.

---

## PORTUGUESE WINE WHITE

**Chardonnay Casa Lantos Lima 1996** 11 D

Has some hint of individuality but is so bereft of wit compared with cava and Chilean specimens £2 cheaper.

---

**Espiga Branco V R Estremadura 1995** 14 C

Great flavour and richness here. Excellent food and person wine (i.e. not cooked persons but live conversational ones).

---

## ROMANIAN WINE WHITE

**Chardonnay Tarnave Region 1995** 16 C

The everyday drinking woman's meursault. It's an opulently textured wine of subtle vegetality, coated but rich fruit and persistence of charm. Great with fish and poultry.

---

**Idlerock Chardonnay 1995** 12 C

---

**Idlerock Oaked Chardonnay, Murfatlar Region 1995** 14.5 C

Chewy in texture with good throughput in flavour and soft, rich fruitiness. Hardly classic but good with food.

---

## SOUTH AFRICAN WINE RED

**Hidden River Pinotage NV** 14 C

**Hidden River Ruby Cabernet NV** 13.5 C

Almost very good.

## SOUTH AFRICAN WINE WHITE

**Cavendish Cape White Jerepigo 1979** 14 D

Delicious old sweetie-poo. Great with a slice of Christmas cake or just a glass to warm the cockles. Tastes like molasses with the added complexity of figs.

**Hidden River Chardonnay NV** 11 C

**Hidden River Chenin Blanc NV** 11 C

**Hidden River Sauvignon Blanc NV** 12 C

**KWV Chenin Blanc 1996** 14 C

Successfully pretends to flavour and style. A good dry elegance of approach, not rich, but not diffident either.

**KWV Sauvignon Blanc 1995** 13.5 C

## SPANISH WINE RED

**Carta de Oro Berberana Rioja 1994** 13 C

Would be at its best with mushroom risotto.

**Don Fabian Tempranillo Navarra 1995** 14 C

**Faustino Rivero Ulecia Rioja 1992** 14 D

Still rates the same as it did when first tasted two years ago (although it costs a little bit more). A food wine of some richness and determination. I like very much the edgy, tannic finish.

**La Mancha** 12 B

Ho hum.

**Stowells of Chelsea Tempranillo (3-litre box)** 14 B

Price has been adjusted to show equivalent per bottle.

**Torres Coronas 1994** 14 D

An excellent accompaniment to roast, herbed lamb.

## SPANISH WINE WHITE

**Castillo Fuentemayor Oak Aged Bodegas AGE 1994** 12.5 D

Interesting, nutty, creamy edge which will go well with food (especially barbecued fish) but is rather an expensive and jejune solo glugging experience.

**Dona Isabella Viura Navarra 1995** 13.5 C

**El Coto Rioja 1995** 13.5 D

**La Mancha** 12 B

Has the merit of being inexpensive but struggles to thrill otherwise.

**Torres Vina Esmeralda 1993** 12 D

**Torres Vina Sol 1995** 13 C

## USA WINE RED

**Blossom Hill, California** 12.5 C

**Fetzer Eagle Peak Merlot, Mendocino County 1994** 14 D

Very smooth and elementally integrated. Perhaps not as exciting as a seven-quid wine might be, but the texture and gentle fruit are solid features.

**Gallo California Zinfandel 1992** 13 C

**Pepperwood Grove Zinfandel, Sonoma Valley 1995** 13 C

Curious rhubarb-crumble edge.

**Sutter Home California Cabernet Sauvignon 1994** 13 C

## USA WINE WHITE

**Blossom Hill, California** 10 C

**Fetzer Echo Ridge Fume Blanc 1995** 14 C

Quiet but quietly impressive. Handsomely textured, gently rich, elegant and stylish.

**Gallo French Colombard** 9 C

---

**Golden State Vintners Reserve Chardonnay 1995** 15 D

Very richly endowed with flavour and a thick texture of some lap-up-able deliciousness.

---

**Montevina Chardonnay, California 1993** 12 D

---

# FORTIFIED WINE

**Calem LBV 1990** 13 E

A sweetie for fruit cakes.

---

**Dom Ramos Manzanilla** 14.5 C

Chilled, well chilled, with spicy prawns, and this wine is utter heaven.

---

**White Jerepigo 1979** 15 D

Delicious with fruit tart at the end of the meal. Thick and honey-rich with a classical cherry centre.

---

# SPARKLING WINE/CHAMPAGNE

**Angas Rose Brut (Australia)** 15.5 D

---

**Carrington Extra Brut (Australia)** 13.5 D

---

**Cava Brut Methode Traditionelle** 14 D

Has elegance and bite.

---

**Chardonnay Blanc de Blancs 'Le Baron' Brut** 13.5 D

Starts crisp then turns soft.

---

**Clairette de Die Methode Dioise Ancestrale, Georges Aubert** 13 D

Good and peachy for sweet-toothed tipplers.

---

**Cremant de Bourgogne Chardonnay Brut** 13 E

---

**Duchatel Blanc de Blancs Champagne** 11 G

---

**Duchatel Brut Champagne NV** 12 F

---

**Graham Beck Brut, Madeba Valley (South Africa)** 13.5 E

Good subtle lemon style – very subtle.

---

**Graham Beck Chardonnay/Pinot Noir (South Africa)** 13 D

It lacks a little zip and personality.

---

**Lindauer Brut (New Zealand)** 13.5 D

---

**'Mayerling' Cremant d'Alsace** 14 E

Like a fine-quality cava. Excellent value.

---

**Nicolas Feuillate Brut Premier Cru NV** 14 G

Difficult to rate such insouciance and style any lower.

---

**Seaview Brut Rose** 15 D

Elegant, purposeful tippling.

---

**Stockman's Bridge Brut (Australia)** 13.5 D

A soft bubbly which is an easy quaffer.

---

**Vouvray Tete de Cuvee Brut (France)** 14 E

---

**Yalumba Pinot Noir/Chardonnay (Australia)** 16 E

One of the Antipodes' finest.

---

# VICTORIA WINE

While examining the retailers' operations in those exotic regions of the world where wine is made, Victoria Wine proved to be a particularly rewarding specimen to study. It is the only chain in this book which employs someone from its own staff to make wines. As Wine Technical Manager, the precise role which Hugh Suter MW performs at Victoria Wine is a little more involved than that, but it has been his job to oversee the production of a number of wines designed to fit the retailer's exact requirements. If any one fact should indicate Victoria Wine's commitment to what might be termed 'bespoke' wines, it is the presence of Mr Hugh Suter.

It is therefore no surprise that the wines produced to a brief or with the retailer's collaboration make a long and impressive list. The company breaks down its involvement in this area into three categories: the house ranges such as the own-label clarets and Vins de Pays where the producer 'will refine the wine until we are happy with it'; wine ranges such as the South African Cape View where 'We know what we want to fill a gap in our range and get involved in everything, supplier selection, blending, naming, packaging'; and thirdly the wines where involvement is 'total', right down to grape selection and vinification methods, such as the Hugh Suter Series of Loire and Californian wines. Thomas Woolrych, senior wine buyer, reckons all told that these wines account for around a third of the retailer's sales. The list also includes innovative concepts such as Ed's Red, Ed's White and Ravioli Red. Clearly, such innovation and Victoria Wine's direct involvement in commissioning and styling wines is important to the company. 'Through research we know what our customers want and thus can set out to produce wines that fulfil a need whether it be a fun wine ideal with pasta, Ravioli Red, or a vintage champagne to celebrate the millennium,' says PR manager, Nicola Harvey.

As with other retailers, this method of sourcing wines contrasts starkly with the more 'off the peg' way of buying wines which until recently was the norm. When a selection of the wines which Victoria Wine has had a hand in developing is lined up in front of you, it is easy to appreciate the idea that there has been something of a revolution in the wine market. The label design and the branding alone, when compared with what one might have seen ten years ago, tells you that something fairly dramatic has happened in the market, before you even begin to discuss how the wines came into being. Mr Woolrych, a veteran of some ten years at Victoria Wine (and who has been involved in wine marketing and in creating the Victoria Wine Cellars upmarket group of shops), sees these wines as reflecting the huge transformation in the marketing of wine over the past ten years. 'The success of these products shows that there is a big audience for new developments,' he says.

Mr Woolrych and I will measure success in different ways. He will ultimately judge a wine in terms of sales and is highly satisfied with the performance of many of these products. I, on the other hand, seek to assess the wines on their taste and style and of course value-for-money. But I have to say that in our different ways we come to similar conclusions on many. Take Hugh Suter's Muscadet de Sevre et Maine for example. This is one of a range of wines from the Loire which Victoria Wine has introduced of late, some made under the supervision of Mr Suter and others from different sources, in an attempt to revive the flagging fortunes of several once-flourishing appellations. Both in terms of how much it flourished and how much it has subsequently flagged, Muscadet is the prime exemplar.

The muscadet here was produced using 20 per cent new wood – American oak, incidentally, rather than French – with slightly cooler fermentation. The result is a fresh and fruity muscadet which shows what the wine could achieve if it came back to form in general rather than in exceptions like this one. Hugh Suter was pretty pleased with the wine himself. I agreed. It notched up 14.5 points in my scoring system and though that may seem modest let me tell you that muscadet has been so wretched for so long, that that rating is a near-miracle. The vinification method – unusual for the region – had not detracted from its 'muscadetness', he explained. 'It respects the tradition,' Mr Suter mused, apologising for the cliche. He soon gave up apologising for cliches. Marketers and winemakers both have cliche-ridden vocabularies; when both are combined the effect is what you would expect . . . a lot of what you expect. But I can forgive the odd hackneyed expression if the substance makes sense and with Mr Suter thankfully it often does. 'It's not over-oaked and it's not ultra-aromatic. It still goes through the [Muscadet appellation] tasting-panel and if it becomes atypical they would not pass it.' (I keep my lips tightly sealed at this point. Wondering, indeed, if the Muscadet appellation tasting panel, for the past twenty-five years, have been equally close-mouthed in order to pass the majority of the vinous products of the region.)

Considering that by his own admission Mr Suter's experience as a winemaker is limited, this wine has to go down as a significant achievement. Having been in charge of quality control at Grants of St James's, he was well versed in matters technical and had naturally as an MW read exhaustively on the subject, but on the practical side he was a novice. Apparently he used to grow grapes and make wine in Guildford and is obviously delighted to have been given the chance by his employers to try his hand in some of the world's more established vineyards. 'They had faith in sending someone who knew a lot theoretically but had never squashed a grape in his life,' he says jauntily. 'They sent me off to do it which was great. It was enormous fun.' His Chardonnay Vin de Pays du Jardin de la France, part of the same series, scored even more highly than the muscadet with 15.5 points. It is rich, ripe and lemony on the finish and terrific value. There is no doubt that Mr Suter is in line for a Croix de Guerre and a peck on both cheeks from whoever's president at the time if there is any justice in the world.

The Cape View range, described by Thomas Woolrych as 'tremendously successful', also performed well in tasting. The 1996 Cinsault/Shiraz, spicy with a savoury tang, is a worthy 16-pointer, while the richly textured merlot scored 15.5. The 14-point Chenin/Sauvignon Blanc is fruity and extremely drinkable with an exotic nip to its finish. Underlining the international nature of the wine business, these wines were made in South Africa to a brief from a UK retailer by a New Zealand winemaker, Chris Kelly, under the direction of Kim Milne, an Australian.

A rather less successful project in my view has been the Slate Valley range, not as the name suggests New World wines, but two wines from the Mosel, an off-dry country wine and a riesling, packaged in clear Bordeaux bottles with Australian-style labels to boot. Somewhere on the bottle it must say it comes from Germany, but you will need your reading specs to see it. On taste alone, the German wine business should not be pinning its hopes of recovery on the riesling, which I gave 11 points; its companion scored 10 points. There is, of course, something defeatist about producing a package that is so entirely unGerman. But the image of German wine is apparently so shameful that it has to be concealed in this way in order for a new wine to stand a chance. Given the level of extraordinarily beautiful riesling the Germans can produce, the trend is humiliating but necessary. Whilst one would have to agree that the extremes of German-style wine packaging and Gothic-nightmare labelling are extremely off-putting to the British consumer, thus making progress in this area important, if the new-style wine flies in the face of this only superficially, then what is achieved but a new generation of alienated drinkers?

On the whole, however, the packaging innovation displayed amongst Victoria Wine's range of bespoke products is rather impressive. The concept and the silk-screened label of Ravioli

Red, for instance, are marvellous. The wine I found rather sweet and simpering, and I would have thought not particularly good with ravioli. I gave it 13 points. On the other hand, I found the Bulgarian Rocky Valley Cabernet Sauvignon to be the perfect pasta wine, full of fruit, flavour, fitness and fatness. Rocky Valley is another European offering at Victoria Wine which is modelling New World garb, but at least in this case the wine does have a certain New World affability about it. I also liked the Coba Falls Chilean Dry White, a wine which Thomas Woolrych himself was closely involved with. It is floral and perfumed, rich and fruity, and it's thunderingly good value. The merlot from the same range, rating 15.5 points, is equally an excellent food wine.

That both Hugh Suter and Thomas Woolrych consider 'packaging to be crucial' is palpably obvious when looking at this line-up. Advances in packaging are a key part of the marketing revolution in wine, sparked in Thomas Woolrych's view by the arrival of the Australians. 'The effect Australia has had on the market has been enormous,' he says. 'It has really changed the way people look at things. The marketing of wine is only just now being treated in the same way as other goods. It could get more professional and in tune with consumers.'

Mr Woolrych is not just talking about Victoria Wine's involvement in creating wines here, but the innovative style of market-led products that this kind of closer collaboration has created. Now, you may say, what business has an expression like 'marketing-led' got to do with me – a wine writer? The answer is this: it may be an odiously fashionable term of big business but *au fond* it means a deep concern with what drinkers like you and me really care about. 'Big Frank's, Ed's Red, Ravioli Red: these are all classic examples of really new ways of marketing wines,' says Mr Woolrych. He makes the telling point that a wine such as Cat's Pee on a Gooseberry Bush – yes, it really does say that on the label – would not have sold nearly so well had it been called New Zealand Sauvignon Blanc – which it is. This reality is at the centre of his discourse on the whole subject and even if it is the most important it is perhaps the least romantic and creative aspect of his work. 'It comes back to commercial realities,' he points out. 'We see opportunities to bring new customers in. To sell more wine.' With reference to Hugh Suter's wines he adds: 'We would only do it if it was going to build sales. We wouldn't do it just because we thought it was a nice thing to do. But it has built sales. It has brought people back to the Loire.' Is it any surprise that wine producers world-wide are so keen to bring their wines to the notice of retail wine buyers such as him? It is part and parcel of the theme of this year's *Streetplonk*: we Brits simply can't keep our noses out of other countries' vineyards and we've been doing it for hundreds of years. Victoria Wine is carrying on a tradition which is not just good business for them, but, in the long term, will ensure survival for many wine areas which, to my way of thinking at least, risk being turned into theme parks by the middle of the next century.

VICTORIA WINE CO
Dukes Court
Duke Street
Woking
Surrey
GU21 5XL
Tel 01483 715066
Fax 01483 755234

## ARGENTINIAN WINE RED

**Balbi Vineyards Cabernet Sauvignon 1996** 15.5 C

This is, likely as not, the most straightforwardly delicious cabernet I've tasted in years. It owes very little to any European or Australian style. It's a deep swimming pool of flavour you simply walk in to up to your nose and let flood down your throat. Victoria Wine Cellars only.

---

**Balbi Vineyards Malbec 1996** 15 C

Oodles of rich, soft, rubberized fruit which just jumps all over the tastebuds. Lively stuff!

---

**Graffigna Shiraz/Cabernet Sauvignon 1995** 15.5 B

Dry, tobaccoey, rich, deep, characterful – this is an excellent red for anyone's money. A superb grilled-food wine.

---

**Libertad Sangiovese Malbec 1996** 13 C

Nice plump texture and soft fruit.

---

**Vistalba Syrah 1995** 14 C

---

## ARGENTINIAN WINE WHITE

**Libertad Chenin Blanc 1996** 14 C

Unusually delicious, cloying edge of the fruit makes this a mannered wine but one of great companionability.

---

**Mendoza White NV** 16 B

A brilliantly priced, spicy, creamy, charmingly textured wine of consummate drinkability. A well-flavoured libation for the throat which is simply bargain bibulosity.

---

# AUSTRALIAN WINE RED

**Basedow Shiraz 1994** 14 D

---

**Brokenback Ridge Shiraz/Cabernet 1994** 13 C

Somewhat simplistic for the money.

---

**Brown Brothers Tarrango 1996** 14 C

The Australian answer to beaujolais: soft, juicy, rubbery fruit with character to counteract the slippery jam of the initial approach. Great fun glugging here!

---

**Corunna Point Red** 

Soft and fruity, simple and very drinkable.

---

**Deakin Estate Cabernet Sauvignon 1995** 14.5 C

Invitingly aromatic, very savourily fruited, and sufficiently dry to catch the flavour nuances of, say, grilled vegetables, casseroled carrots, curried cauliflower and toad-in-the-hole.

---

**Deakin Estate Shiraz 1996** 14.5 C

Real potency to the rich fruit. The jamminess of the '96 vintage is relieved by some earthy edginess.

---

**Hardys Stamp Series Shiraz/Cabernet 1996** 14 C

Getting pricey over £4, this wine. It mixes warm soft fruit with hints of the outback. Not exactly a raunchy wine but a very Aussie one in its kangaroo-pouch finish.

---

**Hardys Bankside Shiraz 1994** 15 D

Soft yet rich and dry. Rather expensive but expressive.

---

**Hardys Nottage Hill Cabernet Sauvignon/ Shiraz 1995** 13.5 C

Okay – but pricey. Wish it was £3.49.

---

**Katnook Merlot Coonawarra 1992** 13.5 E

---

**Lindemans Bin 45 Cabernet Sauvignon 1995** 13 D

I suppose one can imagine toying with a glass, but the wine tries to be liked so unimaginatively, it's embarrassing. I prefer more character in wine, as in people – especially at this price.

---

**Penfolds Bin 2 Shiraz/Mourvedre 1995** 15.5 D

Rich, dry, stylish, this has fluidity of fruit yet tannic firmness of tone. The screwcap is a marvellous taint-free plus.

---

**Penfolds Kalimna Shiraz Bin 28 1994** 14 E

A savoury, rich, deep wine of dry charms and a hint of juicy wit as it coats the throat on the way down. It is expensive, a touch, for the style but I can't gainsay the wine's considerable drinkability.

---

**Penfolds Koonunga Hill Shiraz Cabernet 1995** 14 D

Very tasty, very rich. Very sparky stuff.

---

**Penfolds Old Vine Barossa Valley Shiraz/Grenache/Mourvedre 1994** 16.5 E

The Aussie answer to Chateauneuf-du-Pape? If so, there's something for the Frogs to chew on here: dryness (with a subtle herbiness), richness (with great depth of flavour), balance, style and loads of well-toned fruit. Goes with food and mood. A rousing bottle of ten quid well spent.

---

**Penfolds Old Vine Mourvedre/Grenache/ Shiraz, Barossa 1993** 14 E

Rhone with more sun and more soft texture. Rather expensive, however.

---

**Rosemount Estate Cabernet Sauvignon 1995** 14 D

Stylish and drinkable but a touch expensive.

---

**Rosemount Shiraz/Cabernet 1995** 15 C

---

**Salisbury Estate Grenache 1996** 12 C

So sweet and soupy you could pour it over ice cream.

---

**Saltram Shiraz 1996** 14 D

A bright, cherry-edged wine of great quaff- and ami-ability.

---

**The Cranswick Estate Nine Pines Shiraz 1996** 12 D

My hackles rise as I note the words High Trellis under the word Shiraz on the label. This is not the name of the winemaker (who stood on tiptoe to pick the grapes?). 'Cellar for six years', it says on the back label. Good. That saves you the trouble of drinking this pile of pretension now.

---

## AUSTRALIAN WINE WHITE

**Basedow Chardonnay 1995** 15.5 D

Rich, full, deep, complex, cheeky yet mature, this has oodles of oily personality without a whit of unpleasantness.

---

**Basedow Oscar's Traditional Semillon 1995** 14.5 D

An enjoyable oddball of a bottle. The fruit has an underlying quirkiness which is the sum of some oddly delicious parts. Provokes debate as it quenches thirst. An individual tipple, for sure.

---

**Brokenback Ridge Semillon/Chardonnay 1996** 13.5 C

Decent fish wine, I suppose.

---

**Corunna Point White** 13 C

Rather cosmetic.

---

**Green Point Vineyards Still Chardonnay 1994** 13 E

---

**Hardys Nottage Hill Chardonnay 1996** 15 C

This elegant style of Aussie chardonnay is light years ahead of the blowsy blockbusters of yesteryear.

---

**Jacob's Creek Dry Riesling 1996** 14 C

Lovely friendly riesling which is at its best as a blue-mood lifter. The finish is full of smiles.

---

**Jacobs Creek Semillon/Chardonnay 1996** 13 C

---

**Lindemans Padthaway Chardonnay 1996** 15 E

I've pondered the cost of this wine and retasted it, glass after glass, wondering if its understated deftness was good value and, lo! the bottle was empty and I felt deliciously satisfied.

---

**Moondah Brook Chenin Blanc 1994** 13.5 D

---

**Nottage Hill Riesling 1995** 14 C

Improving nicely in bottle.

---

**Penfolds Barrel-Fermented Semillon 1994** 15 D

Nice wood touches on the fruit – not solid and oaken but soft and balsa. Will develop in bottle well for another year or so.

---

**Penfolds Clare Valley Organic Chardonnay/ Sauvignon Blanc 1996** 15 E

Probably the world's most elegant organic chardonnay/sauvignon blanc link-up.

---

**Penfolds Organic Chardonnay/Sauvignon Blanc 1993** 13.5 D

---

**Penfolds Rawsons Retreat Bin 21 Semillon/Chardonnay/Colombard 1996** 

Richly textured, warmly fruity (some complexity on the finish where the acidity is most pertinent), this is an excellent vintage for this wine.

---

**Rosemount Diamond Label Semillon/ Chardonnay 1995** 13 D

---

**Rosemount Estate Chardonnay 1996** 15.5 D

Opulence vinified. Rather grandly fruity, proud and rich.

---

**Rymill Coonawarra Botrytis Gewurztraminer 1994 (half bottle)** 16 D

A waxily honeyed masterpiece. It'll keep years. Certainly an AD 2000 bottle. Oily custard fruit and texture with a hint of spice. Victoria Wine Cellars only.

---

**Wolf Blass Riesling 1995** 16 D

Big, robust, oily, aromatic, rich (but not cloying), this is an impressively broad shouldered riesling which will work brilliantly with oriental food and rich fish dishes. It really coats the tongue like an emulsion.

---

## BULGARIAN WINE — RED

**Bulgarian Cabernet Sauvignon, Sliven 1992** 14.5 B

Good cabernet style (i.e. dry, blackcurranty, subtly green-peppery).

---

**Bulgarian Country Wine, Merlot/Pinot Noir Sliven** 16 B

Only the Bulgars would stick two such unlikely grapes together and produce a serious wine. This is a really fruity yet dry miracle for the money.

---

**Bulgarian Vintners Cabernet Sauvignon Rubin, Plovdiv 1996** 14 B

Handsome dry edge, characterful and rich, to good, firm cherry/plum fruit.

---

**Bulgarian Vintners Reserve Cabernet Sauvignon 1990** 13.5 C

Like a light port. A light port is where light ships anchor. Tastebuds may prefer dryer docks.

---

**Domaine Boyar Liubimetz Merlot 1996** 16 B

Brilliant value for its richness, texture, depth of flavour, and persistence of fruitiness. An elegant wine of class for the cost of a packet of fags.

---

**Lovico Suhindol Merlot/Gamza Country Wine** 14 B

Touch farmyardy as it impinges on the proboscis but adenoidally it's sleek and purring. The perfect pasta partner. Not at all stores.

---

**Rocky Valley Cabernet Sauvignon, Russe 1996**  

A characterful, opulence-edged pasta plonk with fruit, flavour, fitness and fatness. Has a New World affability I'm not sure about but at the price the fruit is spot-on. Not at all stores.

---

**Rocky Valley Merlot, Russe 1996**  

Here, the New World softly-softly stealth of its cabernet sister is engulfed by the richness of the merlot's leathery indomitability and texture. An excellent wine of polish and pith. Terrific with food. Not at all stores.

---

**Stowells Bulgarian Red (3-litre box)**  

Vague hints of Bulgaria. Price bracket has been adjusted to show equivalent per bottle.

---

**Suhindol Special Reserve Cabernet Sauvignon 1992**  

Seems intentionally made to assume a slight claret-like winsomeness. But that Bulgarian boisterousness won't be quashed! Victoria Wine Cellars only.

---

# BULGARIAN WINE WHITE

**Domaine Boyar Chardonnay/Aligote Country Wine, Pavlikeni 1996**  

Pretty basic but pretty on the tongue and prettily priced. A party plonk, I guess.

---

**Rocky Valley Chardonnay, Russe 1996** 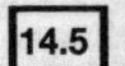 

Very rich on the finish, suspiciously so (as if the winemaker dropped essence of vanilla and apricot in it) but it's eminently well suited to food. With a rich fish stew, for instance, it would be scrumptious. Not at all stores.

---

## CHILEAN WINE — RED

**Altura Cabernet Sauvignon 1996** 14 C

The juicy approach to cabernet. It's a good way to go at this easy-to-swallow price.

---

**Caliterra Reserva Cabernet Sauvignon 1994** 16.5 D

So ripe and gobbet-full of flavour, with the tannins gently ferocious on the teeth at the finish, that it seems to linger an unconscionably long time. Utterly ravishing wine. Victoria Wine Cellars only.

---

**Concha y Toro Casillero del Diablo Cabernet Sauvignon 1994** 15 C

Forget it's cabernet. It's simply a fabulously rich, mouth-gaggingly gorgeous tipple.

---

**Concha y Toro Merlot/Malbec 1996** 16.5 C

Such richness and flavour! It flows like lava over the tongue and then seriously coats the throat with a deep lingering fruity finish. It's simply wonderful.

---

**Cono Sur Merlot 1996** 16 C

Stunning richness, texture and overall style and elegance combined with a rampant confidence. Really impressive.

---

**Cono Sur Pinot Noir 1996** 14 C

Gamy aroma, good texture, wild raspberry edge to the fruit, a dry finish – this is an admirable pinot to please buffs as well as normal human slurpers.

---

**Cousino Macul Cabernet Sauvignon 1994** 12 D

Old-fashioned Chile wine: expensive and awkward with itself. It's neither smooth nor harmonious. Victoria Wine Cellars only.

---

**Don Maximiano Special Reserve Cabernet Sauvignon, Errazuriz 1993** 

Sweet on the finish which rather mars the idea of spending ten quid on a bottle. There are more rewarding four-quid Chilean cabernets all over the place. Victoria Wine Cellars only.

---

**Errazuriz Merlot 1996** 

Totally delicious: textured, dry, multi-layered, gently leathery and enticingly aromatic, rich yet not forbidding, stylish, very classy and overwhelmingly terrific value for money.

---

**La Fortuna Malbec 1996**  C

Not as dry and impertinently stylish as previous vintages, the '96 is rich, deft, dark and the sweet finish turns savoury in the throat. Delicious to simply quaff, this level of fruit.

---

**Stowells of Chelsea Chilean Merlot Cabernet (3-litre box)**  

Price bracket has been adjusted to show equivalent per bottle.

---

**Valdivieso Cabernet Sauvignon, Lontue 1996**  C

What a price for such vivacious complexity and youth! The quality of the fruit and the winemaking is world-class. The flourish, the cheek, of the wine is incredible. A magnificent, rich, chewy finish of spicy cassis!

---

**Valdivieso Cabernet Sauvignon Reserve 1995** 16.5 D

Savoury, rich, beautifully integrated tannins and fruit, and such finesse controlling the power! This is a tremendously well-flavoured wine.

---

## CHILEAN WINE WHITE

**Altura Chardonnay 1996** 

Hints of lemon, nuts and melon combine well and offer a serious contender in the £3.75 chardonnay stakes.

---

**Cabernet Sauvignon Marques de Casa Concha, Concha y Toro 1995** 16 D

When I die, will heaven provide wine like this? It's sinfully drinkable – rich, deep, soft and beautifully polished – so perhaps it belongs in the other place. Victoria Wine Cellars only.

---

**Canepa Oak Aged Semillon 1996** 15.5 C

Delicious, delicious fish wine. Makes a refreshing and interestingly flavoured change from chardonnay and sauvignon. Ripe, fresh and well finished with a keen acidic edge. Elegant, too. But the '97 might be replacing it by the time this book comes out (not tasted as yet). Selected stores.

---

**Carmen Chardonnay 1995**  

---

**Chardonnay Marques de Casa Concha, Concha y Toro 1995** 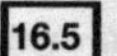 D

Elegant yet humming with flavour and depth. It has an almost casual excellence about it – like Bjorn Borg serving – but it is accurate, deadly efficient, and it hits the spot, beautifully. Victoria Wine Cellars only.

---

**Coba Falls Chilean Dry White NV** 

Very perfumed, almost florally-tarty, and no way elegant. But it's rich and fruity and very refreshingly finished acidically. Brilliant value.

---

**Concha y Toro Casillero del Diablo Chardonnay 1996** 

C

What a price for such divine drinking! The wine has an edge of creamy richness to its nutty-edged acidity and so operating in union are complexity of flavour and texture. It doesn't flag as it reaches the finishing line. A wine which makes the drinker lick her lips and purr with pleasure. One sips this wine and knows what it's like to be a cat stroked under the chin.

---

**Cono Sur Gewurztraminer 1996** 

Not as explosive as some of its Alsatian cousins but is very energetic on the tongue and, in essence, a combination of chardonnay-like richness and subtle muscat grapiness on the finish. Selected stores.

---

**Errazuriz Chardonnay 1996** 

Not as rich and exuberant as many Chilean chardonnays of this year. But it is elegant, decisively balanced, and decently priced for the texture of the fruit and its demurely creamy rich edge.

---

**Errazuriz Sauvignon Blanc 1996** 

Surprisingly delicious and richly textured and yet whilst it runs away in the fruit stakes – way out in front of other sauvignons – it has enough nous to offer a hint of classic crispness amidst all that opulence.

---

**Stowells of Chelsea Chilean Sauvignon Blanc (3-litre box)** 

Price bracket has been adjusted to show equivalent per bottle.

---

**Vina Casablanca Sauvignon Blanc 1996** 15.5 C

Balanced and bonny. Great with charcoal-grilled prawns.

---

## ENGLISH WINE — WHITE

**Mole Valley English Wine** 13.5 B

Falls away at the finish, but an English wine for £2.99 is a rarity. And it is drinkable even if it is horribly naffly labelled. Keep it up, Moley!

---

**Summerhill Dry White** 11 C

Possibly the crassest label yet appended to an English wine (which needs help not hindrance from its marketing designers). The wine is light, faintly floral, ho-hum on the finish, and rather bored with itself.

---

## FRENCH WINE — RED

**Abbaye St Hilaire, Coteaux Varois 1995** 14 B

Good Provencal-like slurping here. The fruit is dotted with thyme bushes which scratch as they go down. A great food tipple.

---

**Big Frank's Best Red Shiraz 1995** 14.5 D

Like a great beaujolais cru ought to be, astonishingly. A rich, fresh, ripe, vivid, very slap-happy wine of developed flavour and vivacity.

---

**Big Frank's Red, Minervois 1996** 13.5 C

Somewhat lighter than previous vintages. Less muscled and rich.

---

**Calvet Reserve 1994** 12 D

---

**Chambolle-Musigny, Premier Cru les Cras 1992** 12 H

Eeh, by gum, this is a tricky wine to rate. Is your £25 better spent elsewhere? Yes . . . but. Not a big but, but it's true the wine does have texture, a hint of the farmyard and, buried deep, a hint of the glories of yesteryear's Musignys. Overall, it's like paying money to watch Roger Bannister race – but race now. Victoria Wine Cellars only.

---

**Charles d'Hauteville Oak Aged Claret NV**  C

Oddly plump bordeaux. To call it dry is almost slander.

---

**Charles de France Bourgogne Pinot Noir 1995** 13 C

Has a reluctant jolliness. Good with food.

---

**Chateau de l'Abbaye de Saint Ferme Bordeaux Superieur 1996** 15 D

Classy act here. The echo of dusty drawers and ticking grandfather clocks as the fruit goes down is splendid. Soft, rich, drinkable, food friendly.

---

**Chateau de la Jaubertie Bergerac 1994** 15.5 C

---

**Chateau de Leret, Cahors 1994** 14 C

This is the essence of good French country wine. It seems to smell and taste of old farmyards, dead crows, furrowed brows (heavy with sweat), and boiled berets. A great companion with burnt sausages. Victoria Wine Cellars only.

---

**Chateau de Vaudieu, Chateauneuf-du-Pape 1994** 13.5 F

Yes, it's lush on the tongue – lush and savoury. But £11!! Victoria Wine Cellars only.

---

**Chateau de Villegeorge, Haut Medoc 1993** 13 F

Too much money, not enough sheer pleasure from the fruit. Victoria Wine Cellars only.

---

**Chateau du Hureau, Saumur Champigny 1995** 14 E

Individual approach to the cabernet franc with a slate edge to dry, wild strawberry fruit. Victoria Wine Cellars only.

---

**Chateau La Claverie, Cote de Francs 1993** 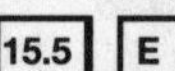 E

Delicious clotted effect to the rich dark fruit as it descends the throat. The texture is elongated and velvety, the flavour ripe and savoury. Victoria Wine Cellars only.

---

**Chateau La Diffre, Seguret, Cotes du Rhone Villages 1995**  C

---

**Chateau La Jalgue, Bordeaux 1996** 15 

If you want a bargain but classic claret style of richness, dryness, flavour yet very little austerity (except on the price tag), this is your wine.

---

**Chateau Mauleon, Cramany, Cotes du Roussillon Villages 1995**  

One of the best reds from France on these shelves. It's the thickness as well as the richness of the dry, herby fruit which wins the day for me. It has lots of flavour and personality but with the guts and lack of pretension to go simply with bread and cheese.

---

**Chateau Michelet, Bordeaux 1995**  C

Touch light on the finish.

---

**Chateau Mirefleurs, Bordeaux 1994**  

Seems to be on song except for a slight blip as it quits the throat.

---

**Chateau Teyssier, St Emilion 1994** 13.5 E

Classy and bold. Lot of money, though. Victoria Wine Cellars only.

---

**Claret, Victoria Wine** 13.5 C

Good texture and classic claret dryness.

---

**Clos des Papes, Chateauneuf-du-Pape 1993** 13.5 G

Put cinders of rich, hot fruit on the tongue. Expensive way to keep warm this winter, though. Victoria Wine Cellars only.

---

**Cotes de Ventoux, Paul Jaboulet Aine 1995** 15.5 C

Big, bruising, earthy, ripe, rich, roustabout but not crude, this is a wine of warmth, savouriness, depth and integrated fruit/acid/tannin. Rusticity yet polished charm.

---

**Crozes-Hermitage La Petite Ruche 1995** 16 E

Curious but captivating depth of style as if Gigondas had met Barolo. The wine is as thickly textured as the Braille-imprinted label and so it's very full and rich, loaded with flavour nuances from blackberry through fig to licorice, and it has a bright touch of sweet fruit on the finish. A compelling bottle. Victoria Wine Cellars only.

---

**Domaine de la Baume Merlot, VdP d'Oc 1995** 17 D

Swims with flavour yet has elegance, finesse, and huge incisiveness of purpose. It is made to be a classy and impressive yet bitingly fruity, beautifully textured, gorgeously concentrated leathery merlot of self evident superiority. This wine is made from estate-owned grapes and vinified using oak (unlike the other Baume merlot at the store), hence the difference in price. Victoria Wine Cellars only.

---

**Domaine de la Fontbertiere, Minervois 1994** 15.5 C

Lovely stuff: vigorous, textured, rich, fruity, characterful, dry and simply great to glug. Victoria Wine Cellars only.

---

**Domaine de la Grande Bellane, Cotes du Rhone Villages 1996 (organic)** 13.5 D

Aromatic, soft, fruity, organic.

---

**Domaine de Peyremorin, Haut-Medoc 1993** 12.5 E

Finish lets it down a bit. Victoria Wine Cellars only.

---

**Faugeres Gilbert Alquier 1995** 13.5 D

Has some tannic assertiveness but rather expensive for the style. Victoria Wine Cellars only.

---

**Fitou Mme Parmentier** 13.5 C

Still going for it, this old-established Fitou. It's even getting tastier as it ages.

---

**Fleurie Duboeuf 1996** 12 E

Selected stores.

---

**French Full Red VdP d'Oc, Victoria Wine** 13 B

Easy enough to drink – and to buy.

---

**Galet Vineyards Cabernet Sauvignon, VdP d'Oc 1996** 16 C

Peppery, blackcurrant aroma leads to suitably well-dressed fruit but it packs a surprise: the earthy tannins are so compacted as to be like velvet. This, with its hint of herby warmth, makes this a hugely approachable cabernet of class, slurpability, and rude food-compatibility.

---

**Galet Vineyards Syrah, VdP d'Oc 1996** 14 C

A soft, soupy syrah but very far from a soppy one.

---

**Gamay de Touraine 1996** 

Like drinkable beaujolais ordinaire used to be: fresh and flavourful, winning and well worth the money.

---

**Gigondas, Les Perdrix 1995** 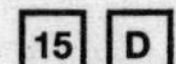

Has loads of rich fruit well attended and balanced by acidity and some urgent unguent tannins. A lovely glug and great with food. Selected stores.

---

**Hautes Cotes de Nuits 1995** 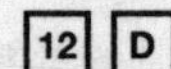

Victoria Wine Cellars only.

---

**Hermitage de Pied de la Cote, Paul Jaboulet Aine 1995** 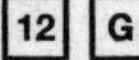

Can't see it myself. Stretches your twenty quid rather too thin. Victoria Wine Cellars only.

---

**James Herrick Cuvee Simone VdP d'Oc 1995** 

Getting on a bit but good until Christmas 1997 when its superb structure and rich fruit will begin to wilt under the tannins. I simply cannot understand Vic Wine customers permitting this under-a-fiver beauty to stay on the shelf for so long. A vivid wine of great class.

---

**La Baume Grenache/Syrah, VdP d'Oc 1996** 13.5 C

Mild-mannered little thing. All freshness, not a lot of texture.

---

**La Baume Merlot, VdP d'Oc 1996** 13.5 B

Soft and light, not as gripping as previous vintages.

---

**La Chasse du Pape Reserve Cotes du Rhone 1995** 13 C

Not in the same league as the '94. Selected stores.

---

**La Cuvee Mythique, VdP d'Oc 1994** 16 D

One of the Midi's most fulfilling reds: characterful, dry, rich, multi-layered, assertive yet soft and polished, witty yet down to earth. It puts scores of fancy bordeaux to immediate shame. Victoria Wine Cellars only.

---

**La Langue Merlot VdP d'Oc, 1996** 13.5 C

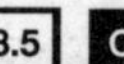

Not especially merlot-like to the palate but who gives a toss? The wine is soft, fresh and ripe but dry, so it has some character to it, and has a decent texture.

---

**Le Baron de Brane, Margaux 1994** 13 E

Trying hard (and soft) but in the final analysis a tenner should buy more thrills. Victoria Wine Cellars only.

---

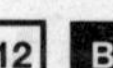

**Le Midi Rouge VdP de l'Aude** 12 B

---

**Merlot Baron Phlippe de Rothschild VdP d'Oc 1996** 13.5 C

Rich, ripe and very ready merlot of richness and savour. Takes itself a touch seriously, I guess, but I've given it the benefit of the doubt. It is well-textured, sweetly fruity, and with a hint of dryness and characterfulness on the finish. I am, however, moved to ponder how much better the wine might have been if the Baron hadn't tried *so* hard.

---

**Merlot Fortant de France VdP d'Oc 1996** 14 C

Good and fruity with lots of muscle and ripe, fresh undertones of plum and dark cherry – plus a hint of herbiness.

---

**Merlot/Cabernet Sauvignon VdP d'Oc, Bouey 1996** 15 B

Excellent value for such soft fruity drinking. Barely nods in the direction of its rustic background. Not at all stores.

---

**Minervois, Caves des Coteaux du Haut Minervois** 13 B

The mild sketch on the label reflects some of the sketchy mildness of the fruit in the bottle. It slips down, yes, and it's cheap but it lacks a bit of 'wow!'.

---

**Montpeyroux, Coteaux du Languedoc 1995** 15.5 C

Lovely texture. This is like a rich country red wine should be: dry, brambly, characterful, smashing to have entertain the tastebuds, great with all sorts of casserole-style foods.

---

**Morgon, les Vignerons du Prieure 1996** 10 D

A drinkable morgon, but at seven quid my eyebrows go up. Victoria Wine Cellars only.

---

**Oak Aged Cotes du Rhone, Meffre 1995** 12 C

Something straining to come out.

---

**Rully Rouge Les Villeranges, Faiveley 1995** 10 E

A point for every quid it costs, more or less.

---

**Stowells of Chelsea Merlot VdP d'Oc (3-litre box)** 14 C

An excellent little tipple for the drinker who finds the commitment to a whole bottle too much. This box, permitting a glass to be drawn off whenever the mood suits, offers a very soft wine of charming texture and fruit. Not at all stores. Price bracket has been adjusted to show equivalent per bottle.

---

**Stowells Vin de Pays du Gard (3-litre box)** 13.5 B

A good fruity party wine. The occasional glass is perfect before settling down to a session of bingo. Price bracket has been adjusted to show equivalent per bottle.

---

**VdP Vallee du Paradis Rouge 1996** 13.5 B

Good glugging here – it's fresh, simple, cherry-bright wine with a hint of earth.

---

**Vieux Chateau Certan, Pomerol 1992** 10 H

---

**Vieux Chateau Gaubert, Graves 1994** 14 F

Expensive but deserving of our attention. It has unique, charcoal-edged dryness of riveting richness. Victoria Wine Cellars only.

---

**Wild Pig VdP des Cevennes 1996** 15.5 B

The back label is the work of an illiterate but the winemaker, not being apostrophically challenged, permits no pause or hiccup to delay the delightful flow of this wine from first sniff to final gurgle gullet-wards. Tastes like a younger brother of Chateauneuf-du-Pape.

---

## FRENCH WINE WHITE

**Baron Philippe Sauternes 1994 (half bottle)** 10 D

---

**Big Frank's Deep Pink 1996** 13 C

Pleasant if not keenly priced.

---

**Big Frank's White VdP des Cotes de Thongue 1996** 14 C

Good lemon-edged style with excellent texture. It keeps the wine stuck to the teeth.

---

**Bois de Lamothe, Cotes de Duras Blanc** 13.5 C

**Bordeaux Sauvignon Calvet 1996** 13.5 B

Peardrop edge to the keen fresh fruit would be fine with shellfish.

**Chablis 1er Cru Vau de Vey, Moreau 1996** 11 E

I cannot find it within the nethermost charitable recesses of my soul to consider ten quid fair exchange for this wine. Victoria Wine Cellars only.

**Chablis, Cave de Chablis 1995** 13 E

Yes, I can drink this with a smile on my face. But then I haven't been asked to cough up eight quid for it.

**Chardonnay Fortant de France VdP d'Oc 1996** 14.5 C

Nutty, with a hint of butter, and a hint of warm southern sun as it goes down. I daresay you could drink this and feel yourself reminded of the Languedoc in early June: equable without being too sweaty.

**Chardonnay VdP du Jardin de la France 1996** 15.5 B

Tremendous elegance for the money: rich-edged, ripe, lemony to finish, stylish, great to glug, good with fish and shellfish. Brilliant stuff at the price.

**Charles de France Bourgogne Chardonnay 1995** 11 C

Not entirely happy with itself. It seems to wear a scowl, this wine.

**Chateau de la Jaubertie, Bergerac Blanc 1996** 14 C

Has some flinty integrity, often a feature of dead poets, and all the wine's wit is in its finish. An attractive, clean wine of clear purpose: to refresh and go majestically with grilled fish. Victoria Wine Cellars only.

---

**Chateau la Tuque Bordeaux 1996** 14 C

Good shellfish style of bordeaux blanc. Has some energy and minerality to the subtly classy fruit.

---

**Colombard/Chardonnay VdP des Cotes de Gascogne, Bouey 1996** 14.5 B

More like a New World style than is usual but this means there is deep flavour and richness to the fruit.

---

**Domaine de Plessis Coteaux du Layon 1995 (half bottle)** 15 C

---

**Fat Bastard Chardonnay VdP d'Oc 1996** 15 D

I went out and bought a few bottles of this wine after I'd tasted it. Its lemon edge and subtle melon richness were perfect for a fish dish I planned to cook. N.B. if a wine writer spends his own money he *really* likes a wine. Selected stores.

---

**French Dry VdP d'Oc, Victoria Wine** 13.5 B

Touch earthy on its approach to the nostrils but it oils the throat agreeably if not in any hugely complex or thrilling form. A very good-value fish wine, though.

---

**French Medium VdP d'Oc, Victoria Wine** 13.5 B

A touch sweeter, that's all, than its dry sister. Makes it better with Chinese food.

---

**Galet Roussanne Barrel Reserve VdP d'Oc 1995** 14.5 C

Makes a great change from chardonnay. The richness of melon with the texture of warm satin. Delicious to sip or slurp with wine. Victoria Wine Cellars only.

---

**Galet Vineyards Grenache Blanc, VdP d'Oc 1996** 14 C

Uncompromisingly characterful, a touch bleak as it gets going, but great with freshwater fish like pike and perch.

---

**Gewurztraminer, Cave Vinicole de Turckheim 1996** 15 D

A good spicy vintage which lathers the tastebuds with hints of rose petals and orange peel. A delicious aperitif, a terrific Chinese food wine.

---

**Hardys Sauvignon de Touraine 1996** 14.5 C

An attractive amalgam of appley acidity and pear/melon fruit. Highly drinkable and untypically subtly delicious.

---

**James Herrick Chardonnay 1996**  C

More lemonic than previous vintages and less like the Old World style – but it will, I feel, pull itself round more richly over the next nine months.

---

**La Baume Philippe de Baudin Sauvignon Blanc VdP d'Oc 1996** 14 C

I see no reason to pay seven or eight quid for sancerre when there's this elegant little thing lurking on the shelves.

---

**La Langue Chardonnay/Viognier VdP d'Oc 1995** 13 D

---

**La Langue, Domaine de Devois Coteaux de Languedoc 1995** 13 C

---

**La Langue Oaked Chardonnay VdP d'Oc 1996** 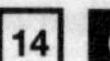 C

Has southern warmth and a soft texture so don't expect tongue-tingling citricity, but then you won't get out of your depth with the flavour, either. All in all, a most engaging chardonnay. Victoria Wine Cellars only.

---

**La Serre Chardonnay VdP d'Oc 1996** 14.5 C

Not a blusteringly rich chardonnay, this specimen has more restraint, a touch of lemon, and a fair level of finesse about it.

---

**Laroche Grande Cuvee Chardonnay VdP d'Oc 1995** 13 C

Improved in bottle a bit since I first tasted it. More excitingly textured and a deeper, creamier edge to the fruit. Selected stores.

---

**Le Midi Blanc VdP de l'Aude** 12 B

---

**Macon-Villages Chardonnay Cave de Vire 1996** 13 C

Nods to the New World but doesn't altogether convince at a fiver.

---

**Montagny Premier Cru Oak Aged Chardonnay 1994** 13.5 D

---

**Muscadet de Sevre et Maine Sur Lie, Domaine de la Roulerie 1996** 14.5 C

Is muscadet back to form? With this example it is – on all fronts and very emphatically. It's keen and fresh, fruity and bold.

---

**Muscat de Beaumes de Venise, Cuvee Antoine 1993** 14 E

---

**Pouilly Fuisse Vieilles Vignes, Domaine de la Soufrandise 1995** 13 G

It's roughly three times more expensive than its soft drinkable style should be. It has touches of opulence to it, but it's the price tag that really sticks in the throat rather than the complexity of the finish. Victoria Wine Cellars only.

---

**Sancerre Cuvee de Chene de Saint Louis 1996** 12 E

---

**Stowells of Chelsea VdP du Tarn (3-litre box)** 14 B

Crisp and clean as it starts work then it waves goodbye with a pleasant fruity lilt. Good to glug, good with grub. Price bracket has been adjusted to show equivalent per bottle.

---

**Vouvray Demi-Sec, Les Girardieres 1995** 15.5 D

It's unique. It's very far from sweet because the richness of the fruit (peachy and melony with a honeyed hint) is saved from being cloying by virtue of the gorgeous pineapple/lime acidity. The lingering pleasure of this wine is enormous. Victoria Wine Cellars only.

---

## GERMAN WINE WHITE

**Bornheimer Adelberg Kabinett 1994** 13.5 C

---

**Bornheimer Adelberg Spatlese 1994** 12 C

---

**Erdener Treppchen Riesling Kabinett 1986** 15.5 C

Astonishingly youthful in spite of its comparatively middle-age. It is light, elegant, touched by honey rather than steeped in it, has good steely acidity and is well balanced. A delicate, slightly off-dry aperitif at a deft price. Don't be put off by the classic plasticine aroma! Victoria Wine Cellars only.

---

**Kendermann Dry Riesling 1996**  C

A big improvement on the '95. Has a rolling polish to its fruit, a hint of strawberry and melon and a good citric finish. The opulence of the texture is excellent.

---

**Slate Valley Dry Riesling, Mosel-Saar-Ruwer 1995** 11 C

If the German wine industry hopes to survive well into the next century it'll have to be more exciting than this for nigh on four quid. Not at all stores.

---

**Slate Valley Medium Dry Country Wine 1996** 10 B

Not at all stores.

---

## HUNGARIAN WINE RED

**Merlot, Danubiana Bonyhad 1993** 13.5 B

---

**Villany Cabernet Sauvignon 1994** 13 B

---

**Chapel Hill Rheinriesling 1996** 13.5 B

Rather weak on the finish but fine with fishy food.

---

**Chardonnay Balaton 1995** 12 B

---

**Hidden Rock Gewurztraminer, Mor 1996** 12 C

Not Hungary's most vivid grape, gewurztraminer. Not entirely a travesty of this exciting variety, but a muted, cloddish one.

---

**Hidden Rock Sauvignon Blanc, Sopron 1996** 13.5 C

Fresh grass, nicely cut, but a short back and side to the fruit so it's at its best with shellfish.

---

# ITALIAN WINE RED

**Amarone delle Valpolicella, Montresor 1992** 15.5 E

Ten quid for layers of figgy licorice fruit, very dry, vivid, characterful, quirky? Yeah, every time – especially with robust food. Victoria Wine Cellars only.

---

**Argiolas Costera Cannonau di Sardegna 1994** 15.5 D

Real style and individuality here from the grenache of Sardinia, cannonau. Has a lovely rich texture and a flavour which leaves a coating of fruity emulsion on the tastebuds.

---

**Barbera d'Asti, Icardi 1996** 14.5 C

The label has chutzpah and so does the wine. Yes, it's light but it's very, very far from insubstantial or ruffled by food. The texture is like biting into soft, ripe plum. Victoria Wine Cellars only.

---

**Brunello di Montalcino, Casanova di Neri 1991** 13.5 G

Dry, rich, edgily herby – has a robust assertiveness which is not entirely convincing for £16. A little more *chutzpah* wouldn't go amiss at that price. Victoria Wine Cellars only.

---

**Cabernet Franc San Simone, Friuli 1995** 14.5 C

Unusually stalky, vegetal Italian red which has the typicity of its cabernet franc grape variety nicely played out, strawberries and pencil shavings, against a warm, jammy background. An excellent grilled veg and melted cheese wine. Not at all stores.

---

**Chianti Classico Castello di Fonterutoli 1995** 15.5 D

Very elegant, untypically unearthy, ripe, soft chianti of great charm – especially in its final parting shot of subtle marzipan and ripe cherries and blackberries.

---

**Chianti Classico Riserva, Rodano 1990** 13 E

Seems very mature as you raise it to the lips and it passes by the nostrils, but there is a youthful tang in the fruit which keeps it vigorous and, whilst dry, rich enough to be an attractive mouthful. Very expensive for the style. Selected stores.

---

**Cortenova Merlot Friuli 1996** 12 C

---

**Dolcetto d'Alba Gigi Rosso 1996** 13.5 C

Very drinkable, if somewhat light on its feet throughout – and I like my grapes well trodden to extract more flavour. Victoria Wine Cellars only.

---

**Montepulciano d'Abruzzo, Cortenova 1995** 14 C

Now this is where Italy's casual vinosity and shoulder-shrugging take-it-or-leave-it fruitiness score: in a touch-of-earthy dry plummy wine with a sheen on the finish which nicely reflects on pasta dishes. Not at all stores.

---

**Ravioli Red Vino da Tavola** 12 C

Very sweet and not, I would have thought, especially good with ravioli. But the concept and label are marvellous.

---

**Rosso del Veneto** 12.5 B

Hardly a winter warmer: soft, cherryish, sort-of-dry, lingers like a snowflake in hell. But has a screwcap and likes being chilled.

---

**Rosso di Montalcino, Casanova di Neri 1994** 14.5 E

Expensive but worth considering. When the lights are low,

the food elegant but impactful, the company dry, fruity and characterful. Victoria Wine Cellars only.

---

**Salice Salento Vallone 1994** 16 C

Prune-edged, rich and chocolatey with almost a licorice undertang. It's a great wine for under a fiver. The texture may lack depth but the flavour gives it its high rating.

---

**Sangiovese di Toscana Cecchi 1996** 13.5 C

What a flirtatious little beast! So juicy!

---

**Valpolicella Pasqua 1996** 13 C

Has a pleasing textural softness, even a hint of luxury, and is so easy on the throat you could barely know it's there – unless you concentrated.

---

**Villa Borghetti Valpolicella Classico, Vigneti in Marano 1995** 13 C

Simplistic.

---

**Vino Nobile di Montepulciano, Antica Chiusina 1991** 15.5 E

Expensive but classy in that classic Tuscan way: burnt, warm earthy undertones to smooth rich fruit which is never underpowered or overripe. Improving nicely in bottle, too. Victoria Wine Cellars only.

---

## ITALIAN WINE WHITE

**Chardonnay delle Colline Pescaresi, Campo del Borgo Reale 1996** 13 B

Some decent lemonic coating to the fruit. Good with grilled or poached fish.

---

**Chardonnay/Pinot Grigio Atesino, La Vis 1996** 15 C

Has complexity and flavour, richness and style, a general thread of citricity running deliciously through it and a solid finish. Victoria Wine Cellars only.

---

**Pellegrino Marsala Superior Dolce NV** 14 D

Molasses with honey. Drink it with Christmas cake and a big grin on your face.

---

**Pinot Grigio Tre Venezie, Ca'Donini 1996** 13 C

---

**Segesta Firriato 1995 (Sicilian)** 12.5 C

A decent enough fish 'n' chip wine.

---

**Soave Classico Superiore, Zenato 1996** 15.5 C

Doesn't do to turn your nose up at the idea of soave when there is this genuinely suave specimen about. Makes a delicious change from chardonnay, many examples of which it knocks into a cocked hat.

---

**Soave, Pasqua 1996** 13.5 C

Apples and pears in decent unison and crisply finished off. A simple fish wine.

---

**Trebbiano del Rubicone, Brioro 1995** 9 B

The kindest thing would be to ask the drain to drink it.

---

**Verdicchio dei Castelli di Jesi, Le Vele Classico 1995** 15 C

Got real personality and spirit, this finely flavoured, cool-headed, sophisticatedly well-turned-out wine. Has delicious nutty fruit with lots of melony, lemony, and peach-edged fruit which always stays clean and crisp. A terrific Italian wine of real class and style under a fiver. Not at all stores.

---

**Villa Romana Frascati Superiore 1995** 11 C

Worthy – the pleasant side of dull if drunk with fish but old-fashioned and expensive.

---

## MEXICAN WINE RED

**L A Cetto Petite Syrah 1993** 14 C

Getting sweeter as it ages. Not, I must say, like some of us. Victoria Wine Cellars only.

---

## NEW ZEALAND WINE RED

**Montana Cabernet Sauvignon/Merlot 1995** 14.5 D

Grass meets wet earth, but the result, though interesting, is not exactly paydirt. A dry, vegetal wine which needs food.

---

**Stoneleigh Cabernet Sauvignon 1994** 13 D

---

**Vidal Hawkes Bay Cabernet/Merlot 1994** 12 E

---

## NEW ZEALAND WINE WHITE

**Cat's Pee on a Gooseberry Bush 1995** 12 D

---

**Church Road Chardonnay, Hawkes Bay 1994** 15 E

---

**Cooks Chardonnay, Gisborne 1995** 15 C

---

**Corbans Private Bin Chardonnay, Gisborne 1994** 16 E

With smoked fish it might possibly be a 20-point treat. Lovely double act of wood and fruit finely interwoven and delightfully textured. Victoria Wine Cellars only.

---

**New Zealand Dry White** 14 C

Good solid fruit, crisp, dry and well-balanced. Difficult for NZ to make good wine at this price. It is an interesting lesson for UK growers who, with the same Muller-Thurgau grape, produce less emphatic wines.

---

**Shingle Peak Chardonnay 1995** 13 D

---

**Shingle Peak Riesling 1995** 12 D

---

**Shingle Peak Sauvignon Blanc 1995** 14.5 D

---

**Stoneleigh Sauvignon Blanc 1995** 15.5 D

---

**Timara Medium Dry 1996** 14 C

Most people won't consider this a medium-dry wine, merely a nicely fruity one. It's at its best with mild Thai food, I reckon.

---

**Vidal Hawkes Bay Sauvignon Blanc 1995** 13.5 D

---

**Villa Maria Chardonnay Private Bin 1995** 13.5 D

Highly drinkable but too highly priced. Victoria Wine Cellars and Wine Shops only.

---

**Villa Maria Sauvignon Blanc 1995** 14.5 D

---

## PORTUGUESE WINE RED

**Alta Mesa Estremadura Red 1995** 15.5 B

Soft, light but thickly textured, well flavoured with plum and cherry, and balanced from start to finish. Good value quaffing here.

---

**Bright Brothers Baga 1994** 15.5 C

---

**Grao Vasco, Dao 1991** 13 C

---

**J P Vinhos Red 1994** 14 B

---

**Jose de Sousa Garrafeira 1990** 13.5 E

---

## PORTUGUESE WINE WHITE

**Chello Vinho Verde 1994** 13 B

Essentially a summer wine for sultry nights resounding to the clatter of cats on hot tin roofs. Victoria Wine Cellars only.

---

**Jose Neiva Aged White 1994** 12.5 B

---

**Quinta de Azevedo Vinho Verde 1994** 13 C

---

## SOUTH AFRICAN WINE RED

**Cape View Cinsault/Shiraz 1996** 16 C

Great new vintage: soft, subtly spicy with a savoury tang on the finish, lovely warm texture and overall classy. Drinkable and distinguished. Not at all stores.

---

**Cape View Merlot 1996** 15.5 C

Superbly richly textured and gently old-car-seaty aromatically and on the finish. Lie back and slurp it. Selected stores.

---

**Clearsprings Cape Red** 14 E

---

**Clos Malverne Reserve Pinotage 1996** 16 D

Wonderfully invigorating and enticing bouquet of chestnuts roasting and cedar wood-smoke. The fruit is less complex and juicier than anticipated but still impressive. Will age interestingly for two years.

---

**De Trafford Merlot 1994** 14 E

Rather an acquired taste with its ripe richness – somewhat terse on the finish but excellent with food. Victoria Wine Cellars only.

---

**De Trafford Merlot 1995** 13 E

Even more sour-faced than the '94. Victoria Wine Cellars only.

---

**Delheim Shiraz 1995** 16 D

Terrific shiraz with a touch of spice and impish acidity which gives the ripe plum fruit great food-compatibility.

---

**Fairview Cabernet Sauvignon 1995** 15 D

The usual high-class act from this estate, though I tend to feel this cabernet is more a glugger than previous vintages. The texture is soft, the fruit aromatic and gently rich.

---

**Long Mountain Cabernet Sauvignon 1995** 14 C

Soft and juicy but with a hint of caramelised fruit on the finish. Drinkable and food-friendly.

---

**Lost Horizons Classic Ruby Red 1996** 14.5 C

Comes in a giant blue cologne bottle but the fruit is in far more conventional shape: rubbery and clean with depth and style. Selected stores.

---

**Simonsvlei Pinotage Reserve 1996** 13.5 C

Odd combination of smells and tastes to which I cannot put an accurate description. 13.5 points about says it all.

---

**Villiera Cru Monro 1995** 14 E

Lovely texture and demurely rich fruit. The elegance of the approach wins it its points. Victoria Wine Cellars only.

---

**Warwick Estate Cabernet Sauvignon 1994** 13.5 E

Good clotted tannins give some style but the ripeness of the fruit is not of the nine-quid variety. Victoria Wine Cellars only.

---

## SOUTH AFRICAN WINE WHITE

**Agulhas Bank Chardonnay 1996** 15 

Great texture, rounded and ripe, and a lovely depth of flavour which is lingering and keen. A very stylish wine with a luxurious edge. Not at all stores.

---

**Cape View Chenin/Sauvignon Blanc 1996** 14 

Fruity, extremely gluggable and adolescent, this is friendliness vinified. Rather interesting, saucy and faintly exotic prickle of flavour on the finish. Not at all stores.

---

**Clearsprings Cape White** 14 F

---

**De Wetshof Lesca Chardonnay 1995** 14 D

---

**Landema Falls Chenin Blanc NV** 14 B

Basic glugging, yes . . . but it's more than that. It's good with a tuna salad or seafish soup,and it's pleasant sipped before more robust fare.

---

**Landema Falls Colombard/Chardonnay NV** 14.5 B

Has bite, personality, flavour and an agreeable balance of rich fruit and pert acidity.

---

**Long Mountain Chardonnay 1995** 14.5 C

---

**Long Mountain Chenin Blanc 1996** 13.5 C

Good fresh fruit, mixing hard fruit flavours with a distant echo of soft, but it does seem a touch pricey at four quid when compared with cheaper brethren on Victoria Wine shelves.

---

**Longridge Chardonnay 1995** 14 E

Expensively cut and priced. Certainly a treat to drink with its poised woody fruit. Victoria Wine Cellars only.

---

**Lost Horizons Sauvignon Blanc/Chardonnay 1996** 13 C

Bit bland on the finish. The blue bottle doesn't help – it is so ostentatious it has to provide good fruit inside. Not at all stores.

---

**Nederburg Chardonnay 1996** 15.5 D

Terrific texture, plump and ripe, with a delicious lemonic edge. Very classy stuff. Not at all stores.

---

**Springfield Special Cuvee Sauvignon Blanc 1996** 16 D

A most interesting sauvignon. One of the most incisive I've tasted from the Cape. Gently grassy and crisp, it has hints of melon and gooseberry. Overall it's better than almost all sancerres. Victoria Wine Cellars only.

---

**Stowells of Chelsea Chenin Blanc (3-litre box)** 12 B

A touch dull even though the suggestion of cream on the meagre fruit hints at a lost opportunity to please. Stowells – you must try harder! Stop being so soft on your wine suppliers. (Price bracket has been adjusted to show equivalent per bottle.)

---

**Table Bay Early Release Chenin Blanc 1997** 13.5 C

Curious fruit which seems fat and blowsy at first sip, then subsides to normalcy as it slips down. Needs food to be at its best.

---

## SPANISH WINE — RED

**Agramont Tempranillo 1995** 

C

Biscuity texture, rich (but not overrich) fruit, lovely plum and blackcurrant flavour, slightly baked and warm. Terrific drinking here.

---

**Campillo Rioja Crianza 1993** 

D

Has flavour and richness of intention.

---

**Campo Viejo Rioja Gran Reserva 1989** 

E

Impressively rich and rioja-rigid but far too pricey.

---

**Castillo de Liria Valencia NV** 

Terrific value: textured, ripe, deep yet never overblown or too eager, this is a hugely quaffable wine of dinner-party poise yet sleeves-rolled-up insouciance.

---

**Chivite Navarra Vina Marcos 1995** 15.5 C

Cherry and ripe plum fruit with a hint of vegetality all parcelled up in rich tannins. A forceful mouthful of fruit. Has great depth of flavour for the money.

---

**Chivite Reserva 1991** 13.5 D

Seems to ask more of us, just a touch, than it is prepared to lavish on us in return.

---

**Dominio Montalvo Rioja 1995** 13.5 C

Bit of soft-heart which isn't altogether ameliorated by the prissy acidity and smidgen of tannin. But richly fruity and certainly a winner with grilled meat and veg dishes.

---

**Don Darias** 14 B

---

**Don Frutos Tempranillo/Cabernet Sauvignon 1996** 12 C

Vegetal edge which doesn't excite this drinker overmuch. Not at all stores.

---

**Ed's Red Tempranillo, La Mancha 1996** 14 B

Great with grub, this wine. It's a touch raunchy but not over-familiar. The fruit is smelly, but not coarse, and the finish is happy.

---

**El Liso Tempranillo 1995** 12 C

Not up to the rich pickings of the past. This vintage seems light and overripe (in the appley sense).

---

**Marques de Aragon Arnacha, Catalayud 1996** 12 C

Curious aroma, odd fruit, rum price. But . . . with grub it might add up to something. Not at all stores.

---

**Miralmonte, Toro 1995** 16 C

Bloody good boozing here! Whacks the tastebuds like a leather clad steel toecap! Rich, soupy, deep, balanced, gently quirky, soft, richly full of itself without being superficially friendly, this is a terrific bottle of peasant plonk with pizzazz and personality.

**Pago de Carraovejas, Ribera del Duero 1994** 18 E

Magnificent aroma, fruit, structure, finish, flavour and so much vivid personality which never gets tiresome that you feel the tenner to be a bargain. The aroma of tobacco leads to richness and the final flourish of savouriness is sublime.

**Puerta de la Villa Valdepenas 1996** 14 B

Ripe cherries cascade over the tongue and all that's missing is the custard. A bright, cheering wine.

**Torre Aldea Rioja 1996** 12 C

Possibly the most eccentrically fruity rioja I've tasted in months. What, I wonder, traumatized its fruit so? Meeting an English wine buyer?

**Torres Coronas 1994** 14 D

Great persistence of flavour which has hints of tobacco. A firm, well-toned wine in fine fettle. Good texture, structure, richness and finish.

## SPANISH WINE WHITE

**Castillo de Liria Utiel Requena, Valencia NV** 15 B

Rich and soft, with a gentle lemony finish. One of the best-value whites on this retailer's groaning shelves.

**Dominio de Montalvo Rioja, Campo Viejo 1994** 12 D

Rather overpriced for such respectable fruit. I want excitement at £5.75!!!

---

**Ed's White 1996** 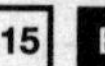

Handsome chewiness to the fruit with a lemony finish. Lovely fish wine and general glug. Very stylish fruit.

---

**Lagar de Cervera, Albarino Rias Baixas 1996** 

I must say I find this wine interesting and not unattractive but absurdly overpriced. It has some individuality, some sticky fruit of rustic yet polished charm, but it seems to me only a real buff would find the money well spent.

---

**Stowells of Chelsea Viura, Manchuela (3-litre box)** 

Has a soft fruity undertone to the generally firm freshness of the style and whilst simple is extremely unpretentious and drinkable. At an equivalent of £3.24 a bottle or 54p a glass it's good value. Not at all stores. Price bracket has been adjusted to show equivalent per bottle.

---

**Vinas del Vero Barrel Fermented Chardonnay, Somontano 1995** 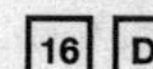

This is a wine! Elegantly wooded, finely textured, delicious from nose to throat, it enjoys fish, chicken, vegetables and soups. It is also, with its aromatic, creamy fruit, very pleasant to sip whilst listening to sexual overtures. Or Bach's. Not at all stores.

---

**Vinas del Vero Macabeo/Chardonnay, Somontano 1996** 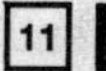

Somewhat feebly fruited, but it tries . . . oh how it tries . . . Not at all stores.

---

## USA WINE RED

**Blossom Hill California** 12.5 C

**E & J Gallo Turning Leaf Cabernet Sauvignon 1994** 13.5 D

**E & J Gallo Turning Leaf Zinfandel 1994** 12 D

**Old Vine Grenache, Collins Ranch 1996** 13.5 C

Very savoury, a touch soupy and easy to get down. Perhaps too soft for my taste.

**Zinfandel Lee Jones Ranch 1996** 13.5 C

Lovely herby aroma, warm and inviting. The fruit is very soft and ripe and somewhat boyish.

## USA WINE WHITE

**Blossom Hill, California** 10 C

**California Sauvignon Blanc, Mohr-Fry Ranch 1996** 15.5 C

It is to sauvignon blanc what Rogers & Hammerstein are to opera: a foot-tapping modern version of the same thing. It's a warm wine relieved by mineral hints, no grass, thank the Lord, and it slips down with well-textured aplomb.

**Essensia Quady NV (half bottle)** 15 D

Rose-essence hints with tangerine peel. Superb with fruit, creme caramel, or to dunk biscotti in.

**Gallo Turning Leaf Chardonnay 1994** 15 D

Improving nicely in bottle and quite delicious. The fruit is rich and full, very opulent and textured, and there is a lovely 'ping' of citric exoticism as it finishes.

---

# FORTIFIED WINE

**Cockburns Anno LBV 1989** 13 E

---

**Delaforce Vintage Port 1975** 12 F

Seems to me bad value when compared with many cheaper LBVs.

---

**Dows Crusted 1991** 15 F

Perfectly rich and ripe and ready to rock the tastebuds and roll effortlessly like oiled velvet over them with hard cheeses or soft cakes. Victoria Wine Cellars only.

---

**Dows LBV 1990** 14 F

To be drunk in front of roaring fires and with rambling grandparents.

---

**Grahams Malvedos 1984** 13.5 G

Not such good value as other Victoria Wine ports which for less dosh offer more posh. True, it's a stridently ripe wine but not quite so marvellously multi-layered or lingering as others. Victoria Wine Cellars only.

---

**Oloroso Seco (half bottle)** 15.5 C

---

**Palo Cortado (half bottle)** 16 C

Remarkable wine. Nutty, very forceful and potently undercut by an exotic richness. Try it with nuts as an aperitif – well chilled. Victoria Wine Cellars only.

---

**Pedro Ximenez Superior Sherry (half bottle)** 14 C

---

**Quinta de Vargellas Vintage Port 1984** 13.5 G

Fruitily wonderful. But is twenty quid worth it?

---

**Quinta do Noval Colheita Tawny 1976 (half bottle)** 16 E

With a texture like cough syrup but with a rousing fruitiness, dry-edged but sweetly coated, of nuttiness, tea-leafiness and faint mustiness, this is a lovely winter warmer. Victoria Wine Cellars only.

---

**Taylors Quinta de Terra Feita 1986** 15 G

Lingering richness and depth and a sweet finish of spiced plum. Very deep flavour. Victoria Wine Cellars only.

---

**Taylors Vintage Port 1985** 13 H

Still seems too young to me. Yes, it's rich and sweet and has paradisical hints. But I'd lay it down for another 100 years. Thirty quid won't buy you a loaf of bread then. Victoria Wine Cellars only.

---

**Warres Traditional LBV 1984** 15 G

Terrifically mature yet brisk and efficient in the fruit department, gorgeously soft and rich, with a lovely finish of liquid chocolate macaroon. Victoria Wine Cellars only.

---

## SPARKLING WINE/CHAMPAGNE

**Asti Perlino (Italy)** 13 C

Good with grapes, over sorbet, on a warm summer's afternoon. A sweet bubbly of nil complexity but some charm.

---

**Cava Brut, Victoria Wine** 16.5 C

Delicious, classy, classic. Hint of fruit (perfect, just as it should be) and great balancing acidity.

---

**Champagne Lanson 1989** 13 H

---

**Cuvee Napa Brut, Mumm NV** 15 E

Lovely lemony finesse – preferable to scores of champagnes.

---

**Cuvee Napa Rose, Mumm NV** 14 E

Lovely rosy-cheeked fruit of style and flavour.

---

**Cuvee Tresor Brut, Bouvet Ladubay** 15 E

Very elegant, subtly lemonic bubbly. Victoria Wine Cellars only.

---

**Deutz (New Zealand)** 15.5 E

---

**Gallo Brut NV (USA)** 10 D

Expensive and crude.

---

**Graham Beck Brut (South Africa)** 13.5 D

Selected stores.

---

**Green Point Brut 1994 (Australia)** 13.5 F

Getting expensive. Victoria Wine Cellars only.

---

**Jacques Monteau Champagne Brut NV** 12 F

Somewhat flimsy of wit for the money.

---

**Lanson Brut Rose (France)** 10 H

---

**Lindauer Brut** 13.5 D

---

**Marquis de la Tour Brut (France)** 13 C

---

**Marquis de la Tour Demi Sec (France)** 11 C

---

**Mercier Brut Rose NV (France)** 12 G

Curious price, this wine. Demands a question mark be put over it.

---

**Millennium Grand Cru Brut Champagne 1990** 12 H

Not worth twenty-two quid. Selected stores.

---

**Moet et Chandon Brut 1992** 10 H

Silly price. Don't pay it. So subtle a wine it's a public nuance.

---

**Pierre Jourdan Cuvee Belle Rose** 13 F

---

**Pinot/Chardonnay Frizzante, Pasqua (Italy)** 10 C

This is semi-sparkling wine which poses a bloody threat to the fingertips as you rip off the metal cap which encloses the cork like a truncated condom. It is hardly worth the bother of entering, so feeble is the wine it protects. Not at all stores.

---

**Pol Roger White Foil** 11 H

---

**Prosecco, La Marca (Italy)** 14 C

One of Italy's closest-kept sparkling wine secrets: Prosecco – soft, nutty, dry(ish), and even an excellent pre-prandial tipple. Not at all stores.

---

**Seaview Brut Rose** 15 D

Elegant, purposeful tippling.

---

**Seppelt Sparkling Shiraz 1993** 15 E

A Lewis Carroll of a wine: puzzling, perverse, immensely witty, deep, packed with incident and ultimately barmy. A shiraz which bubbles? Great to drink with rabbits which have failed to make it down their holes. Victoria Wine Cellars only.

---

**Torre de Gall Cava 1992** 14.5 E

Elegant and subtly rich – and great with smoked salmon. Victoria Wine Cellars only.

---

**Veuve Clicquot La Grande Dame 1989** 13 H

Has hints of class which at £32 it ought to. Are you prepared to pay this much for hints? Victoria Wine Cellars only.

---

**Vintage Champagne 1989, Victoria Wine** 12.5 G

---

# WINE CELLAR

David Vaughan, wine buyer for the Greenalls chain of wine shops, does by his own admission less travelling than many of his counterparts, but what is certain is that he travels more today than he did when he first worked in the wine business as a buyer for Augustus Barnett, that homely chain of off-licences now buried anonymously (some will say amen to that – remember those kitsch radio commercials?) within the embrace of Victoria Wine. The huge difference between what Mr Vaughan did at Augustus Barnett and how a retail winebuyer operates today shows just how the wine market has changed. 'When I was with Barnett in '82 and '83 I was the only buyer and I also did cigarettes as well as wine,' he tells me. 'The only things I did not do were beers and soft drinks. It really was commodity buying. You were not looking at special blends and tended to keep with key suppliers.'

In the case of Greenalls, the key suppliers today still tend to be UK agents rather than the wine producers themselves. While there is much more communication with the producer than there would have been ten years ago, David Vaughan's main point of contact is still the agent. But these agents, he explains, are very different from the wine importers of old. 'They take a proactive approach to their customers,' says Mr Vaughan. 'They take an interest in your business, know it from A to Z. They have looked at your range and are looking at interesting possibilities for you. These types of agent are the ones that have done well over the last few years.'

While Greenalls, which operates the Cellar 5, Wine Cellar and Berkeley Wine stores in addition to food and wine and video outlets, has fewer wines made to order than some of the other retailers in this book, there are still several wines on its list that have been created especially for the retailer. Among them is a range of dual varietal wines from Argentina. These wines, the Viejo Surco Torrontes/Chenin, Sangiovese/Cabernet and Chardonnay/Chenin were blended to Greenalls' requirements by the La Agricola Co-operative in Mendoza. The concept is one which has also been tried in other countries where familiar grape varieties are blended with lesser-known indigenous ones, often to good effect. As far as the retailer is concerned, this marriage serves two functions. The wines are naturally more adapted to UK tastes as they contain grape varieties which are known and liked by UK consumers, and purely from a marketing point of view being able to put Chardonnay or Cabernet Sauvignon on the label helps to sell the wines. With the 1996 vintage, this project is now in its second year and seems to be going well. Greenalls is selling between 4,000 and 5,000 cases a year of these wines. The 1995s were all decent, particularly the Torrontes/Chenin which had a delicious exotic fruitiness – the top-scorer of the three with 15 points.

The La Palma range from Chile was also produced especially for Greenalls by Vina La Rosa. The La Palma Cabernet/Merlot 1995 scored 15.5 points and has now been replaced by the 1996, as has the La Palma Estate Reserva Cabernet Sauvignon. Also from Chile is the Montes Apalta Cabernet Sauvignon 1995 which is a single-vineyard wine bottled specially for Greenalls. Of the three Chileans Greenalls has commissioned, this is the pick of the bunch. I have written of this wine: 'Wonderful old leather and dry cassis shroud holding out against an internal civil war of soft, rich, ripe fruit which deliciously threatens to break through. Great-quality fruit at a great small price.'

Most of the wines that Greenalls has had made to order have been from the New World countries, though its Domaine Blanchard Muscadet-sur-Lie 1995 is also special request. One of the most recent commissions is for its New Zealand Dry White 1996 which has been specially made by the Villa Maria winery.

The company has also had a range of three South African wines made by the flying winemaker, Kim Milne, a Chenin Blanc, a Cinsault/Merlot and a Cabernet/Merlot which are marketed under the Landscape brand.

Although he does not travel as extensively as other wine buyers, David Vaughan regularly goes to wineries to participate in the blending of wines destined for Greenalls shops, something he describes as 'quite normal' in today's wine trade. It may be 'quite normal', but Greenalls actually does very little of this kind of commissioning in comparison with several of its competitors. And I was surprised to learn that David Vaughan was not entirely convinced of the marketing benefits of having wines specially produced for Greenalls customers. While he thought that customers seemed to appreciate it, he wasn't 100 per cent convinced. He did say, however, that he knew that wine writers were interested in wines which have been tailored or developed just for the retailer. 'Whether that means the customers are equally interested I don't know,' Mr Vaughan added somewhat sceptically. I would venture to suggest that if wine writers are interested in such projects it is because they feel their readers will be, and in any case if journalists want to hear and write about such wines, it follows that their readers – all potential or actual Greenalls customers – will then be likely to show some interest themselves. In view of this and the fact that the projects which Mr Vaughan has mentioned have by and large turned out rather well, I would expect to see an increase in Greenalls activity in this area.

The company has a desire to be innovative and bold. As it was when introducing a range of enticing gourmet foods into certain of its wine shops. Surely, an increasing number of tailor-made wines can't be far behind? It would pay, I think, to watch this space.

WINE CELLAR
PO Box 476
Loushers Lane
Warrington
WA4 6RR
Tel 01925 444555
Fax 01925 415474

**SEE STOP PRESS SECTION AT END OF BOOK FOR LAST-MINUTE ADDITIONS TO THIS RETAILER'S RANGE.**

## ARGENTINIAN WINE RED

**Balbi Vineyard Cabernet Sauvignon 1996** 15.5 C

Delicious wine of great bouncy texture and supple fruit rather in the nature of a gamay more than a cabernet. Gorgeous texture. Ripe and raunchy.

---

**Balbi Vineyards Mendoza Rouge 1996** 13.5 C

A good pasta wine. Needs food, I think, to calm its excitability.

---

**Malbec/Tempranillo Bodegas J & F Lurton 1995** 16 C

Wonderful, breezy fruit – it takes the palate and the throat by storm. Flavour, depth, style, richness – an autumnal quartet.

---

**Viejo Surco Sangiovese/Cabernet 1995** 13 C

---

## ARGENTINIAN WINE WHITE

**Balbi Syrah Rose 1996** 14 C

Improving as it ages, this rose. It's really picking up flavour.

---

**Balbi Vineyards Dry White 1996** 15 C

---

**Lurton Chenin Blanc 1995** 14 C

The '96 will probably be in store by the time this book comes out (not tasted as yet).

---

**Viejo Surco Chardonnay/Chenin 1995** 13.5 C

The '96 will probably be in store by the time this book comes out (not tasted as yet).

---

**Viejo Surco Torrontes/Chenin 1995** 15 C

---

## AUSTRALIAN WINE RED

**Angove's Nanya Estate Grenache/Pinot Noir** 13 C

---

**Hardys Bankside Shiraz 1995** 14 D

Ripe but with a curious dry edge to the finish.

---

**Ironstone Cabernet/Shiraz 1994** 15 D

The tannins on the finish give it its most attractive characteristic and make it a terrific contender for roast lamb.

---

**Lindemans Bin 45 Cabernet Sauvignon 1995** 13 D

I suppose one can imagine toying with a glass, but the wine tries to be liked so unimaginatively, it's embarrassing. I prefer more character in wine, as in people – especially at this price.

---

**Lindemans Limestone Ridge Coonawarra Shiraz/Cabernet 1991** 16 E

Nice if you can get it but the '93 vintage will probably be on the shelves by now (not tasted as yet).

---

**Lindemans Pyrus Coonawarra 1991** 15 F

---

**Mount Langhi Giran Shiraz 1994** 12 F

Well, now, what have we got here for thirteen smackers? Blackcurrant and stale tobacco, some attempt at richness, but not a lot of lingering about once it's hit the gullet. Wine Cellars only.

---

**Penfolds Bin 2 Shiraz/Mourvedre 1995** 15.5 D

Rich, dry, stylish, this has fluidity of fruit yet tannic firmness of tone. Terrific screwcap seal.

---

**Penfolds Rawson's Retreat Bin 35 Cabernet/Shiraz 1995** 13.5 C

Usual decent turnout.

---

**Peter Lehmann Grenache, Barossa Valley 1995** 14.5 C

---

**Peter Lehmann Shiraz 1991** 16 D

Wonderful, rich, complex gravy.

---

**Rosemount Estate Cabernet Sauvignon 1995** 14 D

Stylish and drinkable but a touch expensive.

---

**Rosemount Shiraz/Cabernet 1995** 15 C

---

**Yalumba Family Reserve Cabernet/Merlot 1994** 14 E

If it's the family reserve, what's a demotic dick like me tasting it for? Please, Oz, spare us these pretensions! Still, now you've got the bottle open, can I have another glass? Wine Cellars only.

---

## AUSTRALIAN WINE WHITE

**Bridgewater Mill Sauvignon Blanc 1996** 15 E

Very elegant fruit here, not grassy like NZ or minerally like

Loire, but warm with a fresh finish. Stylish and food-friendly. Wine Cellars only.

---

**Hardys Padthaway Chardonnay 1995** 16.5 E

Very impressive aroma, creamy fruit and a rich finish. It's a treat from first sniff to last gentle sip.

---

**Ironstone Semillon Chardonnay, W Australia 1996** 14.5 D

Packed with flavour which crystallizes as it quits the throat. Rather impressive finish, this. Has rich melon and lychee overtones.

---

**Leasingham Domaine Chardonnay 1994** 16 E

Vigour and maturity, great depth and length of flavour, it persists like ogen melon on the tongue and has beautiful balance. Terrific to savour or to enjoy with food. Wine Cellars only.

---

**Penfolds Rawson's Retreat Bin 21 Semillon/Chardonnay/Colombard 1996** 15 C

Richly textured, warmly fruity (some complexity on the finish where the acidity is most petillant), this is an excellent vintage for this wine.

---

**Rosemount Estate Chardonnay 1996** 15.5 D

Opulence vinified. Rather grandly fruity, proud and rich.

---

**Rosemount Semillon Chardonnay 1996** 14 D

Elegance personified.

---

**Rosemount Show Reserve Chardonnay 1994** 15.5 E

---

## AUSTRIAN WINE — WHITE

**Matinee Gruner Veltliner 1995** 15 D

Delicious! What a wonderful change from chardonnay and sauvignon blanc. Has aromatic hints of walnut oil, of fresh cos lettuce and beautiful crisp fruit with a soft edge to finish.

---

## CHILEAN WINE — RED

**Andes Peaks Cabernet Sauvignon 1996** 15  C

Packed with concentrated soft fruit dusted with light tannins giving a textured flightiness to the fruit as it takes off throatward. Knocks many an Aussie red at three times the price into oblivion.

---

**Carmen Cabernet Sauvignon 1993** 13 C

---

**Carmen Grande Vidure/Cabernet 1995** 16 D

Juicy yet savoury, warm yet so easy to get down. Wine Cellars only.

---

**Carmen Reserve Merlot 1994** 16 D

Classy merlot for under a fiver: rich, subtle, leathery softness, dry brambly flavour and a classic lingering finish. Very good value.

---

**Errazuriz Merlot 1996** 17 D

Totally delicious: textured, dry, multi-layered, gently leathery and enticingly aromatic, rich yet not forbidding, stylish, very classy and overwhelmingly terrific value for money.

---

**La Palma Estate Reserva Cabernet Sauvignon 1995** 14.5 C

---

**Villa Montes Domaine Apalta Cabernet Sauvignon 1995** 13.5 C

Getting past it now. Juicy and fresh – hint of tannicity.

---

**Villard Cabernet Sauvignon 1993** 14 D

Hints of lushness are deliciously tempered by soft tannins of great tact.

---

**Vino de Chile Talca** 15 B

---

## CHILEAN WINE WHITE

**Andes Peaks Chardonnay 1996**

Fills the mouth with an opulence of flavour and ripeness which is scandalously stimulating. Be careful if you offer it to the neighbours. They may stay the night.

---

**Andes Peaks Sauvignon Blanc 1996**

Interesting grassy edge to the ripe, rich fruit. Terrific combination of fruit and acid – great fish partner.

---

**Cordillera Estate Oak Aged Chardonnay 1996**

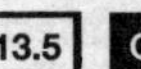


One of the few Chilean chardonnays not to really excite me.

---

**Errazuriz Sauvignon Blanc 1996**

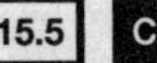


Surprisingly delicious and richly textured and yet whilst it runs away in the fruit stakes – way out in front of other sauvignons – it has enough nous to offer a hint of classic crispness amidst all that opulence.

---

## ENGLISH WINE — WHITE

**Chapel Down Bacchus 1994** 13.5 D

**Downs Edge Vineyards Fume 1994** 14 D

## FRENCH WINE — RED

**Chateau Cardus, Medoc 1994** 12 D

Nice texture, very soft.

**Chateau de Paraza Minervois 1994** 16 C

Superbly well-priced, well-made, hearty brew of style, distinction, individuality and no little class. Rich, dry, very warm.

**Chateau des Mattes, Corbieres Rocobere 1991** 14 C

**Chateau Haute-Roque Faugeres 1995** 16 C

This is more like it! A rich, tobaccoey, herby, deeply fruity wine of character and clout yet real sophistication and depth. One of the best under-a-fiver reds in the shop.

**Chateau Lecugue Minervois 1994** 14 C

Has only hints of rusticality to its surprising, fresh edge.

**Chateau Sainte Agnes Coteaux du Languedoc 1995** 18 D

Brilliant stuff. Rates only a half-point less than last year which was world-class. What did I say last year? 'The flavour just goes on and on. It lingers like a rich remark by Peter Ustinov and it is just as remarkably fat, individual, deep, highly intelligent and immensely rewarding company. Fantastic value at seven quid.' The '95 is not a let-down.

---

**Chateau St Martin de Toques, Corbieres 1994** 16.5 C

Very complex, dry, deeply fruity with a double-edged sword of fruit which strikes the palate all ways. It has a lovely growly-voiced texture which lingers and enriches conversation. It is impossible to drink a glass of this wine and then say something dull or mundane – dry, perhaps, but not boring.

---

**Chinon Domaine La Diligence, Couly Dutheuil 1995** 12 D

Needs a few years to settle down. Wine Cellars only.

---

**Cigala Chapoutier, VdP d'Oc 1995** 

I used to taste d'Ocs like this twenty years ago.

---

**Costieres de Nimes, Maurel Vedeau 1996** 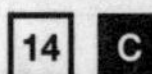

A good rustic undertone combined with a raspberry edge to the fresh finish make this wine, with its alert tannins on the finish, simply terrific with food.

---

**Domaine de Gardie Fitou 1994** 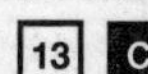

Simple enough: it's fruity.

---

**Domaine de Serres-Mazard, Corbieres 1993** 14 D

---

**Domaine La Croix Belle Le Champ du Coq, Cotes de Thongue 1994** 

Lovely texture of spiky denim and old velvet. The fruit is plum and blackcurrant. The style is Lee Marvin-craggy. The finish is fruity and deeply moving – you want to begin again right away with a fresh glass. Great meaty stuff.

---

**Domaine les Pascales Coteaux du Languedoc 1994** 16.5 C

Lovely tannins, polished yet spicy, which snag food, like hooks in fish, and permit the deep, deep fruit to work with all manner of rich, savoury dishes.

---

**Domaine Salitis Cabardes 1993** 14.5 C

Lovely soft fruit lilt and very supple texture.

---

**Fleurie, Mommessin 1996** 10 E

Disgraceful price for such ordinariness.

---

**Galet Vineyard Bush Vine Grenache 1995** 14 C

Simple and fruity but has a patina of louche, intriguing individuality.

---

**Galet Vineyards Syrah Reserve 1994** 14 D

---

**L'Enclos des Cigales Corbieres 1995** 15 C

A very engaging wine of no little class and terrific fruit.

---

**Louis Jadot Bourgogne Pinot Noir 1994** 10 E

---

**Macon Rouge Cave de Buxy 1995** 13 D

---

**Port Neuf Rouge** 13 B

Soft and very inoffensive.

---

## FRENCH WINE WHITE

**Chateau de Sours Bordeaux Rose 1996** 13.5 D

More generous than many reds, it has elegance to its fruit.

---

**Coeur de Cray Sauvignon Blanc Touraine 1996** 14 C

Clean and fresh with a fruity middle of some style. Much better value than many a sancerre.

---

**Cotes du Ventoux Rose 1996** 12 C

---

**Fat Bastard Chardonnay VdP d'Oc 1996** 15 D

I went out and bought a few bottles of this wine after I'd tasted it. Its lemon edge and subtle melon richness were perfect for a fish dish I planned to cook. N.B. if a wine writer spends his own money he *really* likes a wine. Selected stores.

---

**Port Neuf White** 14.5 B

Terrific value here. Appley but soft, fruity to finish, it has positive, stylish manners.

---

**Pouilly Fume Les Logieres, Guy Saget 1996** 12 E

Expensive for the ill-defined edge to the fruit.

---

**Rivesaltes Hors d'Age (half bottle)** 13 D

---

## GERMAN WINE WHITE

**Erdener Treppchen Riesling Spatlese 1988** 11 C

---

## ITALIAN WINE RED

**Casa de' Monzi Sangiovese di Romagna 1995** 13.5 C

---

**Copertino Rosso Riserva 1993** 14.5 C

**Cortegiara Corvina, Allegrini 1995** 13 C

**Jorio, Montepulciano d'Abruzzo Umani Ronchi 1994** 16 D

Wonderful joyous fruit! Dry, flavourful, rich, riveting, utterly beautifully textured and profoundly fruity. Wine Cellars only.

**Montepulciano d'Abruzzo, Umani Ronchi 1995** 13 C

It's excellent once it's on the tongue but it hasn't a lot going for it before it gets there or after it disappears down the gullet.

## ITALIAN WINE WHITE

**Casal di Serra, Verdicchio Umani Ronchi 1996** 14.5 D

This specimen might change your mind about verdicchio. It's a lovely caressing wine of texture and cosy warmth.

**Chardonnay del Salento, Caramia 1996** 16 D

Great elegance, flavour and lemon-edged finesse. Depth with real style.

**Puglian Bianco Cantele, Kim Milne** 13 C

Mildly attractive but not as positive as it might be.

## NEW ZEALAND WINE RED

**Esk Valley Cabernet/Merlot 1995** 14 E

Expensive but on balance the vegetal aroma, the softness on the tastebuds and the final smack of fruit on the finish gain the wine its rating. Wine Cellars only.

---

## NEW ZEALAND WINE — WHITE

**Brancott Estate 'B' Sauvignon Blanc 1993** 11 F

---

**Esk Valley Sauvignon Blanc 1996** 15 D

Has only echoes of herbaceousness. What most strikes the palate is the sheer luxurious richness of the texture. Wine Cellars only.

---

**Matua Valley Sauvignon Blanc 1996** 14 E

You sip, you smile, you relax. OK, so you've spent nearly eight quid, but you can't complain at being hard done by. Wine Cellars only.

---

**New Zealand Dry White 1996** 13.5 C

Mild, attractively fruited, and not one whit grassy.

---

**Renwick Estate 'R' Chardonnay 1991** 13 F

---

**Villa Maria Chenin Blanc/Chardonnay 1995** 14.5 C

A ripe, rich oriental food wine. It has a very rich texture.

---

## PORTUGUESE WINE — RED

**Alta Mesa Estremadura 1995** 15.5 B

Brilliant summer quaffing: soft, slightly rich and flavourful and exceedingly friendly.

---

**Pedras do Monte, Terras do Sado 1994** 15 C

**Quinta da Lagoalva Ribatejo 1992** 13.5 C

**Quinta da Pancas Cabernet Sauvignon 1995** 15.5 D

Ripe but never puppyish. The blackcurrant concentration is good, and gripping, and the texture is lovely. Wine Cellars only.

**Terras de Xisto Alentejo 1993** 14.5 C

**Tinto da Talha Alentejo 1993** 13.5 C

## ROMANIAN WINE — WHITE

**Block IV Chardonnay 1995** 14 C

## SOUTH AFRICAN WINE — RED

**Boschendal Le Pavillon 1994** 13.5 C

Soft, juicy, ripe – very agreeable qualities in small doses.

**First River Winery Cabernet Sauvignon 1995** 13.5 D

Soft and very giving – but, also, at over a fiver, somewhat of a taker.

**First River Winery Stellenbosch Dry Red** 14 C

Ripe and fruity and with enough oomph to go with food.

**Kumala Ruby Cabernet/Merlot 1996** 14.5 C

**Stellenzicht Shiraz 1994** 13 E

Loadsa fruit. Wine Cellars only.

---

**Welmoed Cabernet Sauvignon 1993** 16 D

Rich and tannic but so beautifully evolved and mature, it teases, enriches and finally invigorates in one smooth progression from nose to throat.

---

**Welmoed Winery Pinotage 1993** 13.5 C

---

# SOUTH AFRICAN WINE WHITE

**Boschendal Le Pavillon 1996** 14 C

Elegant rather than hugely rich but has a prepossessing good nature which lets it finish well.

---

**Bouchard Finlayson Chardonnay 1995** 13 F

Somewhat overpriced, though only a fool would say it was undrinkable. Wine Cellars only.

---

**Kumala Chenin/Chardonnay 1996** 14 C

Interesting coarse finish to the wine. Good for food.

---

**KWV Sauvignon Blanc 1995** 13.5 C

---

**Paarl Ridge Chenin Blanc 1994** 12 C

---

**Stellenzicht Chardonnay 1996** 16 E

The wine is warm and aromatic – with deliciously inviting wood undertones which the fruit has firmly in control. The smoky vanilla edge is subtle yet incisive. Wine Cellars only.

---

**Welmoed Chardonnay 1995** 16 C

What thought-provoking fruit! Rich, ripe, deep, full-flavoured and striking the notes without restraint, it seems as if it must overplay its hand, but the gentle counterpoint of the acids saves the day and the final result is length, elegance and superb value for money.

---

## SPANISH WINE RED

**Casa de la Vina Valdepenas Cencibel 1994** 14 B

---

**Cosme Palacio Rioja 1995** 16 D

Dry yet very fruity, ripe but not blowsy, elegant but not thin, solid on the finish.

---

**Enate Cabernet/Merlot 1995** 14.5 C

Flavour, style, softness, and a very lingering, slightly licorice finish.

---

**Hermanos Tempranillo, Lurton 1994** 14.5 C

---

**Marques de Grinon Rioja 1994** 15.5 C

---

**Marques de Grinon Rioja 1995** 14 C

Too dry? Well, it isn't as firmly fruity as previous vintages.

---

**Ochoa Navarra Tempranillo/Garnacha 1995** 14 D

Seem a touch light compared with previous vintages, but it has a lot of flavour and it's very sure of itself.

---

**Pago de Carrevejas, Ribera del Duero 1994** 18 E

Magnificent aroma, fruit, structure, finish, flavour and so much vivid personality which never gets tiresome you feel the tenner spent will last for ever. The aroma of tobacco leads to richness and the final flourish of savouriness is sublime.

---

**Priorato Novell Scala Dei 1994** 14 C

---

**Torres Gran Sangredetoro 1989** 14.5 D

---

**Vinas del Vero Cabernet Sauvignon 1995** 15 C

The approachable style, hints of tannic depth, and a creamy blackcurrant finish. Great cabernet value.

---

## SPANISH WINE — WHITE

**Enate Macabeo/Chardonnay 1995** 14 C

Lemon-edged fish wine of distinctive manners and incisive finish.

---

**Marques de Grinon Durius 1995** 14 C

A curious thirst-quencher of quiet richness.

---

**Vinas del Vero Chardonnay 1996** 13.5 C

Nice lemon edge to it.

---

## URUGUAY WINE — RED

**Castol Pujol Tannat 1991** 14.5 C

---

## USA WINE — RED

**Benziger Sonoma Cabernet Sauvignon 1992** 13.5 E

Earthy and ripe. Wine Cellars only.

---

**Chateau St Michelle Merlot 1993** 15 E

A gorgeous merlot of insidiously deliciously combined elements (fruit, acid, tannin) which give the wine savour, class and impressive depth. Wine Cellars only.

---

**Clos de Gilroy Grenache, California 1995** 14 E

---

**Columbia Crest Cabernet Sauvignon 1993** 13.5 D

Beginning to dry out on the finish, typical of certain Washington State cabernets. Juicy till this point.

---

**Firesteed Pinot Noir 1993** 14 E

---

**Saddle Mountain Grenache 1994** 13.5 C

Only hints of the saddle and no sign of the mountain. But the grenache is in typical juicy form.

---

## USA WINE WHITE

**Benziger Chardonnay, Carneros 1994** 14 E

Has a lingering finish of creamy, ripe melon with a hint of brazil nut. Delicious. Wine Cellars only.

---

**Chateau St Michelle Chardonnay 1995** 15 D

Lovely texture and soft double attack of fruit and acid. Very stylish.

---

**Chateau St Michelle Riesling 1995** 15.5 D

Brilliant fruit here of sufficient richness to cope with oriental food and enough zip and personality to be a delicious solo companion.

---

**Columbia Crest Chardonnay 1994** 13.5 D

---

**Columbia Crest Semillon/Chardonnay 1994** 12 C

Good texture but has a hint of soap on the finish.

---

**Hedges Fume Chardonnay, Washington State 1995** 12 D

Expensive, ill-balanced, and only a force to reckon with at £3.29.

---

**Robert Mondavi Coastal Chardonnay 1995** 14 E

That elegant richness which marks out Californian chardonnay is present here but with the added texture of ruffled satin. Wine Cellars only.

---

## FORTIFIED WINE

**Quinta do Crasto 1985**  G

Beautiful, with a stunning finish. Quite exceptional.

---

**Quinta do Crasto Late Bottled Vintage 1988** 16 E

Gorgeous ripe fruit – like figs baked in the sun and overflowing with flavour.

---

**Quinta do Noval 1970** 16 H

Chocolate fruit of great richness.

---

**Sandemans 1970** 15 H

---

## SPARKLING WINE/CHAMPAGNE

**Ariston Brut Champagne** 14 G

---

**Champagne Henriot Blanc de Blancs** 14 G

---

**Chardonnay Vin Mousseux (France)** 13 D

---

**Dom Ruinart 'R' Champagne Brut** 12 H

---

**Henri Macquart Champagne Brut** 14 F

---

**Henriot Brut Champagne** 10 G

---

**Quartet, Roederer Estate California** 14 G

A richer style of bubbly which is much tastier than Bollinger.

---

**Seaview Brut** 14 D

---

# STOP PRESS

# MAJESTIC

## FRENCH WINE RED

**Chateau d'Aqueria, Lirac 1994** 17.5 D

Old tobacco, shoe leather, thyme, sage – the lot's stuffed in here – yet it's not remotely rustic on the finish. Rather, it's rich, soft, elegant and classy in a relaxed way.

---

## FRENCH WINE WHITE

**Andante Muscat Gewurztraminer, Ribeauville 1994** 16.5 D

This is a gorgeous blend of muscat and gewurz in which the sensuality of the former melds perfectly with the Reubenesque fleshiness of the latter to produce an exciting aperitif of aroma, weight and style.

---

## USA WINE RED

**Beringer Harmonie Pinot Noir/Gamay 1995** 14.5 D

Intensely serious to sniff, but frivolous at play on the palate, this is a deliciously soft marriage which is eminently quaffable. Better than any number of burgundies/beaujolaises.

---

**Jekel Cabernet Sauvignon 1994** 16.5 E

This is like meeting a member of the cast of Baywatch, any sex it makes little difference, who has a double first and is merely waiting to put on a little fat before becoming a don. An unusual wine, this – it is daft and drinkable, sexy, very witty.

---

## USA WINE — WHITE

**Echo Ridge Fume Blanc 1996** 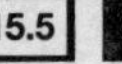

My God! Doesn't it put many pouillys to shame! Rich yet elegant, interesting smoky edge.

---

**Fetzer Viognier 1996**  

Very classy stuff: textured, ripe yet calm, apricoty yet dry. Delicious style.

---

# ODDBINS

## AUSTRALIAN WINE — WHITE

**Southern Right Sauvignon Blanc 1997**

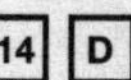


Soft touch on the finish is individual. Perhaps pricey but has gentility and class.

---

## CHILEAN WINE — RED

**Medalla Real Santa Rita Cabernet Sauvignon 1995** 16.5 D

Depth, width, length, angularity, roundedness, and it's not square. What a shape for a cabernet!

---

**Santa Rita Cabernet Sauvignon 1995** 15.5 D

Rich, ripe, warm, beautifully textured and immensely inviting. A comfort wine.

---

**Santa Rita Reserva Merlot 1996** 14 D

Charm, not a lot of substance, but full of charm.

---

## CHILEAN WINE — WHITE

**Andes Peaks Sauvignon Blanc 1997**

Excellent varietal character with hints of gooseberry, raspberry and nuts. Delicious aperitif.

---

**Casa Lapostolle Cuvee Alexandre Chardonnay 1996**

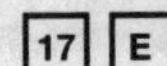


What insouciance! What utter class! What guile, richness, subtlety, elegance and stealth. It lingers like a deeply plucked string.

---

**Concha y Toro Casillero del Diablo Chardonnay 1996**

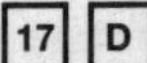


Superb balance! Gorgeous texture, and classy depth without straining for effect.

---

**Santa Carolina Sauvignon Blanc 1997**

Delicious subtlety and stealth. Has crispness and real style.

---

## SOUTH AFRICAN WINE — RED

**Clos Malverne Pinotage Reserve 1996**

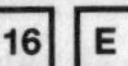


Rivetingly rich and heart-stoppingly deeply flavoured. It's rampant and louche. Delicious!

---

## SOUTH AFRICAN WINE — WHITE

**Namaqua Chenin Blanc 1997**

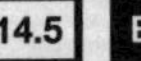


Brilliant little wine: calm, crisp, impishly fruity, full of charm.

---

**Namaqua Colombard 1997** 

Fuller and riper than its chenin sister.

---

## USA WINE — RED

**Franciscan Oakville Zinfandel 1994** 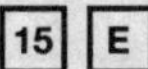

Zipp-pur-dee-do-dah! What a mouthful of warmth, richness and flavour here. This is improving beautifully in bottle compared to when I tasted last year, hence its appearance in this section as well as the main one (rates 14 there).

---

**Franciscan Pinnacles Vineyards Pinot Noir 1996** 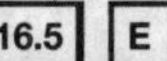

Stunning pinot for the money. Puts the majority of red burgundies to shame. Its truffley, wild strawberry fruit is classic and rich.

---

## USA WINE — WHITE

**Echo Ridge Fume Blanc 1996**  

My God! Doesn't it put many pouillys to shame! Rich yet elegant, interesting smoky edge.

---

**Fetzer Viognier 1996** 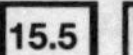 

Very classy stuff: textured, ripe yet calm, apricoty yet dry. Delicious style.

---

# THRESHER

## AUSTRALIAN WINE — WHITE

**Oxford Landing Viognier 1996** 14 D

Delicious apricoty charm.

---

## CHILEAN WINE — WHITE

**Santa Carolina Chenin Blanc 1996** 

Terrific chenin of richness yet dryness. Real class here. The grape really dazzles.

---

## FRENCH WINE — RED

**Cotes du Rhone Villages Sablet, La Ramillade 1995** 

Touches of chocolate, tea and rich blackcurrant underpinned by subtle, soft tannins. Very rounded and supple for a sablet with less of the raucous rusticity of the type.

---

# WINE CELLAR

## AUSTRALIAN WINE RED

**Capel Vale Shiraz 1996** 16 E

Trust Western Australia to rescue the Aussie's sinking reputation. This is not the usual soppy shiraz, soft as a sponge and half as characterful, yet it still has that unique savoury aroma and texture of first class Aussie shiraz. However, what it's got in addition is a dry, herby, slightly Rhone edge to it – so it has some guts. It's immensely quaffable and also good with food.

---

## AUSTRALIAN WINE WHITE

**Capel Vale Chardonnay 1995** 16 E

Beautiful purity of fruit which demonstrates both lightness and guile, yet real impact. It impresses with its class.

---

## USA WINE WHITE

**Echo Ridge Fume Blanc 1996** 15.5 C

My God! Doesn't it put many pouillys to shame! Rich yet elegant, interesting smoky edge. Selected stores.

---

# NOTES

# NOTES

# NOTES

# NOTES

# NOTES

# NOTES

# NOTES

# NOTES

# NOTES

# NOTES